India at 75, Thoughts and Reflections

Edited by Makhan Singh, Steven McCabe
and Beverley Nielsen

Published by Bite-Sized Books Ltd
16 High Holborn, London WC1V 6BX
Registered in the UK. Company Registration No: 9395379

ISBN: 978-1-7395253-2-3

Cover design: Dean Stockton

On 15th August 1947, the modern state of India was born...

...amid celebrations, bloodshed, dire warnings about the impossibility of independence succeeding, and a total confidence amongst the less than 300 million Indians that the future was theirs and they would build a country that would reflect over 5,000 years of history and grasp all that modern life could bring for the 1.3 billion Indians now alive.

Some 75 years later, it is entirely fitting that this book, edited by Makhan Singh, Steven McCabe and Beverley Nielsen, by bringing together distinguished academics, journalists, industrialists and politicians, celebrates the emergence of India as the fourth largest economy in the world and its economic, social and political maturity.

This important book fittingly recognises the giant strides that India has made both domestically and internationally – and looks forward to the next phases of development and achievement.

This edition of *India at 75, Thoughts and Reflections* follows on from the A4 hardback version commissioned by Birmingham City University (BCU) for private distribution to senior government officials, academics and industry leaders both in India and the United Kingdom. The publishers are grateful to BCU for their kind permission to make this paperback edition available to a wider international audience to enable all to celebrate India's 75 years of independence.

Bite-Sized Books – December 2023

Introduction by Anita Bhalla, OBE DL, Chair, Birmingham City University (BCU)

The world that we inhabit now is very different from what it was when India became independent over 75 years ago. Over that period, India has become a symbol for all those countries which have replaced the old colonial-metropolitan relationships with a strong sense of their own identity and their ability to compete in economic, social and cultural spheres with vigour, innovation and creativity.

The various contributors to this book bear testimony to how the achievements of business entrepreneurs, cultural creatives and social reformers have transformed the Indian landscape.

Birmingham is a microcosm of the globalised world known for its rich diversity and is home to the many vibrant communities from the Indian sub-continent. BCU is a major player in the life of the city providing an umbilical cord of connection between the UK and India. Our university provides an academic and professional space where new and exciting economic, social and cultural relationships are nurtured and developed – relationships that are built on mutual trust, respect and admiration.

I warmly commend this compilation and all that it stands for in redefining the British-Indian relationship in the present time.

Welcome by Professor David Mba,
Vice Chancellor, Birmingham City University

During my time at Birmingham City University, I've become quickly attuned to the kinship between BCU and India.

India is a country notable for its intense passion for culture through storytelling, poetry, music and art; BCU is an institution that is founded on creative endeavour, with the Birmingham Society of Artists opening the Birmingham Government School of Design in 1843. And, much like India's transformation since 1947, our University has undergone a dramatic transformation – and, in turn, transformed Birmingham itself – as our renowned Schools of Jewellery, Art and Acting, Royal Birmingham Conservatoire, and the two City campuses have become internationally recognised as Birmingham City University.

There are many reasons the link between BCU and India is so strong and, undoubtedly, that link will only strengthen as the years progress.

We shall continue our knowledge and talent exchange with India, collaborating with the country's foremost academics and industry professionals to unearth new opportunities. We will also welcome more performers, business leaders and statesmen and women to join us at BCU for discussion, networking and celebration.

As Vice-Chancellor of Birmingham City University, I'm delighted to endorse India at 75 as a mark of the astonishing achievements of the country post-independence. I'm also proud of my institution's collaboration with India and am confident we will continue to provide continued mutual benefit to both India and the UK.

Patronage for this book by partners of Birmingham City University

Caroline Rowett, Deputy High Commissioner, British Deputy High Commission, Chandigarh

Looking back to my first year in India, dominated by Covid lockdowns and restrictions, with virtual meetings the only way to connect to people, it was challenging to understand the breadth and depth of the UK–India relationship in northern India.

Things changed in 2022 and I've been fortunate to be able to travel throughout the region. My travels have shown me that the bilateral relationship is strongest in the people-to-people ties – the 'Living Bridge' between our two countries. STEAMhouse India, the Birmingham City University (BCU) partnership with the Munjal Foundation (Munjal Birmingham City University Centre for Innovation and Entrepreneurship) in Ludhiana, Punjab, is a wonderful example of this. I've never experienced anything like the 'Metaverse' lab in Ludhiana.

In 1947 there were 25 universities in India. Television and the internet didn't exist. Today there are over 1,000 universities collaborating with educational institutions around the world. BCU has been energetic and determined in developing its bond with Punjab. I'm sure that the next 75 years will be as exciting and fruitful. I wish I could be there to see the future developments!

Dr Andrew Fleming, British Deputy High Commissioner to Kolkata

There are many links between India and the city of Birmingham, and I think it is wonderful my friends from BCU have put together such an extensive and thought-provoking work in celebration of this fascinating and diverse nation's 75th anniversary. I will restrict my comments to three areas relevant to the states of Andhra Pradesh and Telangana where I have just concluded a most memorable five years.

First – midwifery, because BCU have opened up relations to become a close friend and collaborator of the Hyderabad-based Fernandez Foundation, supporting their mission and bringing respectful midwifery care to India. A succession of practitioners with links to BCU have visited Telangana to support a pioneering programme of training designed to deliver this vision and ultimately mainstream it into the healthcare system.

Outcomes have included not only a better birthing experience for expectant mums but also the hitherto unthinkable scenario of fathers being present at the birth, with a reduction in demand for Caesarean sections and a transformation of the end-to-end pregnancy experience including pre and postnatal care.

Second – film and specifically Tollywood, the Telegu equivalent of Mumbai-based Bollywood and, according to many, the wealthier cousin. This is something few outside India even know about, but something I have tried hard to raise awareness of, exactly because of the kind of collaboration possible with British education institutions with a world-class creative focus like BCU.

Finally – innovation, because the breadth and scale, as can be seen in a city like Hyderabad, is phenomenal. The city boasts more incubators, accelerators and catapults than any other in India (in excess of 80) and in July 2022, the largest incubator (by area) in the world opened in the city. Moreover, in a pioneering move, innovation has been mainstreamed into the state education curriculum in Telangana, meaning children from across the state will be exposed to this concept, enabling them to actively consider a future entrepreneurial career path.

Here are just three areas where the UK–India relationship has delivered in the Telugu speaking region, and I am confident will lead to even greater things in the next 75 years.

Contents

Part One – Historical reflections and cultural context

Part Two – Educational collaborations and partnerships

Part Three – Personal reflections on India at 75

Part Four – India's economic evolution

Acknowledgements

In coordinating and editing a book dedicated to celebrating India at 75, we're aware that any attempt to adequately summarise its progress is a tall order. As many contributors make clear, India's birth as a nation by partition in August 1947 was, to say the least, tumultuous. For the families of the those who died, estimated to be well in excess of a million, as well as the many millions displaced, any commemoration of India's achievement is understandably framed by the suffering and sense of loss. Nonetheless, what we set out to achieve when this book was conceived, was to bring together a collection of contributions by, predominantly, academics from Birmingham City University (BCU), who would offer their thoughts and reflections on what has indeed been possible in the decades since India's relationship with the UK altered by becoming an independent nation.

We believe that what's presented provides a wonderfully informative vista of the development of India in terms of its economy and societal aspirations as well as its culture and technology. This would not have been possible without the willingness of our colleagues at BCU and beyond. We wish to express our profound gratitude to them for the time and effort they have dedicated to writing their chapters. It's worth stressing that without their involvement, this book would not include the diversity of subjects and range of views which, we anticipate, will ensure this book represents a worthwhile addition to the canon of literature written to coincide with the anniversary of India's independence.

A very special thank you to the Vice-Chancellor of BCU Prof David Mba, Mr Pankaj M Munjal, Professor Manoj Ladwa, Caroline Rowett, and Dr Andrew Fleming.

Our sincerest kind thanks to His Excellency, Dr Shashank Vikram (CGI, Birmingham), His Excellency, Dr Aman Puri (CGI, Dubai) and colleagues connected with the Consulate General of India, Birmingham, who have been highly supportive of our BCU work in India.

BCU are developing partnerships with industry, academia and third sector partners within India via the BCU India Group (www.bcu.ac.uk/india-group). This group, founded in 2017 by five staff members - Professor Julian Beer, Anita Virk, Professor Rajinder Dudrah, Dr Vivek Indramohan and Makhan Singh - with the wonderful support of Bharat Sakhuja, a former BCU student. We wish to thank the original founding members of the India Group and our alumni, which is now flourishing with over 100 staff actively involved in engaging with India partnerships.

One of our key partnerships in India is based in Ludhiana. The Munjal Birmingham City University Centre of Innovation and Entrepreneurship (MBCIE), promoted by the Munjal family (Hero Group) and BCU, is our centre based in Ludhiana, engaged in promoting innovation, Industry 4.0 and entrepreneurship. Our warmest and special kindest thanks to the MBCIE India board members: Mr Sunil Kant Munjal, Mr Yogesh Chander Munjal, Mr Vijay Munjal and Mr Suresh C Munjal.

We are very grateful for the warm welcome always received by our esteemed partners when BCU visit India. We would also like to extend our gratitude to Mr Umesh Munjal, Mr Abhishek Munjal and Mr Akshay Munjal for their kindness and thoughts, which have helped shape this book.

In addition, we'd like to express sincere thanks to the following people for without their inspiration, steer, stories and support, this book would not have been created: Mr S K Rai (Vice Chairman, Hero Cycles); Dr Prem Kumar (Executive Director, BCM Foundation), Gaurav Himkar (Hero Motors Company), Mr Sanjeev Sharma (Ronkel MERI), Rowan Kennedy (British Council India) and our colleagues at the university; Professor Rajinder Dudrah for his diligent and, it must be said, always patient reading of drafts of the book. Special thanks go to Prof Hanifa Shah, Jo Birch, Jude Pearson, Dr Nayan Patel, Libby Surplice, as well as to Chris Berry, Fiona Shields, Donna Storrod and Tracey Bradshaw for their wonderful and continued support. We also wish to give thanks to Louise Heath, Contracts Manager, for her patience in dealing with the legal aspects of this book.

Finally, we dedicate this book to those working to make India a country in which every citizen can fulfil their potential and can look forward to a prosperous future for themselves and subsequent generations. As India continues its economic, social, cultural and technological progress, we wish India's citizens and diaspora the very best of luck for the future.

Makhan Singh, Dr Steven McCabe and Beverley Nielsen,

December 2023

Foreword by Pankaj M. Munjal, Chairman, Hero Cycles

To cover a subject as vast as relatively young, post-independence India, let alone its history of millennia, requires courage.

One requires a nuanced understanding of history, culture, religion, society, technology, politics, industry, linguistics and global affairs to try and just define what post-independence India is. This book does a wonderful, nay, courageous job of outlining the most significant and defining subjects that give the most realistic and practical understanding of the phenomenon called India.

The book does an incomparable job of curating subjects that not only take the reader through some traditionally known aspects of India, but also certain nuanced subjects that require one to immerse themselves completely into the India experience to be able to bring them into discourse, to be able to write about it, and to be able to reflect on it. The book and its contributory authors have taken immeasurable effort to stay true to the theme of the book and enrich it the way very few can. As you read through the chapters, you can't help but feel exposed to the quintessential India experience of being sombre, curious, surprised, reflective, pensive, anxious and soothed, all within a single reading session. It makes you enter from the main streets but diverts to traverse through lanes and alleys, and that's where you notice the perspective of this book, which is not accidental.

Much like Indian society, Indian industry had to leave the shackles and legacy of colonial rule behind and create its own policy and enablement structure. What followed was massive progress in phases, with indigenous industrialisation, followed by international partnerships and exports, followed by tremendous value addition through prowess in engineering, IT and manufacturing. This is all reflected in the progress India has made in the 75 years since independence and, in particular, the strides that have been made to develop world-class excellence in engineering and, of course, the now renowned expertise in IT. I feel honoured that the book carries a dedicated section on the history of cycling in India which I have witnessed and participated in through Hero Cycles. Cycling and the bicycle industry was and continues to be a momentous part of the journey towards building the nation, and the book gave me immense joy for it to be recognised as such.

Dear reader, I hope you enjoy the experience as much as I did and that it makes for a read that you will find yourself going back to, for it captures the essence of the subjects it took up so truly, and in a way projects the next 75 years as much as it did the past ones.

Namaste!

About the editors

Makhan Singh is Senior Development Manager – India Partnerships at BCU, with a prime focus on India partnerships in terms of Research, Innovation, Employability and Enterprise. Having travelled, lived and worked in India over a period of 30+ years, Makhan is passionate about India partnerships, continually nurturing strategic partnerships across India. As one of the founding members of the BCU India Group, he is involved in the creation of various projects with India, aligned with the strengths of BCU and working in strong partnerships with organisations in the UK-India bridge.

Makhan commenced his working career within the automotive sector, having worked for companies including Land Rover, BMW, Honda, Britax, Johnson Controls and Keiper Recaro. Makhan has worked with over 30 higher education institutions on a multitude of projects, ranging from higher education business development, HE curriculum development and 'outreach/widening participation' to employer engagement as well as STEM (science, technology, engineering and mathematics) and careers resource development. Having spent three years with the Engineering Employers' Federation and five years working on a UK government funded 'More Maths Grads/National HE STEM Programme', Makhan has worked at national level on STEM educational projects. Having also been part of high-level steering groups (BIS Careers for Science Group), Makhan has presented at various STEM conferences including at the House of Commons in 2010. Makhan is a qualified and highly experienced humanistic psychotherapist and excels in developing partnerships and empowering people. His area of research is emotional nerve intelligence and his work in this field has been published in a number of journals. Additionally, Makhan published his first novel in 2000: The Journey, *Where Seagulls Dare to Fly.*

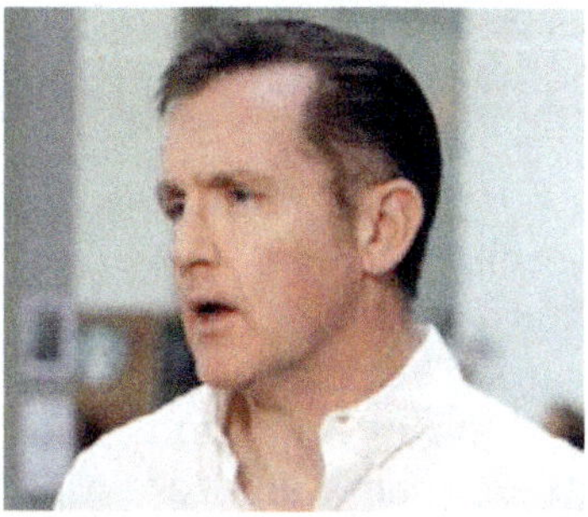

Dr Steven McCabe is Associate Professor at BCU and has been an academic since 1987 teaching economics, business, management and research philosophy. His PhD examined the use of quality management to achieve organisational improvement. Steven writes and comments regularly in the national and international media on politics and the economy. Author of numerous texts on quality management, in recent years he has written on politics and the economy. His co-edited texts include *Brexit and Northern Ireland, Bordering on Confusion* (2019), *English Regions After Brexit: Examining Potential Change through Devolved Power* (2020), *Exploring the Green Economy – Issues, Challenges and Benefits* (2021) and *Green Manufacturing, what this involves and how to achieve success* (2021), *How To Stop Rising House Prices* (2022) and *Another Way, An Examination of Britain's Defence Policy* were published in early 2022. Additionally, Steven has written a number of chapters for texts examining the impact of the pandemic, economics and politics.

Beverley Nielsen is Associate Professor and Director at the Institute for Design, Economic Acceleration & Sustainability (IDEAS) at BCU. She has written and edited books on topics as diverse as Brexit, English regions, the green economy and green manufacturing as well as on redesigning manufacturing. She served as an Expert Commissioner on the All-Party Manufacturing Group at the House of Commons and is an independent district and county councillor in Worcestershire. Alongside her research, previous experience includes her role as Director of FTSE 250 company AGA Rangemaster and MD of interiors business Fired Earth, with over a decade spent at the Confederation of British Industry as Director of the CBI West Midlands. She has an honorary Master's degree and has been recognised as Midlands Business Woman of the Year, West Midlands Business Ambassador of the Year and Woman of the Decade in Enterprise and Leadership.

Opening thoughts by Professor Manoj Ladwa, Chief Executive, India Inc.

Shri Manoj Ladwa presents a book edited by him, "Winning Partnership - INDIA - UK Relations Beyond Brexit", to the Prime Minister, Shri Narendra Modi.

I am delighted to have the opportunity to make an opening contribution to this excellent compendium of reflections and insights to commemorate the 75th year of India's independence.

The wide and varied nature of the essays in this book is testimony to the uniquely multifaceted breadth and depth of the post-colonial relationship between India and the UK, and also signposts the immense opportunities for collaboration in the years to come.

Democratic dividend

The book appropriately seeks to balance the historical and cultural context of the India–UK relationship, along with very clear insights into the evolution of the economic and education systems in India, and its significance in today's much churning world. Especially pleasing to read are the personal experiences from individuals of the Indian diaspora who form what Prime Minister Narendra Modi has eloquently described as the 'Living Bridge' between our two nations. It is in many ways a celebration of our shared and unwavering belief in the power of democracy and the dividends it can deliver for the welfare of our peoples.

India's progress in the past few years is nothing but staggering. According to the World Bank, India's economy has grown eight-fold in 25 years, from US$392.9 billion in 1996 to US$3.17 trillion in 2021, and per capita income during this same period has tripled to around US$7,000. A United Nations Development Programme report in 2020 highlighted that India lifted a record 271 million people out of poverty in under a decade.

Demographic dividend

Further, the World Economic Forum reports that 'By 2030, India will move from being an economy led by the bottom of the pyramid to one led by the middle class. Nearly 80% of households in 2030 will be middle-income, up from about 50% today. The middle class will drive 75% of consumer spending in 2030.' It is therefore not surprising, but nonetheless worth highlighting, that with this impressive trajectory of growth, India will be the second-largest economy (based on GDP in Purchasing Power Parity terms) by 2050 (only behind China).

Also, unlike most other major economies in the world, India has demographics on its side. By 2030, India will still have a median age of 31 compared to 42 in China and 40 in the US. With over a billion people of working age, India will have the largest working-age population in the world.

Digital dividend

India's young people are also driving another revolution: the digital revolution. This will see the country becoming not only a major exporter of technological talent but also of technological solutions for the world. India has the second-largest number of internet users in the world, with 692 million active internet users (351 million in rural areas, 341 million in urban areas); this is expected to grow to 900 million users by 2025. India has already overtaken the US when it comes to digital transactions, with around 346 million Indians using eCommerce, digital payments etc. compared to 331 million in the US.

India boasts one of the world's most powerful digital infrastructure systems, and the digital payments market in India is forecast to triple to US$10 trillion (in value of transactions) in the next five years as per a BCG report. India's tech start-up ecosystem is the third largest in the world in terms of Unicorns and the number of start-ups. The combined valuation of Indian start-ups is US$450 billion, which have created over 770,000 jobs in the past couple of years alone.

India's demographic dividend, coupled with exceptional digital advancement, can only mean great opportunities lie ahead.

Winning partnership

I would like to especially congratulate Makhan Singh, Dr Steven McCabe and Beverley Nielsen and other colleagues at BCU for bringing this wonderful effort to fruition and helping to further strengthen what I have often described as the 'Winning Partnership' between our two great nations.

Special message by Rowan Kennedy, former Acting Country Director, British Council India

In India's 75th Anniversary year, the ties that bind our two countries feel stronger than they have done for some time. Our bilateral relationship is deep, rich, and varied, as the essays in this book make abundantly clear.

The UK university sector has a huge role to play in the development of this relationship. The 2030 Roadmap for India-UK future relations sets out a series of ambitious bilateral goals, and UK universities will be crucial to delivering every one of these - from building our collaboration in education, research and innovation, to driving cooperation on climate, health, and trade and prosperity.

Despite the diversity of the links between our two countries, there is a single thread that runs through them and strengthens them all - and this is the people-to-people links, the huge network of personal, professional and academic bonds between communities, institutions, families and individuals in both countries. It's often referred to as the 'Living Bridge' between India and the UK.

At the heart of the living bridge is the UK's 1.5 million-strong Indian diaspora community; however, its branches extend much further - to the citizens of both countries who travel for study or work; to the researchers who together address the great challenges facing our societies; to the artists who collaborate on cultural projects and the hundreds of thousands of festival-goers who experience and learn from each other's cultures. Universities play a huge part in creating and strengthening these bonds.

The British Council also supports the development of people-to-people connections between our countries - partly, of course, through our work with UK and Indian universities; through our work teaching English and offering UK qualifications; and through our work in arts and culture. This year, in particular, we are proud to be delivering the

India/UK Together Season of Culture, a cultural exchange programme marking the 75th anniversary and celebrating the vibrant cultural bonds between our countries.

Birmingham is a city shaped and defined, to a large part, by its prominent Indian diaspora. I was very struck, on my first call with colleagues from Birmingham City University, at how thoughtfully they have built upon their city's own living bridge to create a comprehensive and far-reaching engagement strategy that is creating impact and new connections right across India.

The essays in this book are a reflection and celebration of that engagement, of course – but also a timely reminder of the importance of the bilateral relationship for both countries, and a useful guide to how to develop the relationship further as we look to the next 75 years. The British Council looks forward to playing a continued part in that development.

Chapter 1

Introduction – India at 75 – an overview

Makhan Singh, Steven McCabe and Beverley Nielsen

A brief history of India's independence - origins

In a book based on examination of India's development over the last 75 years, it would be a serious omission not to examine the origins for the current state. Independence for India commenced on 15 August 1947 when what's referred to as 'British India', which had existed since 1612, was divided into two separate countries. Partition of India created the Dominion of India, now the Republic of India, and the Dominion of Pakistan which was to become the current Islamic Republic of Pakistan, together with the People's Republic of Bangladesh, which achieved independence in March 1971.

Figure 1.1: Map of the British Indian Empire from Imperial Gazetteer of India (Source: Edinburgh Geographical Institute; J.G. Bartholomew and Sons, Oxford University Press).

Figure 1.2: L–R: Muhammad Ali Jinnah, Mahatma Gandhi and Pandit Jawaharlal Nehru (Source: www.outlookindia.com/website/story/opinion- india-of-2019-would-have-shocked-nehru-and-gandhi- not-so-much-jinnah/344819 accessed 8th July).

Simmering tensions between Muhammad Ali Jinnah, leader of the Muslim League, and Mahatma Gandhi and Pandit Jawaharlal Nehru, who were prominent leaders of the Hindu-dominated Congress Party, had led to resentment and, in many cases, conflict between members of the communities they represented. Curiously, Jinnah, who's widely acknowledged to have been responsible for the creation of the Islamic Republic of Pakistan, was a staunch secularist who had spent the early part of his career attempting to allay concerns among Muslims of the need to achieve a separate state. Indeed, in 1916, Jinnah, who was a member of both parties, was able to achieve a common set of demands, the Lucknow Pact, which was presented to Britain, leading him to be hailed as 'the Ambassador of Hindu–Muslim Unity.'

However, throughout the 1930s and 1940s, the relationships between Jinnah, Gandhi and Nehru became increasingly fractious. Jinnah was now calling for a separate homeland for the Muslim minority within India. Though the notion of a two-nation solution had been proposed in the 1920s, the Second World War provided a catalyst for its eventual imposition. As William Dalrymple explains in a seminal New Yorker article, 'The Great Divide, the violent legacy of Indian partition' (2015), Japanese occupation of Singapore and Rangoon, allowing its army to advance rapidly through Burma, now more commonly referred to as Myanmar, towards India, stimulated increased antagonism between Muslims and Hindus. The Congress Party's call for civil disobedience through the 'Quit India Movement' resulted in Gandhi and Nehru being arrested. Jinnah, on the other hand, remained loyal to the British and used his position to rally Muslims to support a separate homeland as a way to provide protection against Hindu dominance.

Violence between Hindus and Muslims increasingly escalated. Tensions were exacerbated by local and regional political leaders. This resulted in communities being divided as well as deaths and serious injury in what is often referred to as 'ethnic cleansing'. Massacres, commencing in Calcutta (now Kolkata) in August 1946, when an estimated 4,000 people were murdered, led to the leadership within the Congress Party, who had opposed partition, regarding it as the only way to resolve a situation that was spiralling out of control. Crucially, the British government, horrified by events in India, decided it could no longer maintain sufficient influence.

Britain's decision to leave India and the Mountbatten Plan

Figure 1.3: Earl Mountbatten of Burma, KG GCB OM GCSI GCIE GCVO DSO KStJ ADC PC FRS.

On 20 February 1947, Prime Minister (PM) Clement Atlee announced to Parliament that British rule would cease on 'a date not later than June 1948'. At this point, there was still a belief that an accommodation between Nehru and Jinnah might be possible to allow power to be transferred to 'some form of central Government for British India'. Nonetheless, as Atlee made clear, if agreement between Nehru and Jinnah proved impractical, the intention of the British government was to transfer power 'in such other way as may seem most reasonable and in the best interests of the Indian people'.

The following month, Lord Louis Mountbatten was sent by the British government to oversee the transition of rule to an independent India. Mountbatten's brief was to oversee the transition of rule to an independent India with as much haste possible[1].

1 In a tragic irony, Mountbatten would eventually be murdered on 27 August 1979 by a bomb detonated on his boat in Mullaghmore, Sligo, in the Republic of Ireland. The

IRA (Irish Republican Army) was then conducting a bloody campaign to reunite the two parts of Ireland that had been created by partition in 1921.

Initial meetings between Lord Mountbatten and political leaders demonstrated to him that the original timetable would facilitate further conflict between Hindus and Muslims. He became convinced that an increasingly bloody civil war would ensue which, he knew, Britain had little willingness to be drawn into, nor to act as a referee. On 3 June 1947, persuaded that a rapid decision might potentially concentrate the minds of Indian political leaders, and to the surprise of all, Mountbatten announced that the transfer of power would take place two months later on 15 August and would create two new dominions. What quickly became known as the Mountbatten Plan or the 3 June Plan was announced and included the following:

> Sikhs, Hindus and Muslims in Punjab and Bengal legislative assemblies would meet and vote for partition. If a simple majority of either group wanted partition, then these provinces would be divided.
>
> Sind and Baluchistan were to make their own decision.
>
> The fate of North-West Frontier Province and Sylhet district of Assam was to be decided by a referendum.
>
> Separate independence for Bengal was ruled out.
>
> A boundary commission was to be set up in case of partition between Hindus and Muslims.

The impact of Mountbatten's decision was to have profound, and immediate, consequences for India. Rather than achieving the sort of compromise he'd hoped for, Mountbatten's decision is remembered by many as the catalyst for the chaos and death which resulted as millions of Hindus fled from the soon-to-be state of Pakistan. Correspondingly, millions of Muslims, who were equally fearful of prospects in the newly created independent state of India, made the journey in the opposite direction. It must be noted that the British judge Cyril Radcliffe, who'd been given the task of drawing the border to create the two states, which was always going to be fraught with challenges and requiring adept sensitivity, had less than six weeks to achieve this objective. It's hardly surprising that Radcliffe was unable to announce the precise location of the proposed border between the two new states of India and Pakistan until 17 August, two days after India's independence had already occurred.

India awakes to 'life and freedom'

The evening before India became an independent state, in India's Constituent Assembly, Jawaharlal Nehru made a speech in which he stated, 'Long years ago, we made a tryst with destiny.' As he asserted confidently, 'At the stroke of the midnight hour, when the world sleeps, India will awake to life and freedom.' Nonetheless, and though this book is explicitly concerned with celebrating the achievements of India in the 75 years since it gained independence on 15 August 1947, 'it would be remiss of us not to acknowledge that the end of rule by Britain was accompanied by a dreadful human cost in terms of suffering and deaths.'

Though exact figures do not exist, it is reliably estimated that 15 million people were displaced by partition. The movement of so many people, because of their religious affiliation to Hindu-majority India and Muslim-majority Pakistan, according to Stanford-based historian Priya Satia, who has studied the partition of India, was accompanied by all the necessary 'ingredients for ethnic cleansing': 'a feeble, polarized police force, absence of troops and an armed and terrified population. The violence marked the crumbling of an old order and abdication of responsibility for minorities by all those with any kind of power' (Shashkevitch, 2019).

In addition to the immense suffering endured by so many who fled homes where their families had lived for generations, never to return, there was widespread violence enacted which, it's estimated, led to the deaths of up to two million people. As many who've studied partition in India will attest, the outcome of the trauma undergone by those who survived its effects has been long term and continues to destabilise relationships between India and Pakistan.

75 years on

If this book is to achieve anything, it's to be sincerely hoped that future generations recognise the futility of conflict and seek to achieve a world in which all citizens are able to enjoy peace and prosperity. Since gaining independence 75 years ago, India has undergone a transition which is as phenomenal as it is impressive. It has established itself as the largest democracy in the world. At the time of independence, India's population was approximately 340 million; this had more than doubled by the time the 2001 census was carried out (Britannica, 2022). Indeed, having surpassed one billion people by the 2001 census, according to the United Nations, it has overtaken China in 2023 to become the world's most populous country (Ellis-Petersen, H., 2023). Though presenting a challenge, one key virtue India possesses is a youthful population. As Figure 1.5 shows, more than half of Indian citizens are under 30 years old. Only a fifth of Indian's population is 45 years or older.

Figure 1.4: India - States and Union Territories

As a number of chapters in this book describe, most particularly 23, India has undergone significant transformation in its journey since gaining independence in August 1947. The creation of government at every level to replace the systems which existed under the British has been a challenge. Indeed, like other politicians across the world, Indian politicians have discovered the seductiveness of power based on making promises to improve the prospects of life for all citizens comes with the risk of disappointment. Nehru's initial optimism of what he wished to achieve was thwarted by the magnitude of altering the basis of an economy that had been plundered by the British, and in large part, improving living standards for citizens since independence has proved intractably difficult.

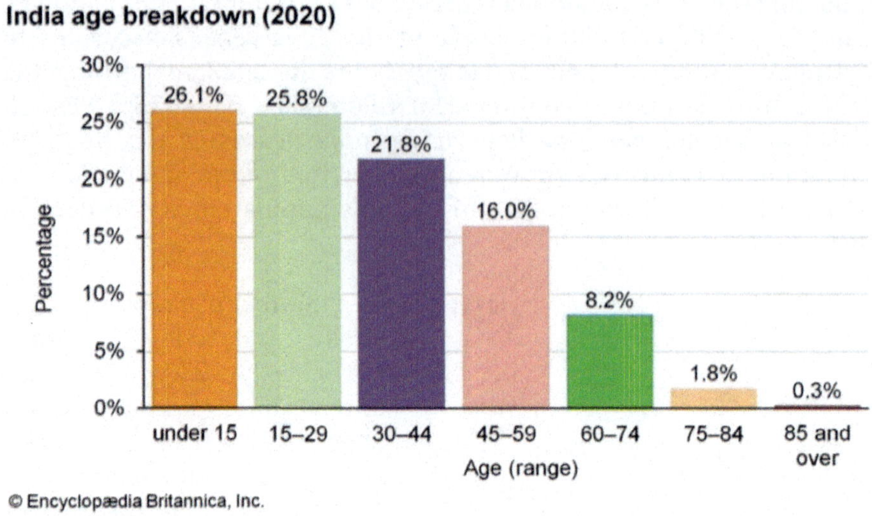

Figure 1.5: Population of India by age group (2020).

Nonetheless, as subsequent chapters demonstrate, from what was a difficult 'birth', India's development has demonstrated what is possible by dedicated and cooperative effort. Success in entrepreneurial effort coupled with innovation in industries, traditional (manufacturing) and contemporary (digital and IT), has proved vital in improving India's economy. Providing well-paid jobs for the growing population of young people in India is essential in raising living standards and providing greater confidence in what can be achieved in the future. India, therefore, though taking pride in what's been achieved so far, surely recognises how much more needs to be done. India at 75 very much represents a 'work in progress'.

An overview of the chapters

In Part One of this book, 'Historical reflections and cultural context', a number of contributors examine the way in which India has developed since independence. In chapter 2, 'A history of railways in India', seminal railway historian and internationally renowned commentator, Christian Wolmar, provides an analysis of the way in which railways in India have proved invaluable in the country's economic and social progress since 1947. In chapter 3, 'India: 75 years of innovation and beyond', Ventakesh Vijay, Makhan Singh, Pratik Dattani and P. Jagadeesh, present an overview of the key sectors which have enabled India to develop expertise and advance knowledge. If a measure of advancement is the way in which health provision improves, then chapter 4, 'The developing landscape of midwifery in India', by Natasha Carr, Maggie Prain, Inderjeet Kaur and Radha Reddy, provides a superb example of the way in which knowledge transfer by academics based in the UK at BCU working in partnership with Indian practitioners is making childbirth a safer experience for mothers and babies. Chapter 5, 'Thoughts and reflections on changes and influences in cinema in India over the past 75 years' by Anita Virk and Swadhin Padhy, is an evocative examination of the role that the experience of Indian films has had on the country's culture. BCU academic, Mark Jeffreys, explains the way in which sport has equally played a crucial role in India's sense of international achievement and pride in chapter 6, 'A reflection of how sport has evolved in *India at 75*', with India sending the largest delegation of athletes to the Commonwealth Games held in Birmingham in the summer of 2022. The final chapter in Part One of this book, 'Cycling evolution – 75 years of changes in India and the world', by BCU academic Andrew Trujillo, analyses why bikes have been so important in providing transport to India's citizens. As he concludes, given ongoing concerns about the environmental devastation caused by global warming, bikes are increasingly likely to enjoy a renaissance in popularity.

Part Two of the book, 'Educational collaborations and partnerships', consists of six chapters in which academic cooperation between India and BCU are explored. Chapter 8, 'The evolution of diabetes and treatments in India since 1947' by Anne Phillips, Wasim Hanif, Martha Stewart, Jayne Robbie and Theresa Smyth, demonstrates how such collaboration has reduced the incidence of diabetes among Indian citizens. The way in which cultural collaboration is being achieved is powerfully described by Louise Lansdown, Lamberto Coccioli and James Bunch, in chapter 9, 'Learning from each other: the partnership between Royal Birmingham Conservatoire and the A R Rahman Foundation' and demonstrates that music continues to create ties between India and the UK. Culture and the role of poetry and the Indian diaspora is examined in chapter 10, 'Celebrating the multilingual poetry of India and its diaspora at 75 years of independence', by Vivek Sachdeva and Gregory Leadbetter. As Sachdeva and Leadbetter beautifully conclude, poetry can connect across cultures. In chapter 11, 'A personal reflection of India's growth in its private higher education provision since independence', BCU's Panchalingam Suntharalingam examines the phenomenal growth in private providers of higher education in the last three decades. As Suntharalingam shows, seeking a UK memorandum of understanding is seen as being vital in achieving international recognition of courses by students. The importance of community radio to provide a link between citizens is abundantly clear in chapter 12, 'Radio in India', by Sam Coley, Arul Aram and R. Lavanya, who describe the recent growth in provision. Using empirical experience of involvement in the operation of Anna Community Radio, they present insights into what has been possible. In the final chapter of part two, 'Memories of academic international engagement; cross-cultural knowledge sharing and future possibilities in a post-pandemic world', BCU academic Jacqueline Norton writes a passionate personal reflection on how valuable international partnerships have been. Using interview data from those she has worked with in the Tamil Nadu region, Norton provides utterly persuasive evidence of the symbiotically beneficial relationships that have been created.

Part Three of the book, 'Personal reflections on India at 75', includes four chapters in which there are compelling accounts of the way in which change has occurred among Indian citizens and the diaspora since independence. In chapter 14, 'Reminiscing about Indian film in Birmingham', BCU's Dharmesh Rajput allows the reader to appreciate the way in which Indian cinema has provided a link between the families of those who arrived in Birmingham seeking employment and the country still regarded as 'home'. In chapter 15, 'The modernisation of India and its impact on fashion', BCU academic, Jasbir Kaur, considers how rapidly Indian fashion has developed in the last three decades. Kaur provides a summary of the influences creating the catalyst for change and how the development of the sector has created employment and, significantly, been essential in enabling the country's journey towards modernity. In chapter 16, 'Women in India at 75 – a contemporary examination of women in India from the perspective of the British Indian diaspora', Beverley Nielsen interviews a number of women whose success proves their capability and ability to work at the highest level of every sector, whilst considering the progress made in promoting women's rights and independence in India today. In chapter 17, 'Indian Muslims: a personal reflection', Imran Mogra provides a potent examination of the way in which leading Indian Muslims have contributed to the country's development. As the history of India's independence starkly shows, such contributions, essential as part of post-independence healing and recovery, are rightly celebrated by Mogra.

Part Four of this book, 'India's economic evolution', presents a number of contributions analysing progress that has been made since independence in enhancing the country's financial and, as a consequence, potential social prospects. In chapter 18, 'What is this India business? Influences and competitive advantage', publishing executive, Paul Davies and Steven McCabe examine what engagement in business in India consists of. In chapter 19, 'Solar villages – a smart sustainable future for rural India', BCU's Cham Athwal provides an overview of his research that analyses the way in which sustainable forms of energy can prove vital to economic development in rural areas.

The issue of India's agricultural sector and continued importance to the country's citizens is considered by BCU's Navjot Sandhu, Javed Hussain and Shishank Shishank in chapter 20, 'Changing landscape of Indian farming: smart agriculture as a way forward'.

The critical aspect of technological and innovative development is dealt with in subsequent chapters included in part four. In chapter 21, 'The Indian National Innovation System: historical perspective and key characteristics', Danilo Sartorello Spinola and Rituparna Kaushik describe how immense strides in product development and technical improvement have been possible because of government commitment to innovation. In chapter 22, 'The Indian automotive industry, an overview' Alex De Ruyter in examining India's automotive industry explains how car production has become a significant element of the country's quest to become a developed country.

In chapter 23, 'Reflecting on India's economic and technological revolution', seminal economic expert, Vicki Pryce, with BCU's Steven McCabe and Beverley Nielsen, consider how economic progress has been engendered through a combination of political will and a series of deliberate policies. Unfortunately, like all ex-colonial nations, the transition has not proved as straightforward as would have been anticipated (and hoped) at the birth of India as an independent nation in August 1947. However, as Makhan Singh, Steven McCabe and Beverley Nielsen contend in the final chapter of this book, 'Conclusion – What's the future for India?', there's an abundance of evidence to suggest India's future looks bright. Crucially, they believe, the combination of education and research expertise by academics working in collaboration with industry will provide a platform for progress at an increasing rate. Indeed, as many commentators argue, by the time the country celebrates the centenary of independence in 2047, it's more than likely that India will be regarded as a developed nation that has vastly enhanced the quality of life for its citizens.

References

Britannica (2022), 'India, Facts', Britannica Online, https://www.britannica.com/ place/India/Resources-and-power, accessed 10 July

Dalrymple, W. (2015), 'The Great Divide, The violent legacy of Indian partition',

Ellis-Petersen, H., (2023) 'India overtakes China to become world's most populous country', The Guardian 24th April 2023

New Yorker, 22 June, https://www.newyorker.com/magazine/2015/06/29/the-great- divide-books-dalrympl, accessed7July

Shashkevitch, A. (2019), 'Stanford scholar explains the history of India's partition, its ongoing effects today', Stanford News, 8 March, https://news.stanford. edu/2019/03/08/partition-1947-continues-haunt-india-pakistan-stanford-scholar says/#:~:text=Although%20the%20agreement%20required%20no,died%20 in%20 the%20ensuing%20violence, accessed 7 July

Part One

Historical reflections and cultural context

Chapter 2

A history of railways in India

Christian Wolmar

Introduction

Nowhere in the world is the history of a nation's rail network so entwined with the wider story of its development than in India. While the role of, say, the building of the Transcontinental linking the two coasts of America or Russia's Trans-Siberian in opening up Siberia in the history of these two nations cannot be underestimated, the way that India's economic and cultural history is so bound up with that of its railways makes it quite impossible to disentangle the two.

Indeed, it is unimaginable to think of India without reference to its railways. With – pre- Covid – 25 million passengers a day, more than any other country, that symbiotic relationship remains. The railways have played a vital role in the nation's history since the day in 1853 that the first train clanked its way on the 21-mile track between Bombay (now Mumbai) and Thane, a line that is now merely a small part of the vast network of that city's heavily used suburban system. The beginnings were indeed modest, as apart from that inaugural line run by the Great Indian Peninsula Railway, over the next couple of years, there was only the addition of the much longer East Indian Railway, which ran Howrah, on the other side of the river from Calcutta, and Burdwan, with the aim of serving the coalfields of West Bengal. That line was largely intended to carry coal and cotton, and this was typical of other early lines which ran inland from ports largely to enable exports of raw materials – and later imports of manufactured goods, notably clothing from Indian cotton.

That helps debunk the oft-used trope that Britain gave India its railways out of some sort of altruistic philosophy of helping native peoples to develop their land. In fact, it was Lord Dalhousie, the governor general of India between 1848 and 1856, who instigated the creation of the Indian railway system set out in a series of reports that made no attempt to hide the commercial, military and indeed imperial ambitions underpinning the idea. He designed the initial route map, ensuring the selected lines were the most useful for imperial purposes, and he even determined the somewhat eccentric gauge of the tracks, which remains the same today. He also created the system that ensured it was Indians who underwrote the construction of these first railways. The early rail companies were established in London and needed to attract.

UK investors. Therefore, they offered a 5% guarantee for their shareholders if income from the railway was insufficient, with the Indian, not the UK, government having to make up any shortfall. Therefore, while the capital was indeed British, it was serviced by taxing the local population.

The expansion of the railways – not yet a network as the various initial lines were unconnected – was initially slow, and it was not until the rebellion of 1857 that the pace accelerated as the British realised the railways would play a vital role in enforcing their rule. Always outnumbered and only able to afford relatively small garrisons, the colonial rulers realised the railways would, in an emergency, play a vital role by transporting troops and military equipment rapidly across the country. The rebellion stimulated the imposition of rule by the British government, rather than the East India Company, and ministers realised that building railway lines was a cheaper and more effective way of maintaining control over the subcontinent than establishing and maintaining a huge military presence. As a result of this change, many stations in big towns were designed as fortresses, to be easily defended in the event of an insurrection.

Of course, the Indian people benefited greatly from the arrival of the 'Iron Horse'. They may not have been the intended beneficiaries but in a vast country like colonial India – which included what is now Pakistan and Bangladesh – the creation of a fast, efficient transport system inevitably attracted large numbers of users given the alternative was the tortuously slow oxcart that could barely manage three miles per hour. For example, pilgrimages, which might have taken weeks to undertake, became far easier and this led to massive crowds arriving at the most revered religious sites. But more widely, Indians were ready to embrace this new form of transport.

This was despite the conditions they had to put up with in the trains. There seemed at times an almost perverse unwillingness by the railway companies to provide even basic facilities. Not only were there no toilets during the first couple of decades of the railways, but third-class passengers were often locked into their compartments and could not get out to relieve themselves at intermediate stops. It was not until the turn of the century that the issue of toilets in third class was properly addressed and sanitary facilities became universal on trains. In fact, conditions generally for passengers in third class were so bad that fatalities during the summer heat were not uncommon in the overcrowded compartments. It was not unusual for 12 or 14 people to be crowded into compartments that were designed to hold six or eight comfortably. The contrast with first class, which was used almost exclusively by Europeans, and which provided comfortable sofas and spacious compartments, as well as menus that would not have been out of place in the Ritz, could not have been greater. To make matters worse, even though fares in third class were low, it accommodated all but 10% of travellers - with most of the rest in second, leaving only a tiny minority in first – and consequently was the mainstay of income for the railways as it was highly profitable.

Figure 2.1 Matheran Steam Railway.

The poor conditions of rail travel for Indians and the effective bar preventing them from obtaining managerial or even good blue-collar jobs in the service of the railway were undoubtedly key factors in the growth of the independence movement that dated from the last years of the 19th century. It was hardly surprising that the railways, where the first trades unions were established, were a source of industrial trouble, too.

Throughout the back end of the 19th century and the first half of the 20th, the rail network continued to be extended and modernised. While some of the new lines were built for military purposes such as those on the north-west frontier, or for the use of Europeans escaping the summer heat of the Deccan Plateau such as the branch to Simla, a comprehensive network was created. Most of India is geographically easy territory for railway construction, and as well as the private companies, several rulers of the semi-independent states established networks. With roads remaining poor or even non-existent, the railways were the only viable way of travelling long distances – and even many short ones – on the subcontinent. It was not always efficient, often slow and occasionally unsafe but in general the railways were at the heart of the Indian transport system.

Nevertheless, the railways remained very much a colonial project. Gradually the individual railway companies merged or were taken over by the state, but many decisions were still taken by boards in London or by the colonial government. The most egregious aspect of the colonial policy in relation to India was the failure to use the railways as a key economic driver in the way that had happened elsewhere. As the largest industrial enterprise in the country and its largest employer, the Indian Railways should have been the key stimulus for the economic take-off that was occurring in many other countries in the interwar period. The supply chain should have been used as a way of creating a wider industrial base that would have, in turn, led to widespread employment and technology transfer. The railways undoubtedly contributed to improving agricultural output and greatly improving the nation's food security. But unlike in many other countries, they did not affect the basic structure of the economy. As a result, both nations lost out. If the British had, for example, allowed a far greater mingling of the races on the railways, and consciously built up a local managerial class of Indians able to run the system, the bonds between the nations today would be far greater.

Instead, until independence in 1947, virtually all the locomotives and most of the rest of the manufactured equipment needed to run the railway were imported from the UK. And in terms of the personnel, the local workforce was confined to the lower- paid jobs with managers almost exclusively chosen from the European or, at times, Anglo-Indian communities. The Victorian-era colonial ethos that the 'natives' were not capable of undertaking the senior jobs remained. So, for example, Indians were not allowed to drive the faster locomotives on express trains or manage the larger stations, being confined to goods trains and running small rural halts.

This would all change at independence. Nehru rightly saw the railways as an essential component of an independent India's economic take-off and provided the money needed for both modernisation and expansion. The notion that Indians would not be able to run their own railway network without the help of their colonial masters was rapidly debunked. Indeed, after the chaos and destruction of partition, the railways were in a terrible state of repair, and it took a heroic effort by the newly established Indian Railways to transform the network into a workable state.

Figure 2.2: New Delhi Railway station board in English, Hindi and Urdu.

Figure 2.3: A Train at Kanpur Central Railway Station, Kanpur.

This massive organisation employed a million workers and it had to quickly fill the managerial posts vacated by the Europeans who, for the most part, quickly departed to the UK. Considerable efforts were made to standardise and, in particular, 'Indianise' the rail system. The distinction between first- and second-class refreshment rooms, an inherent form of apartheid, was abandoned and all now had to offer Indian food. Distinctions, encouraged by the British, such as having different water taps for Hindus and Muslims, were abandoned and the conditions for the workforce, who previously had been subject to dismissal for the most minor transgressions, were greatly improved. The process of Indianisation was, however, at times overly bureaucratic and the workforce over the first decade after the creation of Indian Railways increased to 1.7 million.

Crucially, though, the Indian railway network not only survived the departure of the British but thrived. As I wrote in *Railways and the Raj* (Wolmar 2017), 'the fact that the railways not only held together in this time of turmoil following independence, but actually flourished in the post-Partition period, was the most powerful rebuke to the British who had so long resisted the Indianisation of the railways'. The hasty departure of the top layer of European management actually inspired their replacements to adopt a 'can-do' spirit to show the British that their skills had been greatly underestimated.

The symbiotic relationship between Indians and their railways has not only ensured their survival but their continued expansion. Major new lines were being added to the system at the same time as other countries around the world were paring back their networks. While slowly a network of highways is, belatedly, being constructed, the railways remain as heavily used as ever and considerable investment is being made to improve them with new rolling stock and, even, new high-speed lines.

As a fully nationalised integrated concern, Indian Railways in a way harks back to the past. Attempts to privatise parts of it have been firmly resisted, and there is now acceptance that this is unlikely in the near future. Rail freight transport in India is profitable, but passenger services have to be subsidised, not least because rail fare rises are deeply unpopular and therefore resisted by politicians. This has resulted in underinvestment in the system, though there are plans for new major investments in the coming decade. The system is undoubtedly a bit ramshackle in places, but appearances can be deceptive.

A first-time visitor to an Indian railway station might only see a vast number of people seemingly in perpetual but not necessarily purposeful motion. There are hawkers and hustlers everywhere, the smell of dal and chai is never very far away, and there is a permanent queue at the ticket office – despite today's widespread computerisation of the system. The second-class carriages, with their bars across the permanently opened windows through which hands stretch out to the food and chai sellers on the platforms, may look rather grim – though Indian Railways is just embarking on a massive replacement programme for them – but, in fact, these huge 24-carriage-long trains are the backbone of the nation's transport system and, by and large, the system works. As my friend the author Rajendra B Aklekar put it, India functions even if it does not always look like that'. As I've previously described, my own personal experience of riding the system is that 'the seat you reserved is available, the dabba wallah brings you your lunch and the train leaves and arrives safely and on time.' What is there not to like?

Reference

Wolmar, C. (2017), Railways and The Raj: How the Age of Steam Transformed India, Atlantic Books, London.

About the contributor

Christian Wolmar is a writer and broadcaster specialising in transport. He has written more than 20 books including *Railways and the Raj, How the Age of Steam Transformed India* which was published by Atlantic Books in 2017. His latest book *British Rail, A New History*, is published by Penguin.

Chapter 3

India: 75 years of innovation and beyond

Ventakesh Vijay, Makhan Singh, Pratik Dattani and P. Jagadeesh

Introduction

Since the start of civilisation, India has been a place of invention and creativity. From the discovery of 'zero' to the founding of the world's first university, from shampoo to Snakes and Ladders, India has been at the forefront of numerous innovations. The world's first higher education institution, Takshashila University, was founded in India; chess is thought to have originated in eastern India; and the word shampoo, which originates from 1762, is derived from the Hindi word 'chmpo'. The shampoo was first used as a head massage in the Mughal Empire's eastern territories. Ayurveda, known to be the world's oldest healing/medicinal system, is an ancient Indian medical practice that goes back to the Iron Age.

India has made significant progress in agriculture, heavy industry, irrigation, energy production, nuclear power capabilities, space technology, biotechnology, telecommunications, oceanography and science education/research over the previous seven and a half decades. India has become an IT giant with one of the world's largest scientific personnel and railway networks. The new India is on the verge of making a quantum leap ahead in science and technology. On 15 August 1947, the nation gained independence from British sovereignty, and over the last 75 years, India has surmounted several challenges, and Indians have achieved global prominence in various sectors, setting new standards in physics, mathematics, medicine, chemistry, literature, music, cinema, sports and space exploration. Over the years, India has seen various transformations, and Indians have seen significant changes in their lives, from the political arena to social life. This has been aided by investment in scientific research and the establishment of eminent centres of research including the Indian Institutes of Technology.

Significant contributions to science and technology

India has benefited from the contributions of many creative minds in science and technology, enhancing its global standing. India boasts the world's second-largest population of scientists and engineers, and Indian scientists have devised various initiatives to improve the lives of the world's population due to technological developments and scientific achievements. The following subsections provide examples of excellence over the past 75 years.

Figure 3.1: Science and Technology Heritage of India Gallery - Science Exploration Hall - Science City - Kolkata.

Agriculture – food grain production hits a new high

Even though there was some slowness in harnessing the advancements of the late modern age, India's sovereign republic was allowed to construct a complete agricultural strategy, India has made great progress in food security since its independence. The Indian population has increased more than threefold, while agricultural goods output has increased fourfold. It is interesting to note that India used to rely on imported commodities and supplies to meet its basic needs until the 1960s. Moreover, the extreme drought of 1965 and 1966 persuaded India that it needed to transform its domestic policy and stop depending on international assistance and foreign goods for agricultural production. Significant policy reforms were made in India to achieve agricultural goods self-sufficiency. The Green Revolution in India began with this event. It all began with the choice to increase production by combining significantly greater, disease-resistant crop varieties with increased farming knowledge. Punjab, often known as the breadbasket of India, was at the forefront of the country's Green Revolution. India's Green Revolution technique was adapted to rice production after its agricultural policy success in wheat. Indian farmers created wells to extract groundwater due to a lack of irrigation infrastructure. When the benefits of modern technology reached their limitations in the states where it was first adopted in the 1970s and 1980s, the technology was shifted to Bihar, Odisha and West Bengal in eastern India. Improved seeds and new technology had the most significant long- term benefits in irrigated agriculture, representing nearly a third of all harvested crops. Farmers began to accept superior technologies and methods in dairy production, fishery and cattle to supply the diversified food requirements of an expanding population. Improved seeds and farming technology, like rice, are now largely dependent on India's infrastructure investment, such as irrigation facilities, flood protection systems, reliable energy production capability, all-season rural and urban key roadways, and cold rooms to protect quality.

Education

Literacy growth is widely regarded as a sign of increased educational attainment. The spread of education at all levels in India has helped to increase the country's literacy rate. Over 50 years, the number of literate people in the country has grown tenfold, from 57 million in 1951 to 570 million in 2001. Some of the educational achievements in India include the following:

Mathematics

Srinivasa Ramanujan was a mathematician, and he is widely regarded as the finest mathematician of the 20th century. Srinivasa Ramanujan made significant contributions to analytical number theory by working on elliptic functions, continuous fractions and exponentials. His published and unpublished works have influenced some of the world's most brilliant mathematicians.

Science and engineering

Indian scientist Dr Shanti Swarup Bhatnagar was highly respected. Science and engineering had always attracted him since he was a child. Along with Homi Bhabha, Prasanta Chandra Mahalanobis, Vikram Sarabhai and others, Shanti Swarup Bhatnagar made substantial contributions to India's post-independence technological and scientific infrastructure, as well as the creation of its science policies.

Physics

One of India's most well-known scientists is C. V. Raman whose intellectual prowess was obvious from a young age. In 1930, C.V. Raman received the Nobel Prize in Physics for his groundbreaking work on light scattering. He was the first Asian and non-White individual to be awarded the Nobel Prize in Physics. When light passes through a transparent substance, he noticed that part of the deflected light changes wavelength. The Raman Effect causes this phenomenon, known as Raman scattering. Raman also researched musical instrument acoustics. He was the first to analyse the harmonics of the tabla and mridangam drum tones.

Palaeobotany

Birbal Sahni was a well-known Indian palaeobotanist who specialised in studying Indian subcontinent fossils. In Lucknow, Uttar Pradesh, Sahni established the Birbal Sahni Institute of Palaeobotany. He was a geologist with a passion for archaeology and an innovator in palaeobotanical institutions in India. He was widely feted and honoured. In 1936, he became the first Indian botanist to be elected a Fellow of the Royal Society of London, the highest scientific honour in the UK.

Chemical industry

According to the India Brand Equity Foundation (www.ibef.org) in 2019, India's chemical sector (which includes fertilisers and pharmaceuticals) was valued at USD 178 billion, and it is expected to rise to USD 304 billion by 2024–25, with an annual growth rate of 9.3%. India is Asia's third-largest chemical producer and the world's sixth-largest, and India is rated 14th in terms of chemical exports.

Chemical and pharmaceutical works

Prafulla Chandra Ray, a well-known professor and pharmacist, founded Bengal Chemicals and Pharmaceutical Drugs, India's first pharmaceutical enterprise. Prafulla Chandra was employed as an Assistant Professor of Chemistry at Presidency College Calcutta in 1889. His papers on exceptional nitrite and related compounds gained him widespread acclaim. His teaching ability was crucial since he motivated a fresh era of Indian researchers to establish an Indian chemistry school. Among his students were Meghnad Saha and Shanti Swarup Bhatnagar, two well-known Indian scientists. Prafulla Chandra played a key role in the growth of India's industries. He built India's first chemical industry with extremely minimal materials and from his home. The Bengal Chemical and Pharmaceutical Works Ltd was founded in 1901 due to this vision.

India is commonly known as 'the pharmacy of the world' today. This is due to the supply of affordable, effective drugs and vaccines to different countries of the world, which we saw most recently during the Covid pandemic. The journey started with the establishment of Hindustan Antibiotics Limited in 1954, followed by Indian Drugs and Pharmaceuticals Limited with Soviet assistance. Also, the council of the Central Drug Research Institute was expanded further for private sector laboratories, which played a genesis role in creating an environment for Indian pharmaceutical research to flourish.

The Patent Act of 1970 recognised only process patents, which meant Indian companies could make copies of patented drugs using alternative processes. It enabled India to supply cost-effective drugs to Africa and other markets in need, which could not afford expensive American or European products.

Energy production

By 2025, India will become the world's largest power user/consumer and third-largest exporter of green energy, with green energy contributing 38% of total energy output (136 GW out of 373 GW). India's installed renewable energy capacity, is the fourth- greatest globally, with the fourth-largest wind and fifth-largest solar capacity. In 1992, India became one of the first countries to create a Department of Non-Conventional Energy Sources, which was named the Ministry of New and Renewable Energy in 2006.

Figure 3.2: Green energy, windmills – panoramio

This is a monument to India's goal of promoting renewable energy sources since the beginning of sustainable development. Since then, the Indian government has undertaken actions to stimulate the development and use of renewable energy to aid the country's growth and prosperity. India was named a 'Global Champion' for energy change at the United Nations High-Level Dialogue on Energy. The country has developed numerous groundbreaking projects which have resulted in these achievements. Looking ahead, India is on the way to becoming a global leader in the battery sector too, with large-scale energy storage facilities in the pipeline across the country, including using British Intellectual Property from Sheffield-based Faradion.

Nuclear power capability

India has a nuclear energy system that is virtually self-sufficient. As part of its vast infrastructure development aim, the Indian government is dedicated to improving nuclear-generating capacity, with lofty goals for expanding nuclear-generating capacity.

Astrophysics

Meghnad Saha was as born in the Dacca district which is now part of Bangladesh, and had established himself as a distinguished physicist by 1920. He made contributions to the thermal ionisation of elements, leading to the development of the Saha equation. This formula is among the simplest basic strategies for analysing star spectra in astrophysics. The Saha equation, which explains his theory of the high-temperature electrostatic interaction of chemicals and its utilisation of stellar atmospheres, is fundamental to modern astronomy; further elaborations of his concepts have contributed to a deeper explanation of stellar environment pressure and temperature variations. The temperature of various stars can be determined by evaluating their wavelengths and then applying Saha's equation to determine the ionisation energy states of the different atoms that build up the star. He also devised a method for determining the mass and intensity of sunbeams. He was the most influential river designer and engineer in India. He was the first person to sketch out the Damodar Valley Project design. He was a driving force behind establishing scientific organisations across India and technology-based national financial management.

Space technology

Indian astronomers have found one of the universe's furthest star galaxies, marking a watershed moment in space exploration.

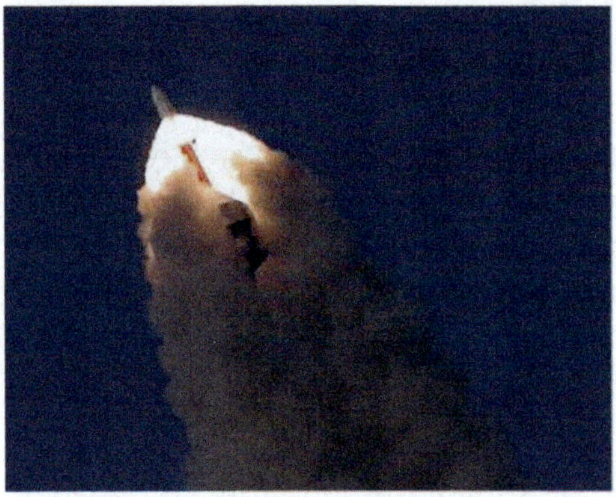

Figure 3.3: The Crew Escape System test Satish Dhawan Space Centre, Sriharikota, Andhra Pradesh.

Solar astronomy

Arvind Bhatnagar made substantial contributions to solar research and established several planetaria throughout India. The Udaipur Solar Research Centre and the Mumbai Nehru Planetarium were founded and directed by him.

Indian space programme

Vikram Sarabhai was a well-known scientist from India. He is widely regarded as the founder of India's space exploration. One of several initiatives which he coordinated included the launch of India's first spacecraft, Aryabhata, in 1975. Sarabhai, like Bhabha, was concerned with making science's practical applications more accessible to the general public.

As a result, he recognised a once-in-a-lifetime chance to employ space research to help the country flourish in. communication, atmospheric science, satellite imagery and teaching. In 1975–76, the Satellite Instructional Television Experiment (SITE) trained five million people in 2,400 Indian communities.

To promote science among college students, he founded the National Science Museum in Ahmedabad in 1965. He and his wife, Mrinalini

Sarabhai, founded Darpana Institute, a non-profit dedicated to the performing arts and disseminating India's ancient culture due to their shared cultural interests.

He was a scientist, an inventor, an industrialist and a visionary, among other things. He received the Bhatnagar Memorial Prize for Astrophysics in 1962, the Padma Bhushan in 1966, and the Padma Vibhushan later. He was Chairman of the Atomic Energy Commission from 1966 to 1968, Deputy Chief and Chairman of the United Nations Conference on Peaceful Purposes of Interstellar Space from 1968 to 1969, and President of the International Atomic Energy Firm's 14th General Conference from 1969 to 1970.

Dr. Vikram Sarabhai

Chandrayaan-1, India's first lunar exploration mission, made it possible for the Indian Space Research Organisation to go beyond the geostationary orbit in 2008. India emerged as only the fourth country to hoist its flag on a lunar surface. The Magalyaan-1 Mars orbiter mission made India the only country in the world to reach Mars on its first attempt, and only the fourth to reach the surface of Mars at all. The Indian Space Research Organisation also demonstrated its capability of handling complex missions by successfully launching a record 104 satellites in sun-synchronous orbits, through the PSLV-C37 mission in 2007.

Figure 3.4: The Secretary, Department of Space, Chairman, Space Commission and Chairman, Indian Space Research Organisation (ISRO), Shri A.S. Kiran Kumar releasing the Compendium on Indian Space Industry.

Oceanographer

Aditi Pant is a well-known oceanographer from India. In 1983, she was a member of the Indian Antarctic expedition, and she was the first Indian woman to explore the continent (along with Sudipta Sengupta). Dr Aditi received the Antarctica medal from the Indian government, as did Dr Jaya Naithani and Dr Kanwal Vilku, for their excellent contributions to the Antarctic programme.

Summary

As one of the oldest civilisations in the world, with an inspiring cultural history, it comes as no surprise that India, as of 2021, has the third-highest number of incubators in the world with over 250 incubators being present. Many significant inventions have come out of India – indeed, over the past 75 years, India has seen an exponential growth in innovations and inventions. It will be very intriguing for our children and future generations to observe what the next 75 years will bring.

About the contributors

Dr Venkatesh Vijay leads the Knowledge-Based Engineering lab in BCU. His expertise involves virtual reality, augmented reality, mixed reality, artificial intelligence, embedded systems and developing educational tools using a gaming environment. Vijay has secured and been part of several successful grants in the field of visualisation, decision support systems and virtual/augmented reality. Currently, Vijay is working on the STEAMhouse India initiative established by the Munjal family-run BCM Foundation and BCU at Ludhiana (India), namely the Munjal Birmingham University Centre of Innovation and Entrepreneurship, to promote innovative education, industrial innovation and start-ups in the region.

Pratik Dattani is managing director of economic consulting firm EPG, specialising in market entry advisory and strategic communications, with offices in the UK, India and Uganda. Pratik is additionally UK Director for the Federation of Indian Chambers of Commerce and Industry. He sits on the board of leading think tank Bridge India and is co-founder of a charity advisory initiative, helping major donors give better. Earlier, he worked at FTI Consulting and Deloitte in London and Abu Dhabi, with a focus on international arbitration. He was formerly chair of a non-profit organisation with several thousand members. He read Economics at Warwick University, where he was awarded the Prize for Excellence, and LMU University of Munich. Pratik has published academic research on behavioural economics and social impact and contributed to various books.

Dr P. Jagadeesh is Assistant Professor in Saveetha School of Engineering, Saveetha Institute of Medical and Technical Sciences. He received his B.Tech degree in ECE from Bharthiyar College of Engg. Tech. Karaikal, Pondichery University; M.Tech degree in VLSI Design from VIT University, Vellore, Tamil Nadu; and PhD from Saveetha School of Engineering, Saveetha Institute of Medical and Technical Sciences. He has published 40 papers in Scopus-indexed journals, participated and presented 12 papers in international conference proceedings. He also filed for two patents in 2020. He received the Research Excellence Award 2021 from InSc Awards and the Dr Sarvepalli Radhakrishnan Best Teacher Award from society for learning technologies in 2021. His research interests include medical image processing and pattern recognition, and ASIC design using Verilog HDL.

Chapter 4

The developing landscape of midwifery in India

Natasha Carr, Maggie Prain, Inderjeet Kaur and Radha Reddy

Summary

Presenting the historical perspective of morbidity and mortality in India, this chapter demonstrates the evidence for the need and development of midwives. A case study of the Fernandez Foundation, Hyderabad, reveals an effective model of midwifery education, in line with international midwifery standards, to provide respectful maternity care.

Introduction

The Republic of India is the seventh-largest country in the world and the second- most densely populated. The birth rate has decreased to between 1.6 to 2.0 births per childbearing woman (National Family Health Survey, NFHS-5, 2019–21), comparable to the UK statistics of 1.58 average births per woman (Office of National Statistics ONS, 2021). However, due to the extensive population growth, India's citizens will grow at a greater rate. Yet, most women do not experience the care and support offered by midwives during this time. Childbirth is a very different experience for many women. This chapter provides the current position of midwifery provision in India and why midwives trained to a high standard can impact women and family health. A case study of the Fernandez Foundation will be used to illustrate how respectful maternity care can be facilitated by midwives trained using the International Confederation of Midwives' definition of midwifery (ICM, 2017).

Evidence for effective midwifery care

Most maternal and newborn deaths occur on the day of birth, with more than 40% happening in these first 24 hours (Lawn et al., 2014). As such, focusing on the provision of high-quality assessment and care during this time has the potential to save the highest number of women, neonates and stillborns (Lawn et al., 2014).

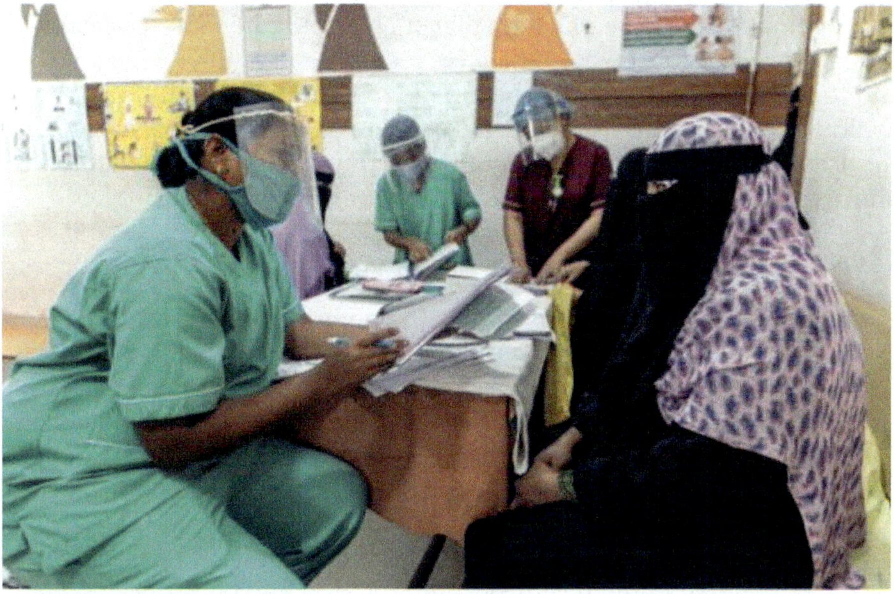

Figure 4.1: Taking a detailed history to risk assess, plan, and provide appropriate maternity care.

The United Nations Fund for Population Activities (UNFPA) estimates that a country's cadre of midwives, trained to international standards of competency and properly regulated, could provide care for as much as 8% of essential newborn and maternal services (UNFPA, 2014). Unfortunately, India does not currently have a cadre of midwives trained to international levels of competence. Therefore, it is crucial to comprehend and enhance India's midwifery education, regulation and practice, because professionally trained midwives will make an impact (Homer et al., 2014). Homer et al. (2014) found that by providing family planning advice, there were fewer pregnancies, resulting in a reduction of 57% of all deaths related to childbirth. Furthermore, the addition of midwifery care could avert 83% of all maternal deaths, stillbirths and neonatal deaths. Midwifery care has the most significant effect when provided within a health system, with effective referral and transfer mechanisms to specialist care. India does have a functioning health system, but midwifery needs a higher priority.

India's neonatal mortality rate has improved since 1970, with 84 per 1,000 live births reduced to 20:1,000 live births in 2020 (UNICEF,

2022). The government of India recognises a role for midwifery to reduce this further. Nadda in 2018, the Minister of Health and Welfare, while acknowledging the advances in healthcare, suggested that further improvements could be made by placing the midwife more centrally in the care process for most women. He recommended 85% of secondary and tertiary centre care could be moved to midwifery, resulting in both health and economic benefits. Launching guidelines for midwifery services which adopted the Sustainable Development Goals aimed to improve the health indicators for maternal and infant mortality.

The challenges in India

Mayra et al. (2021) summarised that Indian midwifery education faces multiple challenges: a lack of qualified educators, an incongruity between theory and practice in learning, a lack of practical experience, and gender-based discrimination and stigma. Currently, India does not have a cadre of competent, independent midwives (ICM, 2013). Midwifery education is provided as part of a three-year diploma course called General Nursing and Midwifery (GNM) or a four-year BSc nursing degree. Ideally, the ICM recommends a course duration of three years for a direct-entry midwifery programme following appropriate school education or an 18-month training programme for registered nurses (ICM, 2021). ICM education standards (2021) also recommend that midwifery educators are qualified according to the ICM definition of a midwife and demonstrate competency in practice, generally accomplished with a minimum of two years of full-scope practice. Future students can learn from their example, with students having sufficient midwifery practice experience in facility- based and community care settings, including women's homes, to attain the current ICM Essential Competencies for Midwifery Practice.

The solution

The National Health Mission (NHM), launched by the government of India, has initiated operational guidelines to implement midwifery education (2018). The Indian Nursing Council (INC) and State Nursing Councils play vital roles in regulating nursing and midwifery education in India, overseeing registration, licensing, inspection and examination. These roles are duplicated at the national and state levels with significant variation in inter- and intra-state-level maternity care (Government of India, 2018).

Figure 4.2: Midwives and educators at Fernandez Foundation.

In India, nurse-midwives join the workforce after completing two to four years of mandatory pre-service education, which aims to provide nursing and midwifery professional skills.

The midwifery profession in India is underdeveloped; concerning the ICM aspirations, it is still dominated by nursing. This model leads to approximately 32,000 pregnant women dying each year during pregnancy, childbirth and the postnatal period. Additionally, 59,000 newborns die each year in the first month of life, the time when midwives can make a difference (Government of India, 2018). The government of India's decision in 2018 to initiate midwifery care across the country to strengthen the response to maternal and newborn morbidity and mortality will provide safe and fair practice for women. The government issued national guidelines for midwifery to expand the reach of professional midwifery and its transformative model of care, compliant with international standards issued by the INC. In addition, the government is strongly dedicated to the Social Development Goals, with its 'sab ka Saath, sab ka Vikas' or 'development with all, and for all' policy initiatives.

The Social Development Goals align with developing a professional midwifery workforce following a midwife's ICM scope of practice (2017). To improve the health of the family and the wider community, the midwife has a vital role in public health for childbirth and sexual, reproductive and childcare education. Woman are central to developing family health and reducing mortality, hence needing support to achieve this role. In addition, women are often responsible for the nutrition and hygiene needs of the family. Thus, higher levels of education among mothers will positively impact children's nutrition and reduce child deaths and maternal mortality

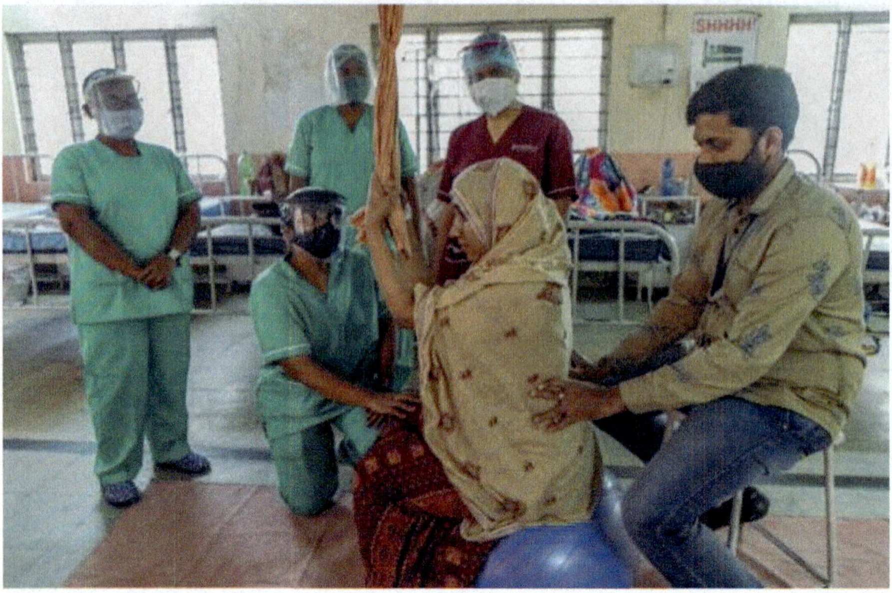

Figure 4.3: Facilitating family-centred care and education; note partner involvement.

India is progressing to reduce the under-five mortality rate, which declined from 125 per 1,000 live births in 1990–91 to 50 per 1,000 live births in 2015–16. The Maternal Mortality Ratio of India has shown a decline from 212 in 2007–09 to 167 per 100,000 in 2011–13 (United Nations, undated). Furthermore, by 2030, India's Social Development Goals aim to:

reduce the global maternal mortality ratio to less than 70 per 100,000 live births, as maternal mortality is a strong indicator for measuring the attention paid to the healthcare of women;

end preventable deaths of newborns and children under five years of age, with all countries aiming to reduce neonatal mortality to at least as low as 12 per 1,000 live births and under-five mortality to at least as low as 25 per 1,000 live births;

ensure universal access to sexual and reproductive healthcare services, including family planning, information and education, and the integration of reproductive health into national strategies and programmes.

Specifically focusing on maternal health programmes (antenatal to postnatal care), key initiatives have been instigated. Pradhan Mantri Surakshit Matritva Abhiyan, under the NHM, was launched to provide comprehensive and quality antenatal care universally to all pregnant women, including second/third trimester appointments (National Health Mission, 2022), and a focus on nutrition with a variety of programmes being formulated such as Village Health and Nutrition Days (outreach services for comprehensive maternal and child healthcare:

take-home rations

integrated child development services

supplementation of iron and folic acid

POSHAN Abhiyan (India's flagship scheme to improve the nutritional outcomes of adolescents, children, pregnant women and lactating mothers) (POSHAN 2018)

Although institutional births (i.e. those not occurring at home) have increased following incentive schemes aimed at reducing maternal morbidity, mortality and sepsis, the rates have not reduced proportionately. Hence, the government has introduced programmes such as the LaQshya-Labour Room Quality Improvement Initiative, aimed to improve quality care services to mothers during the intrapartum and immediate postpartum period (NHM, 2017), Surakshit Matritva Ashwasan (SUMAN), to promote delivery of and provide access to free and quality care services (https://suman.nhp.gov.in/).

Initiatives are not enough without the appropriately trained midwives and maternity staff. Appropriately trained midwifes are essential to improve the mortality and morbidity rates and truly make a difference and this is where the evidence base lies (Homer et al., 2014).

Fernandez case study

The Fernandez Hospitals provide care exclusively for women and newborns in Hyderabad, Telangana state, and are dedicated to improving the health and welfare of mothers and newborns. Desiring to provide compassionate, evidence-based care to mothers and incorporate midwifery into maternity care delivery, the Fernandez Foundation has been educating midwives for over a decade, using an 18-month model of education, being leaders in promoting woman-centred, respectful quality maternity care and providing jobs with salaries and working conditions in respected careers for women, all assisted by UK midwives. They also prepare midwifery educators as part of a countrywide expansion of training, improving education, maternity and public health (Table 4.1). This is especially important as the State of Telangana had experienced an extreme shift to over-medicalisation with a 58% Caesarean section rate in public facilities and a 75% Caesarean section rate in private facilities. This situation highlights the need to have an alternative model of delivery of care (Government of India, 2018). In addition, Kruk et al. (2018) showed that India had almost double the number of deaths due to poor-quality healthcare than deaths due to the non-utilisation of healthcare services.

Fernandez's model of midwifery education has been recognised by the government, with the consultant in maternal health and director of midwifery being core members of the 'National Midwifery Task Force' set up by the Ministry of Health, which is summarised as follows (Government of India, 2018, p. 319):

> In 2011, the Professional Midwifery Education and Training Programme was conducted by the Fernandez Hospital.
>
> In 2014, Fernandez Hospital was given accreditation to provide the Post-basic Diploma in Nurse Practitioner in Midwifery (NPM); this was made available to ten students.
>
> In 2017, the government of Telangana initiated a tripartite partnership between the state government, UNICEF and Fernandez Hospital to train nursing students in midwifery using 18-month courses based on ICM competencies.
>
> Training is supported by the NHM.
>
> A total of 126 midwifery posts were created by the state government; however, the national regulatory framework was lacking until recently for those midwives trained to be independent.

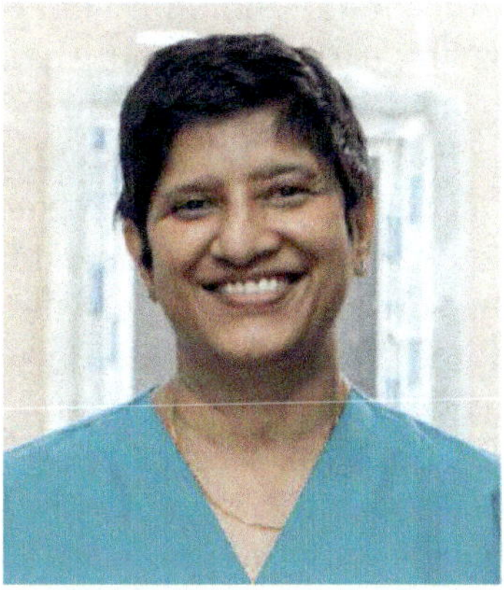

Figure 4.4: Indie Kaur, Director of Midwifery

Now backed by the Ministry and the INC, midwifery has been brought centre stage at a national level through the publication of Midwifery Guidelines (Government of India, 2018), following a landmark policy decision. It is recognised that midwifery-led care plays a crucial part in promoting physiological birth, reducing over-medicalisation, and providing dignified quality care to mothers and babies while contributing to the Social Development Goals. The new guidance discusses woman-centric care with respectful maternal and newborn care using new specialist Nurse Practitioners in Midwifery in line with global standards and The Lancet Series on Midwifery (2014). They have 18 months of training as per international standards (ICM, 2021) and the introduction of midwifery-led units at public health facilities. This regulation allows nurse-midwives to practise autonomously and provide all midwifery care. Currently, the INC regulates midwives in India and is in the process of amending the 1947 Act. Under the new amendment, INC will be renamed the Indian Nursing and Midwifery Council (Government of India, 2018) with a revised national curriculum. This is yet to be enacted but is in the public domain for consultation. The draft Bill has included midwifery, which improves the current Act, which only consists of the term 'nursing', standardises entry and exit requirements and brings regulation under centralised governmental control (Mathew, 2020; Akhter, 2021).

Figure 4.5: Dr Evita Fernandez and members of medical staff at the Fernandez Foundation.

Fernandez the institution mirrors the aspirations of national midwifery training in India and has the necessary infrastructure such as maternal and child health labs, classrooms, and other facilities (Government of India, 2018). The training is further strengthened by partnerships with international and national institutions of repute for expertise, observerships, faculty learning, research activities, innovations and partnerships with BCU in the UK. In addition, Fernandez conducts the education of midwifery educators aligned to the WHO Midwifery Educator Core Competencies (2013) and recognises that the key to a competent workforce is education. Completion of a recognised midwifery education programme has not always been the case in India, although now there are excellent strides forwards with the publication of the scope The government of India is developing a pool of midwifery educators compliant with the INC. The Fernandez Foundation uses practical apprenticeship-style training, supported by midwives from the UK. It is one of six institutes selected in India for the national midwifery educators training programme and the first to launch. The government of India has recognised the Fernandez Foundation as a National Midwifery Training Institute and in collaboration with the WHO is training 30 midwifery educators across five states.

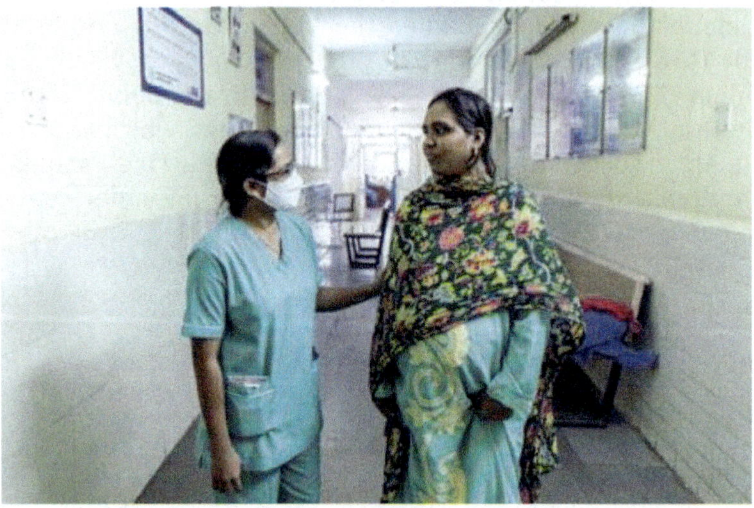

Figure 4.6: Educating, empowering and advocating for women.

Name of the programme	Batch	No. of trainees	Status
Nurse Practitioner Midwifery Educator (NPME) training			
NPME programme for govt. of India in collaboration with WHO	1	29	Completed 6-month residential training and currently undergoing 12-month internship
NPME programme for govt. of Telangana in collaboration with UNICEF	1	11	Completed 18-month training and they are mentoring NPM trainees in Telangana
	2	11	Started their training in Feb 2022
	Total NPME trainees to date	**51**	
NPM training			
Govt. of Telangana in collaboration with UNICEF	1	30	Midwives are currently posted in 16 public hospitals across 12 districts of Telangana
	2	50	To be posted in various public health hospitals from April 2022
	3	136	Currently undergoing clinical training; will be posted in Aug 2022 after their final examinations
	4	200	Currently undergoing theory sessions
Govt. of Andhra Pradesh	1	60	Currently undergoing theory sessions
	Total NPM trainees to date	**476**	

Table 4.1: Numbers of midwifery educators (MEs) trained for both government of India and government of Telangana (ME:trainee ratio 1:10) by 31 March 2022

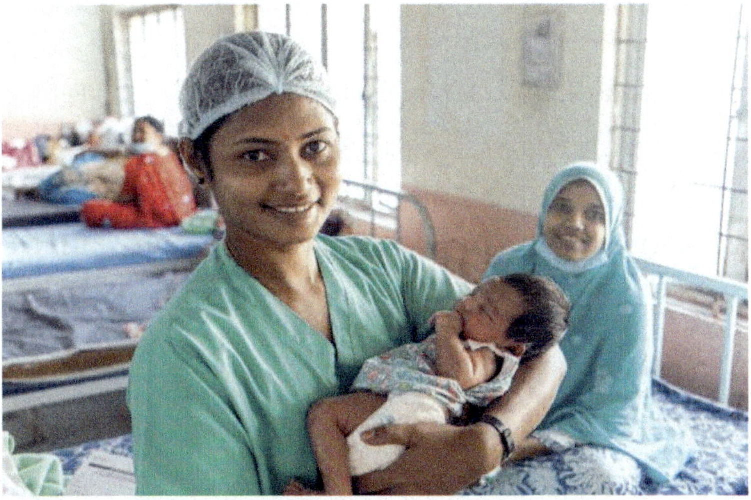

Figure 4.7: Caring for mum and baby in the postnatal period; part of the midwife's role.

Conclusion

Looking to the future development, the Director of Midwifery at Fernandez has stated that India needs to look at midwifery independently from the nursing profession. Striving for a direct-entry curriculum, which is successful in other countries such as the UK, will enable midwifery to actualise its autonomy (Akhter, 2021). However, to achieve this, India's midwifery education institutions need to also be at the same level as their UK counterparts, where degree-level qualification is the basic level of education.

References

Akhter, S. (2021) 'Until India sees professional midwifery as a separate entity, it will struggle to gain the autonomy it deserves: Inderjeet Kaur', https://health.economictimes.indiatimes.com/news/policy/until-india-sees-professional-midwifery-as-a-separate-entity-it-will-struggle-to-gain-the-autonomy- it-deserves-inderjeet-kaur/86493739

Government of India (2018) Operational guidelines on midwifery services in India, MIDWIFERY_GUIDELINE.pdf (nhm.gov.in)

Government of India (2021) Scope of practice for midwifery educators and nurse practitioners midwife, 1626159560175927057460ed39c8888fe.pdf (indiannursingcouncil.org)

Homer, C.S.E, Friberg, I.K, Dias M.A.B., ten Hoope-Bender, P., Sandall, J., Speciale, A.M. and Bartlett, L.A. (2014) 'The projected effect of scaling up midwifery', The Lancet, 384(9948), https://doi.org/10.1016/S0140-6736(14)60790-X

ICM (2011) International Confederation of Midwives Global Standards for Midwifery Regulation, GLOBAL STANDARDS FOR MIDWIFERY REGULATION ENG (internationalmidwives.org)

ICM (2017) Definition of a Midwife, https://www.internationalmidwives.org/assets/ files/definitions-files/2018/06/eng-definition_of_the_midwife-2017.pdf

ICM (2021) Global Standards for Midwifery Education global-standards-for-midwifery-education_2021_en.pdf (internationalmidwives.org)

Kruk, M.E., Gage, A.D., Joseph, N.T., Danaei, G., García-Saisó, S. and Salomon, J.A. (2018) 'Mortality due to low-quality health systems in the universal health coverage era: a systematic analysis of amenable deaths in 137 countries', The Lancet (Supplement).

Lawn, J.E. et al. (2014) Every Newborn – An Executive Summary of the Lancet's Series. May 2014.

Mathew, A. (2020) 'Health Ministry to repeal Nursing Act, replace Indian Nursing Council with govt-controlled body', National Herald

Health Ministry to repeal Nursing Act, replace Indian Nursing Council with govt- controlled body (nationalheraldindia.com)

Ministry of Health and Family Welfare, Government of India, (2022) SURAKSHIT MATRITVA AASHWASAN (Suman). An initiative for zero preventable maternal and newborn deaths. https://suman.nhp.gov.in/ accessed 17/10/22

Ministry of Health and Family Welfare, Government of India (2022) Labour Room Quality Improvement Initiative. https://nhm.gov.in/New_Updates_2018/NHM_ Components/RMNCH_MH_Guidelines/LaQshya-Guidelines.pdf, accessed 1/10/22

Mayra, K., Padmadas, S.S., Matthews, Z. (2021) 'Challenges and needed reforms in midwifery and nursing regulatory systems in India: implications for education and practice', PLoS ONE 16(5), e0251331, https://doi.org/10.1371/journal. pone.0251331

National Family Health Survey, India (NHS-5) (2019–21). Database to strengthen India's Demographic and Health Policy Programmes http://rchiips.org/nfhs/ factsheet_NFHS-5.shtml

ONS (2021) Maternal Death https://www.ons.gov.uk/aboutus/transparencyand governance/freedomofinformationfoi/maternaldeath Accessed 11.4.22. Updated 2021.

POSHAN (2018) Poshan Abhiyaan or National Nutrition Mission https://www.niti. gov.in/poshan-abhiyaan, accessed 11.4.22

The Lancet (2014). Midwifery: an executive summary for The Lancet's series. http:// www.thelancet.com/series/midwifery

UNFPA (2014) The State of the World's Midwifery – A Universal Pathway, A Woman's Right to Health, https://www.unfpa.org/sowmy-2014, accessed 11.4.22

United Nations in India (undated) SDG 3: Good Health And Well-being (un.org), accessed 11.4.22

UNICEF (2022) UNICEF Data Warehouse. Monitoring the situation of children and women
https://data.unicef.org/resources/data_explorer/unicef_f/?ag=UNICEF&df=GLOBAL_DATAFLOW&ver=1.0&dq=IND.CME_MRM0.&startPeriod=1970&endPeriod=2022, accessed 13.3.22

WHO (2013) Midwifery educator core competencies 13012 WHO Midwifery educator core competencies_Dec4th, accessed 13.3.22

About the contributors

Natasha Carr is a Senior Midwifery Lecturer at BCU. She is a practising midwife who is passionate about maternity education and the care of women, babies and families. She is the course lead for the midwifery programmes at BCU. Natasha has experienced a variety of roles and positions in both the National Health Service and the education sector. She has been course lead for supervision of midwives, professional midwifery advocacy and undergraduate midwifery education. She has taught across both undergraduate and postgraduate courses, designed curricula and undertaken overseas education provision. Clinically, while starting her career in the NHS as a nurse in intensive care, midwifery soon became her passion and has remained so for many years. She continues to undertake clinical midwifery infant screening as a Newborn and Infant Physical Examination Practitioner and in her role as a Professional Midwifery Advocate.

Since 2019, Natasha has been involved in supporting education of midwives and development of midwifery in India at the Fernandez Foundation, Hyderabad. Recent activity has involved visits to India to teach and assess midwifery educators and students, working alongside local midwives and other international educators and midwives.

Natasha has a Master's degree in medical ethics and law, and is currently undertaking a PhD investigating the experience of midwives who have made errors in practice.

Maggie Prain is a Senior Midwifery Lecturer at BCU. She is a practising midwife who is passionate about maternity education and ensuring the midwives of the future are equipped with skills to excel. Throughout her

18 years working in the NHS as a nurse and midwife and then 19 years working at BCU, Maggie has enjoyed a variety of roles as Course Lead for Examination of the Newborn and Infant Screening for the past six years. Prior to this, she was the course lead for the postgraduate midwifery education provision for six years. Clinically she achieved a senior midwifery management role with responsibility for implementing research into practice.

Since 2019 Maggie has taken a keen interest in supporting midwifery education in India, specifically students and midwifery educators in the Fernandez Foundation. She has recently returned from an international midwifery education visit to the Fernandez Foundation where she has been teaching midwifery educators, supporting student midwives and auditing midwifery education across Telangana. Maggie is committed to ensuring that the philosophies of respectful, safe and compassionate care of women are provided internationally.

Maggie is currently undertaking a PhD investigating back pain in pregnancy. She is proud to have successfully completed the Advanced Higher Education Aurora Leadership Programme, progressing gender equality in education, and acts as a mentor inspiring leaders of the future. She continues to undertake clinical midwifery infant screening.

Inderjeet Kaur is Director of Midwifery at Fernandez Hospital, Hyderabad. She has spent the last five years in India training professional midwives and providing clinical leadership to midwives in the Fernandez Foundation and the government of Telangana and India. She is passionate about reducing maternal mortality via midwifery training and respectful humanised care for Indian mothers. Her background as a consultant midwife for public health with Barts Health NHS Trust in the Royal London Hospital and Newham generated an interest in improving health and outcomes for women from marginalised societies. She is highly qualified with a strong academic and professional background in clinical leadership and strategic change management. She is also a member of the East London Saving Lives (ELLY) team and as a team leader she has provided maternal obstetric midwifery training in India. Her work in India was published in the September 16 MIDDIRS. The team has organised several multi-collaborative training workshops in South India and now Fernandez Hospital has home-grown trainers in obstetric emergencies.

Inderjeet is passionate about reducing health inequalities of vulnerable women. She has successfully launched, in partnership with My Body Back Project, the world's first maternity clinic in the Royal London Hospital to support women who have experienced sexual violence. She has previously successfully developed a seamless pathway of care for women with complex social needs in a deprived East London area, reducing inequality of healthcare and ensuring access specially to refugee and migrant groups. This initiative won a British Medical Journal award. She received the Chief Midwifery Officer Gold Award for outstanding contribution to the midwifery profession, maternity services and ultimately the lives of women and babies around the world in November 2019.

Dr Radha Reddy is a medical doctor with an MD in Community Medicine and ten years' working experience in public health especially in handling government projects. She has held leadership positions with responsibility for quality improvement and successful change management initiatives. She has experience as state nodal for Karnataka Health Department in planning, budgeting and execution of the National Urban Health Mission (NUHM) and handling an estimated annual budget of more than 100 crores for the project. In particular, Dr Reddy played a key role in the nationwide launch of NUHM in 2014. She subsequently worked as a State Consultant in Maternal Health (part of UNICEF) for the government of Telangana, where she was instrumental in improving the quality of care in maternity areas and implemented specific projects such as a midwifery programme and standardisation of labour rooms across the state and initiated respectful maternity care workshops both at the state and district level.

Currently, Dr Reddy is Head of Public Health and Maternity Services in the Fernandez Foundation and is part of the government of India's national-level steering committee for midwifery and closely associated with the midwifery educators project at national level with the Fernandez Foundation as a partner.

Chapter 5

Thoughts and reflections on changes and influences in cinema in India over the past 75 years

Anita Virk and Swadhin Padhy

The journey: Anita Virk – personal reflections in the UK: partition through to the present

The journey of Indian cinema has come a long way over the last 75 years, depicted from ox-driven carts to jeeps, aeroplanes and space travel. Badged originally as 'Bollywood', Indian cinema has dazzled and hypnotised audiences globally by its enchanting musicals and more recent modern era cinema through platforms such as Netflix. It has influenced the Indian diaspora as well as several generations growing up in India. Indian cinema is one of the largest entertainment industries in the world, having created a unique identity over the past 75 years. It has grown exponentially, attracting major international studios to invest in Indian content. In particular, the unique use of songs and dance has attracted a loyal and devoted fan base. Sharing stories and experiences, we will explore how Indian cinema has inspired and preserved India's rich and diverse culture. It has been a strong catalyst for change as well as societal transformation. As one of Bollywood's most celebrated stars Shahrukh Khan said: 'Cinema in India is like brushing your teeth in the morning. You can't escape it.' (www. brainyquote.com)

1950s

Like many Indians, my father emigrated from India shortly after partition (in 1951). These migrants were seeking a new and better life and opportunity. For many, life was challenging – leaving behind parents, brothers, sisters and extended family. To fill the void, they immersed themselves in Indian film and music and the escapism it offered. During this era, vinyl was the only medium. Like many, including my father, they cherished the vinyl they possessed, often wrapped carefully in old newspapers. During the 1950s, going to the movies in the UK was not a readily available option with cultural challenges for young Indian men going out alone. They would eat at home and sing ghazals (poetic songs) with the few friends they met at the factories.

1960s and 1970s

To many south Asians, in the late 1960s and 1970s, Indian cinema provided an unlikely refuge. As this community grew, many Indians invested in cinemas such as The Ritz in Coventry, well before there were mosques, mandirs or gurdwaras there. Sundays at The Ritz on Foleshill Road started to showcase Bollywood films. It became a social hub for Indian immigrants but more importantly a place where Muslims, Sikhs and Hindus could gather to experience communal harmony and seek respite from what seemed like a different world.

The 1970s provided a more risqué genre of female roles and sensual content styled movies. The music matched the newfound emancipated female roles portrayed by Zeenat Aman. Favourites included *Satyam Shivam Sundaram* (transl. The Truth, the God, the Beauty), a 1978 Indian Hindi-language romantic drama film produced and directed by Raj Kapoor and written by Jainendra Jain, starring Shashi Kapoor and Zeenat Aman. Followed by *Qurbani*, (transl. Sacrifice), a 1980 Indian action thriller film produced, directed by and starring Feroz Khan (under the banner of FK International). The film co-stars Vinod Khanna, Zeenat Aman, Amjad Khan, Shakti Kapoor, Aruna Irani, Amrish Puri and Kadar Khan. Qurbani was famous for its music, especially the Bollywood disco song "Aap Jaisa Koi" sung by Pakistani popstar Nazia Hassan and produced by Biddu, as well as the song "Laila O Laila". Zeenat Aman changed the concept of the Hindi film heroine. It was refreshing for audiences to view a female in Indian cinema who was not playing the obedient wife or coy, pure heroine. Audiences liked the fact that she was always the woman in charge, and quite happy to play the less-than-pure heroine. This was the disco era and the music and costumes in retro style wowed cinema audiences. The dramatic make-up and outfits to match were now a mix of traditional with modern. Many women of this era were influenced by cinematic icons and styled their eyes with dark kohl and retro polo necks during the day and for an evening out would don their saris.

The 1970s also saw some in the community acquiring video players. The VHS recorder became very popular and Indian cinema viewing habits changed. Audiences were no longer squashed in the cinema with broken samosas on the floor. Now we were in our homes with food and drink while still maintaining the community spirit with Indian movies bringing us together.

Figure 5.1: Anita Virk, aged 11, with the famous Bollywood superstar Sanjay Dutt and her older sister Rajan - Mumbai 1982 Copyright is of the author.

Figure 5.2: R–L: Anita Virk with Gopi Puthran (film director - Mardaani 2) and Swadhin Padhy (Ronkel Media Education & Research Institute) Visit to BCU in February 2020 as part of an India–UK arts knowledge exchange project. During their visit, the university hosted the screening of Mardaani 2 at the Midlands Arts Centre (MAC), Birmingham. The film marked the directorial debut of Gopi, who was the writer of the first Mardaani film, produced by Yash Raj Films. Copyright is of the author.

From a personal perspective, one of my father's younger brothers decided to remain in India. He left Punjab to move to Bombay (Mumbai). Dharmendra (known as the He-Man of Bollywood) was a huge influence on many Indians, including my uncle. My uncle enjoyed the Indian cinema so much that it later became his career and passion, leading to him becoming a proficient filmmaker, having produced such iconic films as *Benaam*, released in 1974.

1980s and 1990s

During this era, audiences in the UK began to gain more choice in their viewings, and as technology evolved so too did the terrestrial television channels. The introduction of Channel 4 was a welcomed change among the South Asian communities as it became a channel which seemed to champion Indian cinema, especially with films such as Sholay and later Dil Se. With the advent of DVDs, communities no longer needed to venture out to cinemas to watch Indian films. Also, low-cost travel enabled more and more Indians to revisit their roots, and for the first time since migrating, to view Indian cinema in India.

2000 and beyond

As cinema screen developed new technology and better experiences for audiences, such as more comfortable seating, more food options and greater film choice, there was a revival in cinema-going audiences as opposed to viewing at home. Indian cinema also began to change, and the films that were being produced became less linear and more modern in their outlook. *Kabhi alvida naa kehna* became one of the first films of this era to discuss the topic of extra-marital affairs and it gained a wide populist audience. This era also began to see more film festivals being showcased in and around the UK – which encouraged second- and third-generation Indians to visit the cinema and to watch Indian films, as opposed to Hollywood movies. Indian cinema continued to evolve; with such platforms as Netflix investing millions into Indian cinema, time will tell if we are, once again, going through another phase where audiences will prefer to stay at home, watching Indian motion pictures from the comfort of their own armchairs.

Swadhin Padhy, Ronkel Media Education & Research Institute: changes and influences in cinema in India over the past 75 years

As they say, change is the only constant, and the films of India have also undergone immense change, especially since its independence.

Era of Nehruvian socialism

The 1950s was termed the golden age of cinema. After independence it was the era of Nehruvian socialism. Naturally Nehru and Mahatma Gandhi's concept of the 'welfare state' was portrayed in Bollywood films. The most acclaimed directors of the time were Mehboob Khan, Bimal Roy and Guru Dutt, who brought new depth to established themes tackling a sophisticated mix of characters, plots, ideas and morals. Their films were lyrical and powerful, dealing with socially meaningful themes like exploitation of the poor by rich landlords in Do Bigha Zameen, the importance of sacrifice and honour in Mother India, which also became the first Indian film to be nominated for an Oscar, survival in the big city in Boot Polish, untouchability in Sujata, dilemmas faced by modern Indians in Andaz, and materialism versus spiritualism in Pyasaa.

One of the most prominent filmmakers of this time was Raj Kapoor. His career spanned the first four decades following independence from 1947 to 1988, coinciding with Nehruvian socialism. In his films Awara, Shri 420 and Mera Naam Joker, his protagonists are underprivileged and drawn inexorably to the city only to discover the pervasive corruption and danger that lurks beneath its glossy surface. In the end these protagonists succeeded professionally while maintaining their moral integrity.

Drawing on these themes, directors were able to create commercially successful movies. This immense fecundity of Bollywood increased its audience base internationally. Lovers of Bollywood cinema spread across the Indian subcontinent into Russia and China.

Middle cinema

Late 1960s and early 1970s Hindi cinema witnessed the dominance of romantic movies with actors like Rajesh Khanna, Shashi Kapoor, Dharmendra and Asha Parekh becoming household names. Hrishikesh Mukherjee and Basu Chatterjee were pioneers of Indian middle cinema. Their films reflected the changing middle- class ethos with light-hearted stories of middle-class families often in urban settings featuring marital and love relationships. Films like Anand, Chameli Ki Shaadi, Golmal and Chupke were hugely successful.

Angry young man

In the mid-1970s, with the increasing popularity of Amitabh Bachchan, a new kind of hero emerged who was identified by his rugged machismo. The boy image of a hero no longer interested the public. This rugged machismo was termed the 'angry young man'. As this was a period of rising worker, peasant and student unrest, this image of the hero worked well alongside the prevailing conditions in society. These films addressed endemic corruption, promoting the victimised working-class hero challenging the status quo, reflecting the anger and frustration of an entire generation exploited by those in power. Films in this category include *Zanjeer, Sholay, Kaala*

Pathhar and *Deewar.* Amitabh Bachchan turned out to be the biggest superstar the country had ever seen, continuing to inspire millions of people across the globe.

New wave

Bhuvan Shome (1969) by Mrinal Sen pioneered the Indian new wave. This film made 'art cinema' palatable to wider audiences. The themes included monotony, solitude, camaraderie and compassion. The psychology of Bhuvan Shome, a 50-year-old played by Utpal Dutt, whose character is widower and dedicated civil servant in transition from a solitary existence into a companiable routine after meeting Gauri, a friendly village girl. It highlights the rural–urban divide in India. Some films in the 1980s dealt with sensitive socio-economic issues while also becoming commercial successes. For example, Govind Nihilani's *Akrosh,* winner of the Golden Peacock Award, features a lawyer defending a man under arrest for killing his wife. As the case proceeds, the harsh truth about life for scheduled tribes in India becomes clear to the lawyer and audiences.

Scheduled Castes and Scheduled Tribes are officially designated groups of people and among the most disadvantaged socio-economic groups in India. The terms are recognized in the Constitution of India and the groups are designated in one or other of the categories.

Shyam Benegal, Ketan Mehta and *Basu Chatterjee* are some of the prominent names of the Indian New Wave. Shyam Benegal's *Ankur* is the story of a happily married Dalit couple whose life changes after the landlord's son seduces the Dalit wife. This film takes up many social issues like casteism, religious differences in India, and the way the rich exploit the poor. Ketan Mehta started a trend in making socially conscious political films through *Sardar* and *Mirch Masala*, which became commercially successful, with other films like *Ardha Satya, Chakra, Maro Charita* and *Samskaara* in this category.

Psychology started to play a central role in the films of the New Wave. Another important part of the New Wave was *Saraansh*, directed by Mahesh Bhatt. This film explored a couple coping with loneliness and anxieties of old age and the utter aimlessness of their lives after the death of their only son, a victim of arbitrary violence. It focused on the importance of finding new meaning and purpose in life despite one's age.

Revival of romance

The late 1980s saw the revival of romance depicted on screen as a culture war between a Westernised vivacious young couple and their traditional parents, with the protagonists attempting to maintain their individual identities while fulfilling their duty towards their family. Films like *Maine Pyar Kiya, Qayamat Se Qayamat Tak, Dilwale Dulhania Le Jayenge* and *Hum Aapke Hain Kaun* are in this category.

With liberalisation, privatisation and globalisation from the late 1990s, Hindi cinema increasingly started to cater more to the English-speaking Hindi audience rather than the whole of India as was previously the norm. The needs of unprivileged Indians were no longer the focus of movies. Films were extensively shot in foreign locations and Indian audiences got to explore the world through cinema. Filmmaker Yash Chopra became one of the pioneers setting this benchmark. Because of his films, Switzerland turned out to be the most sought-after honeymoon destination for Indians. *Dilwale Dulhania Le Jayenge* is still running in Maratha Mandir (a single- screen theatre in Mumbai) despite being released 27 years ago.

Cinema declared as an industry

The early years of the 21st century witnessed many dramatic developments in Indian cinema, with movie making at last declared an industry by the Indian government in 2001 followed by the gradual corporatisation of film entertainment and media. Banks, insurance companies and the Federation of Indian Chambers of Commerce and Industry were persuaded to support the industry.

The rapid proliferation of 'multiplexes' and digital cinema theatres, first in metropolitan cities, then more widely, providing a livelier experience to cinema- goers, contributed significantly to the growth of the entertainment industry. Small budget films began to be released in multiplexes where ticket sales were stronger than in single screens and attracted upper middle-class families with more disposable income.

Small budget experimental films

This gave rise to small budget experimental films on subjects rarely portrayed in mainstream cinema. Young directors like Nagesh Kukunoor (*Hyderabad Blues, Bollywood Calling, Iqbal*) and Anurag Kashyap (*Black Friday*) have been able to make a mark thanks to the multiplex phenomenon with films like *Being Cyrus, Mixed Doubles* and *Joggers Park* released in these outlets.

Directors like Tigmanshu Dhulia and Vishal Bhardwaj changed the trend with films like *Makdee* and *Paan Singh Tomar*. The society and culture of rural India along with the drawbacks affecting the lives of innumerable Indians became the concern of the filmmakers.

The themes grew bolder, including homosexuality and old age featuring in Being Cyrus; *My Brother Nikhil* covering HIV and AIDS; *Salaam-Namaste* on live-in relationships; Black and Iqbal about communication with people of disabilities; Bombay and Roja about religious fundamentalism; and *The Legend of Bhagat Singh* focusing on nationalist history. Films on patriotism like *Lagaan* and rural development like *Swadesh* were also becoming popular.

Women-centric movies

In addition to this, the importance of the roles of women in Bollywood films started to increase. In the 1980s, in the 'Action Era of Bollywood', women lost strength and space to the 'hero', being reduced to a glamorous prop, dancing around trees, being kidnapped or killed. But as the status of women started to reform socially, Bollywood gave more importance to their roles. Their marital, professional and personal struggles at different ages started to be portrayed vividly.

Films like *English Vinglish* show how sweet and caring housewife and caterer Shashi is mocked by her family for not knowing English. Later, while learning English, she rediscovers her worth as a woman. In *Queen*, Rani is a small-town girl who discovers herself by going on honeymoon alone after being jilted by her fiancé just before the wedding. The film *Piku* portrays the father–daughter relationship in a new light. Despite the generational challenges, the love and sense of responsibility in the relationship keep it going with the daughter making sacrifices for her father as she takes care of him. Fashion tells the story of small-town girl Meghna Mathur who sets out to fulfil her dream of becoming a supermodel. In her journey, she is sucked in by the corrupt world of haute couture, paying a hefty price but rising again like a phoenix after her downfall. The film *Thappad* depicts a housewife's retaliation after she is taken for granted, abused and disrespected. The bravery of women in different fields also started to be recognised in films like *Neerja,* where a courageous flight attendant risks her life to save the passengers.

The true power of cinema

With his humorous and entertaining way of telling meaningful stories with a strong message, filmmaker Raj Kumar Hirani through his films, *Munna Bhai MBBS, Lage.*

Figure 5.3: Shuddhi: A New Beginning (official poster) Copyright is of the author.

Raho Munna Bhai and *Three Idiots*, tapped the true power of cinema. His film *Lage Raho Munna Bhai* presented the philosophy of Mahatma Gandhi in a new light and reminded the entire nation of the relevance and impact of Gandhian philosophy. His next film, *Three Idiots*, was revolutionary in encouraging Indian youths to go against the popular norms and pursue their own passions and interests, giving Indian parents a different perspective and propelling them to support their children in pursuing their respective dreams. The entire education system and culture started changing after the film, with Indian youths today feeling free and confident in selecting a career of their own choice. Because of his high-impact films, Raj Kumar Hirani is now one of the most celebrated filmmakers in the country.

Similarly, filmmaker Rakeysh Omprakash Mehra wove his magic through the film *Rang De Basanti*, which explored the current relevance of the philosophy of one of the most revered 'Indian Freedom Fighters', Bhagat Singh. The film redefined and rekindled the feel of patriotism among young people, helping them to realise their true power and how their energy can be channelled into nation building. A direct impact was seen in the 1999 Jessica Lall murder case, where civilians joined hands in silent protests to demand justice, which acted as a trigger to bring the culprit to justice.

Case study: new era experimental filmmaking

One such film writer and director who's changed the way Indian cinema was made is Sanjeev Sharma. His films have gone beyond entertainment and acted as a strong catalyst for direct individual and societal transformation. In all his films, he casts non-actors, often real people from the world his stories are set in, with his films empowering these individuals. He started his filmmaking journey by casting real-life prisoners in his short film *Shuddhi: A New Beginning*, taking them on a journey of reformation through art and creativity with a one-month sentence reduction for all the prisoner participants.

He continued his efforts to utilise films as a catalyst for societal change with his feature film *Road to Reform*, where he again empowered more than 200 prisoners by using them as actors.

Figure 5.4: Road to Reform (official poster) Copyright is of the author.

The film was very well received and upon screening, a decision was taken by the Hon'ble Chief Minister of Rajasthan to establish a placement division in the Prisons Department so that reformed prisoners would have a job available when they get out of prison.

About the contributors

Anita Virk has over 25 years of achievement in the financial sector and approaching seven years in higher education (Head of Compliance and Funding Assurance at BCU). Anita has held various strategic roles based in the City of London and internationally in locations including Sydney, New York, Hong Kong, Singapore and Buenos Aires. She has developed industrial partnerships and is passionate about empowering women and has partaken in areas of research related to emotional nerve intelligence and supported work published in several research journals. Anita holds an international MBA awarded in the Netherlands. Anita's passion for Indian cinema has been inspired by her late father and an uncle and aunt as filmmakers in Mumbai. Anita has frequented many film festivals and produced a short film for Cannes Film Festival in 2007. Having travelled and worked in over 50 countries, Indian heritage and cinema remains at the core of her influences.

Swadhin Padhy, Academic Director at Ronkel Media Education & Research Institute, is an IITian (An alum of one of the Indian Institutes of Technology) with three Best Actor Awards in theatre. He is also the Production Head at Ronkel Brothers Production which is known for its path-breaking projects and innovative storytelling. For the first time in the history of Indian cinema, a road has been named after a film, Road to Reform, in which Swadhin was also the Chief Assistant Director. Legendary actors Padma Vibhushan, Amitabh Bachchan and Randeep Hooda are a few of the renowned actors to have worked with the production company in the past. Swadhin started his journey with theatre where he honed his craft as a writer, director and actor. He then started his film career as an assistant director and producer in charge of the prestigious film Shradhanjali, https://www.imdb.com/title/tt7915600/ which was made to actualise the vision of Shri Narendra Modi. Since then, he has been actively involved in challenging projects which are 'out of the box' and attempted for the first time in Indian cinema. He is also a passionate educationalist who devotes most of his time interacting, guiding, motivating and nurturing the future aspirants of cinema.

Chapter 6

A reflection of how sport has evolved in India at 75

Mark Jeffreys

Summary of chapter

This chapter investigates the history of Indian sport and reflects on the sporting journey since 1947. The chapter will explore the successes on the international stage while considering the challenges for India to become a global sporting nation. The role of cricket as India's preeminent national sport will also be examined?

Introduction

When investigating the role of sport within any country, it is important to understand the history that has led to the engagement and cultural interest in particular pastimes, and how the diversity of sports characterises and mirrors the culture of the country as a whole. This chapter will aim to provide a context to the social and cultural influences on sport and reflect on how sport has evolved since gaining independence from Britain in 1947.

The chapter will reflect on some of the highlights that have taken place in that time, and will also investigate some of the challenges the country faces in developing an infrastructure for India to become a global sporting nation. Cricket, which has become such an integral part of the Indian culture, will be considered, as will the way that sport has become a way for Indians to display their national pride.

Transition into independence

Sport has been found to have played a part in Indian life for a long time before British rule. Sen (2015) reports that wrestling has a very long tradition as a sport in India with references to the sport going back to at least the 13th century. He also refers to sports such as archery and shooting which still exist today along with sports such as kabaddi which now have a large television following. It is also evident that British rule and British colonial policy had a profound effect on Indian sport, especially through sports such as cricket and soccer. It was not only in the playing of the sport, but Sen (2015) also points out that the way the European-style clubs were formed was also important. Some of the Indian elite saw the development of such clubs as an opportunity to enhance their social status and enhance relationships with their colonisers. It is also evident that the British were keen to develop an elite caste of Indian rulers who were familiar and comfortable with European culture. We are also reminded, however, that the cultural influence through sport was not just one-way. Polo, which had been a traditional sport in India, became a firm favourite with British soldiers who saw the sport as an excellent form of entertainment.

Current popular modern sports in India include athletics, badminton, basketball, boxing, cycling, football, gymnastics, shooting, table tennis, tennis, squash, volleyball, weightlifting and wrestling. Indigenous sports that remain popular include snooker, chess, kho-kho, gillidanda and polo. Cricket has proved to be by far the most popular sport. On a global stage, India started to participate in the Olympics held in Paris in 1900. While still under British rule, a single Indian athlete, Norman Pritchard, won two silver medals in athletics and became the first Asian to win Olympic medals. However, it was in Antwerp in 1920 when India first competed in the Olympics as a nation and has competed in every summer games since. In 1927 the Indian Olympic Association (IOA) was formed with a remit of promoting sports in India and selecting teams for the summer games. The first gold medal success came in Amsterdam in 1928 where the hockey (field hockey) team defeated the Netherlands in the final.

Figure 6.1: India national football team at Olympics 1948.

Following independence in 1947, the 1948 games witnessed the largest contingent of Indians to compete in summer games with 79 athletes participating (the previous largest contingent had been 27). The 1948 games in London saw the Indian hockey team continue their dominance of the sport and defeated Great Britain in the final and secured the first gold medal for India as an independent nation. Hockey has continued to be India's most successful Olympic sport with eight gold medals in total between 1928 and 1980 (Majumdar, 2006).

The Tokyo 2020 games (held in 2021) saw a new record of 124 athletes represent India and gained seven medals in total which is the best team performance in its Olympic history. As a country India is ranked 58th overall against all Olympic nations. India has also competed in the Asian Games since their inception in 1951 winning a total of 672 medals and ranking fifth overall in the medals list behind China, Japan, South Korea and Iran. Athletics has proved to be the sport where most medals have been won within the games. New Delhi has also hosted the Asian Games on two occasions, the inaugural games in 1951 and again in 1978. The most successful event for India was the 2018 games in Jakarta with a total of 72 medals.

Figure 6.2: XIX Commonwealth Games-2010 Delhi Winners of Discus (Women's) Krishna Poonia of India (Gold), Harwant Kaur of India (Silver) and Seema Antil of India (Bronze) during the medal presentation ceremony of the event.

The other major multi-sport games that India competes in are the Commonwealth Games (formerly known as the British Empire Games). India sits fourth in the all- time medal table behind Australia, England and Canada, with shooting as the most successful sport. India hosted the Commonwealth Games in 2010 in Delhi. The Delhi Games are reportedly the most expensive games ever, costing approximately US$7.5 billion (Madhavan, 2012). Delhi hosted over 6,000 athletes from over 70 nations and dependencies. The 2010 games also saw India achieve its best result at a Commonwealth Games, finishing second overall behind Australia. The UK has the sixth-largest Indian diaspora globally and Birmingham, which hosted the Commonwealth Games in 2022, has the largest Indian diaspora in the UK outside of London.

Policy and challenges

When examining the sporting landscape in India from a policy perspective, Chelladurai et al,(2010) identify that it must be remembered that India is a vast and complex country. It has a population of nearly 1.5 billion, a relatively high population density covering over 3 million square kilometres, with 18 official languages. They also suggest that India's performance in international competition doesn't reflect the size, population and economic status of the country. When comparing India to the UK (Great Britain for international sport purposes), for example, and taking two important indices (GNP and GDP), we can see that India compares very closely. At the time of writing India's GNP is US$2.73 trillion and ranks seventh globally against the UK's US$2.77 trillion and fifth ranking, whereas Indian GDP is US$2.69 trillion and ranks as the fifth-largest GDP while the UK's GDP is US$2.65 trillion and ranks sixth. However, the difference in Olympic performance is stark.

Following the 1996 Atlanta Olympics where Great Britain only won a total of 15 medals with a solitary gold medal, Prime Minister John Major decided that money from the National Lottery would be specifically channelled towards supporting Britain's elite Olympic sports to support medal chances. Funding increased from £5m for the Atlanta Games to £54m for the Sydney Olympics in 2000. In the Olympic cycle leading up to the Tokyo 2020 Olympics (held in 2021), UK Sport, the government agency which distributes the money from the exchequer and lottery funding, spent £354m on the Tokyo Games.

The result of this funding and the focus of UK Sport in distributing the money directly to the National Governing Bodies of Sports and setting specific medal targets is that Great Britain's Olympic performance has improved significantly. The medal haul has increased from 15 in 1996 through to 67 in Rio in 2016 and 64 in Tokyo in 2020. The overall medal position has improved from 36th in 1996 to second in 2016 and fourth in 2020. This compares to India's ranking of 67th in Rio and 48th in Tokyo.

Therefore, success at a global level in events such as the Olympic Games can be seen as being developed by political will alongside targeted funding, more than just having sporting talent within the country. There is undoubtedly the sporting talent within India's population, but that talent may not to date have been recognised and fully developed. India has, however, recognised the importance of having a National Sports Policy (NSP). The first NSP was published in 1984. This policy sought to promote the development of a sustainable infrastructure for sport, greater participation in sport and physical activity, the training of physical education teachers and the development of sports coaches. It also financially supported the Netaji Subhas National Institute of Sport, at Patiala, and the Lakshmibai National College of Physical Education in Gwalior.

Figure 6.3: The Minister of State for Youth Affairs and Sports and Information and Broadcasting (IC), Col. Rajyavardhan Singh Rathore with the Indian Kick Boxers, who represented India at the 2018 World Championship in Argentina, in New Delhi.

The second NSP was published in 2001. The focus of the 2001 policy was primarily on finding and nurturing sports talent and achieving excellence at the national and international level alongside promoting greater mass participation in sport. This was to be done by focusing on a number of key areas: the infrastructure for sport, the role of sport governing bodies, competition structures, sport science support and the mobilisation of resources to support performance. The policy also recognised the importance that sport can play as a diplomatic tool and how it can support international friendship and cooperation through sporting competitions and other exchange programmes.

The policy which is overseen by the Ministry of Youth Affairs and Sports is certainly a step forward towards creating the right type of infrastructure to create a better culture for sport; however, it also needs to be remembered that although the policy is created at a national level, responsibility for the delivery of sport sits at a state level, and so it is difficult to evaluate the effectiveness of the policy as a whole, as there are potential significant differences in its delivery.

Cricket

English (2013) identifies that cricket is the most popular sport in India and coverage of the various formats dominates its media. He acknowledges that in India, cricket may be considered as akin to 'religion' and that it has become the country's best- known global brand name. From its introduction to India during British rule, cricket soon became a favoured sport of the Indian people and in the early 20th century, sport and especially cricket also became a mechanism for revolt against the British colonisers.

Figure 6.4: Indian cricket players

Sen (2015) also states that following independence from Britain in 1947, rivalry with Pakistan soon replaced competition against the British colonisers. Cricket matches became an opportunity for Indians to express their patriotism as it surpassed all other forms of sport to emerge as the national pastime.

Successes such as the World Cup victories in 1983 (immortalised through the film *83*) and 2011 alongside (co-)hosting the event in 1987, 1996 and 2011 have helped to cement the place that cricket holds in the culture of the nation. The World Cup is due to revisit India in 2023, where the hosts will be one of the firm favourites to win the title on home soil.

In my experience of visiting India, once the term sport is mentioned, it is cricket that immediately comes to the heart of the conversation in the same way that when you speak to any New Zealander about sport it is rugby and the All Blacks that dominate the discussion.

When looking at the current world rankings it is clear to see why. At the time of writing, India lies fourth in the one-day international format of the game, second in the Test format, and first in the T20 format, demonstrating that they are truly a world- class team and able to compete against the best in the world. Alongside the current international scene, it is also worth noting that the Indian Premier League (IPL) is seen as the premier club competition across the world, with many of the world's best cricketers competing for one of the ten teams involved in the league. With a brand value of over US$6 billion, the IPL can be seen as a template that other sports can and are starting to follow, such as the pro kabaddi league and football's Indian Super League (ISL). These other sports are, however, yet to draw the international audience that the IPL has been able to develop. The IPL is also investigating the launch of a women's competition in 2023. This would reflect well as the rise of female sport globally is one of the biggest-growing markets and audiences across many sports (KPMG, 2016).

Conclusion

It is evident that sport has played an important part in the culture of India and can often be seen as a source of national pride when teams from India compete and succeed

against the best in the world. However, it is also evident that India has not competed on a global basis in the way that a country of its size, population and economic status can do. Following the development of the NSP in 2011, it would seem appropriate for the government to evaluate the place of sport within the culture of the nation and develop a focused plan to ensure that sport can deliver the potential for the nation.

References

Chelladurai, P., Shanmuganathan, D., Jothikaran, J. and Nageswaran , A.S. (2010) 'Sport in Modern India: Policies, Practices and Problems', The International Journal of the History of Sport, 1743–9035

English, P. (2013) 'It's not just cricket: content in the sports pages of The Hindu and The Times of India', South Asian History and Culture, 4(3), 351–365

Government of India (2001) National Sports Policy, http://yas.nic.in/vsyas/nsp2001. htm

KPMG (2016) The Business of Sports: Playing to win as the game unfurls. Available online at https://assets.kpmg/content/dam/kpmg/in/pdf/2016/09/the-business-of-sports.pdf, date accessed 5 May 2022

Madhavan, N. (2012)'Unlike Delhi CWG, London Olympics well within budget'. Available online at https://www.businesstoday.in/opinion/perspective/story/unlike- delhi-cwg-london-olympics-well-within-budget-36234-2012-10-25, date accessed 5 May 2022

Majumdar, B. (2006) 'When North–South Fight, the Nation is out of Sight: The Politics of Olympic Sport in Postcolonial India', The International Journal of the History of Sport, 23(7), 1217–1231

Sen, R. (2015) Nation at Play: A History of Sport in India. New York: Columbia University Press

About the contributor

Mark Jeffreys is Director of Sport and Physical Activity at BCU. Mark has worked in sport and education for over 30 years and is passionate about the role that sport can play in the development of individuals and in societal good. Mark's role at BCU involves the development and delivery of the university sport strategy which aims to encourage as many students and staff as possible to become engaged in sport and physical activity. Alongside his role at BCU, Mark is active within the sports 'industry'. He is an independent board member of England Squash and is the Senior Independent Director at the British Equestrian Federation where he also chairs the World-Class Performance Management Group. Mark also sits on the talent and performance groups for England Squash and England Lacrosse. He also chairs the United Communities Activity Network, a sports-based charity in Birmingham. Mark is a former junior international rugby player and has coached at international level.

Chapter 7

Cycling evolution – 75 years of changes in India and the world

Andrew Trujillo

Summary

This chapter hopes to give an insight into the development of the bicycle industry in India over the past 75 years. Although the focus of all these chapters is India, this chapter aims to compare the experience that India has had with other cycling realities in diverse parts of the world.

Introduction

Bicycles often give an excellent insight into a society and a glimpse to a time and space. Although these machines can be eminently utilitarian devices, they too can make personal, environmental and status statements or they can be fashionable toys for old and young. However, bicycles have a habit of subtly weaving into the fabric of a society, often reflecting but also driving changes.

Historical context

The initial stages of development of bicycles was mostly centred in Europe; this chapter is too short to elaborate on all the phases of the development of bicycles, but we can briefly touch upon the most prominent events. It seems that bicycles first made their appearance due to environmental factors, a somewhat ironic motive given that they are championed for their environmental credentials today. The first two- wheeled machines that required balancing were developed in Germany by Baron Karl von Drais, partly in response to the climactic effects of the explosion of Volcano Tambora in Indonesia. This event caused worldwide changes in light and temperature levels in 1815 due to the very high levels of volcanic ash in the atmosphere, which led to severe shortages of food due to crop failures. In these circumstances, many horses were slaughtered due to lack of feed. Von Drais seemingly developed his running machines for transportation to replace horses to some extent. Further developments primarily in France, the UK and the

US eventually saw the addition of pedals and cranks, tubular frames, tensioned spoked wheels, the use of bearings etc.

Many of the first bicycles were quite dangerous, and the quest for speed made them 51 more so; the poor quality of many road surfaces also made riding bicycles of any kind less than comfortable or convenient (Wilson, 2004). It was not until 1885 that the Rover safety cycle was invented in Coventry in the UK's West Midlands. To all intents and purposes, it was the true precursor of the modern diamond frame bike, with similarly sized smaller wheels, handlebars, rear driven wheel through a chain and a tubular frame laid out in a familiar way. With the introduction of the pneumatic tyre in 1888, the modern bicycle was born. The pneumatic rubber tyre helped overcome some of the comfort issues associated with poor road surfaces, although tarmac and other forms of improved road surfaces were instrumental. Soon after, the British brought the first bicycles to India, around the 1890s.

After World War 2, India began to focus on the manufacture of bicycles with production increases every decade (see Table 7.1). Cycling has now become almost synonymous with everyday living for many people in India. What began with a series of cottage industries, many of which were sited in the city of Puna, has gone on to become many large multinational manufacturing enterprises. At the time of writing, India is the second-largest manufacturer of bicycles in the world, a position that it took in 1992 and is now the third-largest exporter.

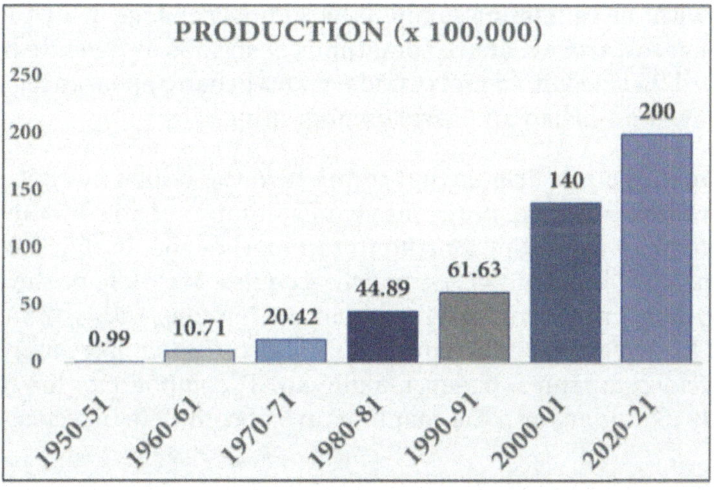

Table 7.1: (Puneeth and Nethravathi, 2021).

Popularisation

It was not really until mass production methods pioneered by Henry Ford were widely introduced in most non-automotive industries that the price of bicycles allowed these machines to become more affordable. This led to significant democratisation of the bicycle.

The popularity of bicycles in India and many parts of the world has seen ebbs and flows, sometimes with the use of these two-wheeled machines being seen mainly as inexpensive and utilitarian transport and others as a fashionable accessory. There have been numerous periods where bicycles have been popularised for use in both the country and in cities, only for people to succumb to the charms and status of motorised vehicles. Despite this though, many still appreciate the bicycle for its convenience, the health and environmental benefits it confers and the relatively small footprint it requires for storage and road use. It is not unusual to see hundreds of bicycles parked outside of large railway stations in Amsterdam or outside cinemas in Jaipur, the main difference being that most Dutch bikes are locked and most bikes in India are not. As I stated at the beginning, bicycle usage can offer interesting social insight.

The market in India was for decades dominated by what are called standard bicycles: low-cost, tough bicycles, which accounted for 90% of the market up until the 1990s and which in many ways remained unchanged. However, these machines now account for 66% of the market with the remaining segment heralding a change in attitudes and the market towards what are sometimes described as juvenile bicycles: a standard bicycle with a more modern and urban appearance aimed at a younger, semi-urban and rural demographic.

There are numerous brands that compete in the Indian market, most of which are home-grown. In recent years a number of non-Indian brands have sought to carve out a niche in the market too. By far the largest brand in India is Hero Cycles, which accounts for 40% of the market share. Other important players include Hercules, Atlas, BSA, Avon, Firefox, La Sovereign and Cannondale. Hero Cycles, like many of the other cycle companies, began making small components for bicycles, gradually extending into the manufacture of complete bicycles. (KPMG, 2021)

Bicycles and development

Many developing nations have found that bicycles are one of the most effective means of increasing the living standards of the poorest people, with several charities in different parts of the world seeing that those in possession of a bicycle not only reduce transport outgoings but also increase productivity by discernible amounts (*https://worldbicyclerelief.org/*). This is not only true of developing nations, but historically in developed nations bicycle usage is seen to be the means of going to and searching for employment, with numerous politicians exhorting working-class people to 'get on their bikes and find a job'. For many, bicycles are not only a means of transportation but also a means of personal freedom and independence. It is not unusual for bicycles to have been the means of young folk to meet and court, or to extend the reach of their horizons.

India's first cycling global explorers – forgotten heroes

Indians did indeed seek to broaden their horizons in spectacular fashion, and in 1923 an expedition of Indians departed from Mumbai (or Bombay as it was then known) on what would become an international and quite colossal journey that spanned 27 countries and some 40,000 miles: through Punjab, Baluchistan, the Middle East, Europe, the USA, Japan and Southeast Asia. The cyclists were Adi Hakim, Jal Bapasola and Rustom Bhumgara. They chronicled the whole extraordinary four-year expedition. This journey which took place in a changing world gives not only a glimpse of life in India but of a world in a bygone era. They returned in 1928 to a great welcome in Mumbai. Along the way they had received many warm receptions, and quite a few hostile ones, were awarded 26 medals, delivered public lectures, and collected 146 autographs from kings, the Pope, prime ministers, presidents, industrialists, majors and even Zhang Zuolin, the warlord of Manchuria. Their expedition inspired several other great expeditions at the time. Many of these are only recently being brought to the attention of Indians, as sadly the recognition for these amazing adventurers was not given for long, perhaps because India was still being ruled by the British and they did not see the value or relevance of these achievements by people that they did not see as part of their own at the time. However, the spirit of adventure and desire for freedom did stay on with these three men; for instance, Bhumgara joined the independence movement and later assisted in the Indian National Congress (Das, 2022).

Cycle culture

Cycling culture varies from nation to nation. For instance, some view their bicycles as tools; the Dutch will have bicycles for varied purposes: less expensive or older bikes to commute to the railway station, and more refined and expensive bikes for use at the weekend and recreation. The Dutch have also begun to replace their cars with cargo bikes that easily can carry children and some goods. Colombian rural folk (as many other rural folk elsewhere in the world) will often be seen carrying heavy loads, or complete families on the handlebars, rack and wherever else adults and children might be accommodated. Luis Herrera, a notable professional Colombian cyclist of the 1980s, began as a gardener carrying a heavy petrol mower on the rack of his bicycle, adding to the myth that it was this that helped him develop almost superhuman abilities to scale Colombian and later French mountains in competitions.

In India for decades, most bicycles were mainly items of transportation, mostly rural, hardy, and dependable, relatively affordable items. Indian society has changed though, with a greater number of segments in the market catering for the different aspirations and pockets. Children's bicycles have increased in popularity, However, it is the trend for hybrid bicycles, mountain bikes, road racing bikes and other speciality bicycles, that gives a hint to the changes in Indian society. Many of these categories mirror the trends that exist in Europe and the USA. Yet they also show a change in the mindset of the buyers and the kinds of cycling that are done; most of these new categories are about bicycles used for leisure, fitness or exploration. The Covid pandemic if anything has increased interest in the use of these myriad of bicycles. (KPMG, 2021)

Pedicabs or cycle rickshaws

However, it would be odd to not mention pedal-powered rickshaws or pedicabs in the context of India. Though quite obviously not two-wheeled bicycles, these pedicabs do borrow much from the technologies and principles of bicycle design. Although cargo bicycles, trikes and even quads have existed alongside the standard bicycle, it is in Asia where the pedal-powered pedicab rickshaws have really become popular forms of transport, with India being notable in their widespread use. Mostly used in Indian smaller and medium-sized cities and towns, these machines form an integral part of life in India. They are derived from simpler machines that trace their origins and name to

Japan (Britannica, 2019), which are two-wheeled (side-by-side) carriages and are drawn by a person that holds on to two shafts. Pedicabs offer numerous advantages, but some disadvantages too. As with other pedal-powered machines,

pedicab rickshaws are silent, do not pollute, and for relatively short journeys on flat terrain, are excellent transportation devices, so much so that many European and US cities have fleets of these machines, mainly in tourist areas to whisk people from one place to another. In India their purpose is simple: they provide a form of taxi service and are very well suited to that task (Tiwari, 2014). The downsides, however, are that these machines are comparatively slow, and when available in large numbers can lead to congestion, particularly if used in mixed traffic unsegregated conditions. It is the case that many of these (and their motorised cousins) are restricted in use in some larger cities in India. However, it is important to note that cycle rickshaws are poorly understood in India (often not included in analysis or not distinguished from bicycles), and their benefits are not fully appreciated with perhaps too strong an emphasis on electrically assisted 'replacements'.

Future trends

'Alas, it is always dangerous to prophesy, particularly about the future.'

Anon. Quote used in the May 1961 edition of The Canadian Journal of Economics and Political Science, (subsequently attributed to other people)

With bicycles and the technology that is currently changing the industry, the most notable trends are electrification and the huge increase in light mobility vehicles. This is true throughout Europe, and it would not be unreasonable to suppose that India will also be following these trends. Electrification, in this context, means the addition of electric motor assistance and battery power to conventional bicycles and cargo bikes, trikes and quads. The biggest issue with this particular trend is that both electric motors and lithium-ion batteries are expensive, making the final bicycles harder to afford in wealthy countries, let alone poorer ones. The trend for light mobility vehicles is one that saw a huge increase due to the different lockdowns caused by the Covid pandemic. The explosion of home deliveries and collections has meant that many organisations have sought vehicles that are environmentally friendly, not too expensive to purchase and run to deliver food and parcels. There have been some changes to the materials used in the construction of bicycles, with most European bicycles now being made of aluminium, although in India there is still a large market for steel-framed bicycles.

The more 'exotic' composite frames, particularly of carbon fibre and Kevlar, have become more widespread (for racing bicycles) but do tend to be expensive and are aimed mostly at the high-end segment of the market, with bicycles costing thousands of pounds. However, carbon fibre is not the most environmentally friendly of materials so it would be possible to envisage more sustainable materials to be used in future as an alternative or to complement carbon fibre.

Conclusions

Bicycles and pedal-powered machines are one of the most efficient machines that have ever been invented (Wilson, 2004); they are very versatile and deserve to be taken seriously as a means of generating employment (in manufacture and in their use), as well as being excellent in terms of their environmental and health benefits. Silent, with a small physical footprint (bicycles) and relatively affordable, they must surely be one of the best inventions ever made, or at least they are in the eyes of the author. Comparatively low tech to produce, they have enabled India to become a manufacturing powerhouse of these vehicles, not only satisfying local demands but also international markets too. Although technology is evolving the flexibility of the original idea allows for the mass customisation of these products. India is well placed in this regard.

Undoubtedly with a world experiencing problems associated with global warming through the production of greenhouse gases and reliance on fossil fuels, expansion of the production and use of bicycles must surely be an important tool in the armoury of any person, organisation or government that is seeking to make a difference and reduce the production of greenhouse gases. It is a real triumph that this humble machine has taken over the world, and it is creditable that India is now one of the world's leading producers.

References

Anon (n.d.) History, https://cyclingfederationofindia.org/history/#:~:text=Cycling%20as%20a%20sports%20was [Accessed 8 April 2022]

Britannica, The Editors of Encyclopaedia. 'rickshaw'

Das, A. (2022) 'India's Mini-Craze for Bicycling Around the World', Atlas Obscura, https://www.atlasobscura.com/articles/indians-who-cycled-around-the-world [Accessed 8 April 2022]

Encyclopaedia Britannica (2019) https://www.britannica.com/technology/rickshaw- vehicle. [Accessed 1 April 2022]

KPMG (2021).. Pedalling India' s Growth Cycling into the future. [online] Available at: https://assets.kpmg/content/dam/kpmg/in/pdf/2021/06/world-bicycle-day-e-bikes.pdf.

Puneeth B. R. and Nethravathi P. S. 2021. Bicycle Industry in India and its Challenges – A Case Study. International Journal of Case Studies in Business, IT and Education (IJCSBE). 5, 2 (Aug. 2021), 62–74. DOI: https://doi.org/10.47992/ IJCSBE.2581.6942.0120

Robinson, A. (2013) 'Built by bicycle: Andrew Robinson mulls over a study of India's adaptation of low-tech inventions', Nature, 498(7453), 168, https://link.gale.com/apps/ doc/A334042521/AONE?u=uce&sid=bookmark-AONE&xid=b4fcd600 [Accessed 08 Apr 2022]

Sahapedia (n.d.) Pune's Cycles Museum: Ride into the Past on Two Wheels, https:// www.sahapedia.org/punes-cycles-museum-ride-past-two-wheels#:~:text=While%20this%20particular%20bicycle%20has [Accessed 8 April 2022]

Singh, S. (1990) 'Bicycle Industry since Independence: Growth, Structure and Demand', Economic and Political Weekly, 25(34), M98–M109, http://www.jstor.org/ stable/4396675

Singh, D.R., Mishra, S. and Tripathi, K. (2021) 'Analysing acceptability of E-rickshaw as a public transport innovation in Delhi: A responsible innovation perspective', Technological Forecasting and Social Change, 170, p. 120908

Tiwari,G.(2014)'Theroleofcyclerickshawsinurbantransport:todayandtomorrow', Transfers: Interdisciplinary Journal of Mobility Studies, 4(1), 83+, available:

https://link.gale.com/apps/doc/A397135159/AONE?u=uce&sid=bookmark-AONE&xid=f425460b [Accessed 08 Apr 2022]

Unventured (2020) A Brief History of the Bicycle. https://unventured.com/a-brief- history-of-the-bicycle/ [Accessed 8 April 2022]

web.archive.org (n.d.). Wayback Machine, https://web.archive.org/web/20101226075146/http://www.worldbicyclerelief.org/_images/pdfs/tsunami_measurement. pdf [Accessed 8 April 2022]

Wilson, D.G. (2004) Bicycling science. Cambridge (Massachusetts): MIT Press

World Bicycle Relief (n.d.). World Bicycle Relief | Global Bicycle Charity, https:// worldbicyclerelief.org/

R, P.B. and S, N.P. (2021) 'Bicycle Industry in India and its Challenges – A Case Study', International Journal of Case Studies in Business, IT, and Education (IJCSBE), 5(2), pp. 62–74, https://zenodo.org/record/5205299#.YlAWVdPMLQY [Accessed 8 April 2022]

About the contributor

Andrew Trujillo is a Lecturer in Product & Furniture Design at Birmingham City University as well as Interior Architecture & Design. He was awarded the 2022 Steamhouse Fellowship at BCU. Andrew is an Industrial Designer specialised in Transportation and has more than 30 years of experience in the Marine and Automotive industries.

Andrew to cycle in Colombia where he grew up, probably aged 8. He says: "My passion for cycling really ignited when a scheme was set up in Bogotá in the 1980s, the Ciclovia, the closing of most major roads in the city on Sunday mornings. It meant that at least on one day of the week there was an opportunity to cycle the length and breadth of the city without fear of being knocked down by a car." Andrew began cycling on road racing bikes, he took to cycling on country roads. It helped that Colombians love cycling and are immensely proud of their professional cycling teams and cyclists that often have been seen to be battling with some success in international events such as the Tour de France, Giro d'Italia (Italian Tour) and la Vuelta a España (the Spanish Tour). His life has in many ways had this cycling thread running through it. Andrew came to study in the UK, and his trusted bike was his primary means of transport and recreation. Andrew has examined human-powered vehicles as part of his research and has built a tilting pedal-powered trike.

Andrew later moved to the Netherlands where cycling is part of everyday life and learnt how cycling networks effectively operate in catering for cyclists and their needs. At present, in addition to his role as a lecturer, Andrew designs cargo vehicles and cargo bikes that are human powered with additional electric and other power sources too.

Part Two

Educational collaborations and partnerships

Chapter 8

The evolution of diabetes and treatments in India since 1947

Anne Phillips, Wasim Hanif, Martha Stewart, Jayne Robbie and Theresa Smyth

Summary

This chapter considers and reflects upon the evolution of diabetes and treatments in India since 1947 and the emerging new opportunities currently becoming available within India. As science and healthcare approaches evolve, responding to diabetes challenges in India has created opportunities for partnership knowledge exchange between India and the UK.

Introduction

Diabetes is a major health issue that has reached alarming levels globally. India has the second-highest number of adults diagnosed with diabetes (Diabetes Atlas, International Diabetes Federation (IDF), 2021). The incidence of Indian citizens diagnosed with diabetes is calculated to be 75 million people in India; however, an additional 40% of adults in India have impaired glucose tolerance, which is a predictor for development of type 2 diabetes (Vijayakumar et al., 2019). One in six people (17%) with diabetes in the world are from India (IDF, 2021). Type 2 diabetes, which is a predictor for cardiovascular disease, is the most prominent presentation in India. Type 1 diabetes is autoimmune and insulin-dependent, and this affects about 1 million people in India; these are mostly children and young adults.

Emergence of diabetes care in India

Management of diabetes within India has faced many challenges and developments. The highest incidence of diabetes in India is in Tamil Nadu, (formally known as Madras State until 1969) and Kerala (formally Malabar until 1956) and the lowest incidence is in the northern states of Rajasthan (formally Rajputana until 1949) and

Haryana (formally East Punjab until 1966) (Arokiasamy, 2018). Over the last 75 years, from an initial paucity of medically trained staff, there has been a rise in doctors specialising in diabetes care, along with the first diabetes specialist nurse being appointed in 2001 at Christian Medical College (CMC) Vellore (Sharma et al., 2020).

Conversely, the unaffordability of many anti-diabetes medications and innovative medications and devices create inequity among many communities. Since the first use of insulin in India by Dr Bose, a diabetologist in The Calcutta School of Tropical Medicine in 1924, many children and young people's lives have been saved.

Figure 8.1: Dr J.P. Bose.

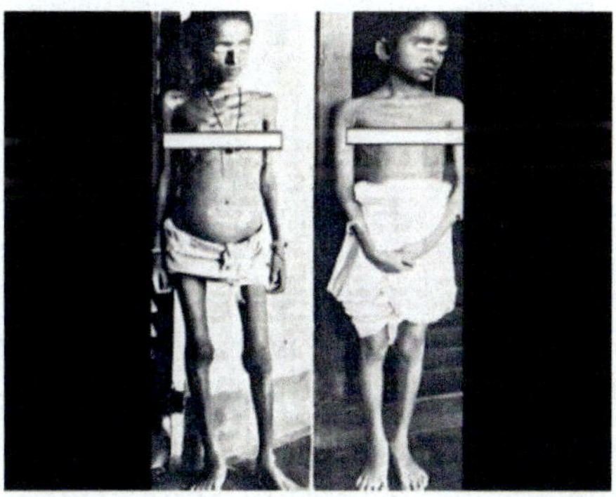

Figure 8.2: A young Bengali girl being treated with insulin by Dr Bose.

Insulin is still often unaffordable to those most vulnerable; the Indian government does provide older insulin preparations to the most in need. However, different insulins and newer therapies are not funded which restrict people's choice and glucose control so non-government organisations and foundations have arisen across India to fund insulin for those who need this essential life-saving medication. Diabesties is one such foundation run for people with type 1 diabetes by people with type 1 diabetes (www.d1abesties.com/). Diabetes was previously seen as a condition of India's urban middle class, and it received little state medical attention in the decades immediately following India's independence in 1947 (Arnold, 2009). However, it did gain traction in the extensive emerging medical literature, generated by Indian and British doctors, pathologists and medical researchers, who were beginning to understand the condition not just in terms of class susceptibility and the consequences of colonial modernity, but also in relation to ethnic and environmental characteristics (Arnold, 2009). Despite the discovery of insulin in the early 1920s, prophylaxis and treatment of diabetes in India suggested a continuing belief in a culturally distinctive approach to the condition.

Elevated susceptibility to diabetes

India has become known as a 'diabetes capital' of the world, despite maintaining high rates of under-nutrition (Wells et al., 2016). People of Indian descent have lower birthweight, develop diabetes at a young age which indicates reduced metabolic reliance (Wells et al., 2016), and have a lower body weight than other populations. There is a strong genetic susceptibility with increased risk of insulin resistance and relatively higher ratio of fat to lean mass to any given BMI (Body Mass Index).

Diabetes is known to inversely affect populations from lower- and middle-income countries (IDF, 2021). There is an exponential rise of diabetes in rural and semi-rural communities across India. This is coupled with diversity in educational attainment across rural communities, urban and inner-city communities and inequity in access to healthcare across India. Dr Viswanathan Mohan, a leading diabetologist based in Chennai (formally Madras Patnam), has driven improvements and access to diabetes care, (Figure 8.3). His services have 50 outreach diabetes centres in 21 states across India. His work is recognised as a Centre of Excellence in Diabetes Care by the

International Diabetes Federation, and he has established a large diabetes research centre in Chennai.

Dr Mohan (cited in Fralick et al., 2022) recognised that paradoxically people belonging to middle-income groups in India (about 70–80% of the population) are affected most by the cost of their anti-diabetes medication. These medications are 'out of pocket' so have to compete with their household and family expenses. Older anti- diabetic medications are inexpensive and available in most parts of India (Chow et al., 2018); however, the newer agents are more expensive and hence are unaffordable for the majority in India. Fortunately, this has been offset by the introduction of generic drugs by innovative Indian pharmaceutical companies such as Lupin Healthcare. When patents for diabetes medications treatment expire, lower-cost, generic versions become available, increasing their accessibility and affordability across India, thereby reducing the economic divide and improving accessibility.

A partnership approach

Kasthuri (2018) recognised the 'Five A's' in healthcare across India: Awareness, Access (or lack of it), Absence (of clinicians), Affordability (cost of healthcare, in particular insulin) and Accountability (or lack of it).

Figure 8.3: Dr Viswanathan Mohan

BCU established a partnership with Lupin Healthcare to train physicians specialising in diabetes throughout India in order to address regional variations in diabetes care due to shortages of trained healthcare professionals.

Kasthuri's (2018) concepts undoubtedly underpinned this partnership. Together with reciprocity, we at BCU recognised the need to respond with appropriate erudition and realistic suggestions to accord with medical doctors and their teams and multi-cultural experiences to improve health outcomes for people with diabetes. This enabled an online course in Advancing Diabetes Care to be designed, created and delivered from 2019 under the medical directorship of Professor Wasim Hanif.

All the students study across India and this enables their diabetes service to be nurtured while they learn. Our approach is student-led with purpose, needs-based and justified due to the escalation and multiplicity of diabetes care across India. Looking upstream, we also envisioned our students, who work in every region across India, to develop themselves as leaders in diabetes care for policy, research and dissemination among their medical, team and patient communities.

Developing a diabetes specialist workforce has increased access for populations most at risk. The doctors have reached out into their communities and have made significant developments during their programme. Previously they worked in relative isolation, so together we recognised that policy and networking opportunities stimulate students' engagement, growth and outreach. Collaboratively, the students and our team worked synergistically to influence each other reciprocally. Small steps can make big changes. Students networked with each other and formed their own support and clinical supervision partnerships. This has been hugely appreciated with students sharing their best practice initiatives and ideas in their developing services and programme via a group WhatsApp.

Service developments have been enabled with student feedback highlighting this:

> *'Thank you for your education and vision which has developed me and my teams service for ladies with gestational diabetes. Our service has been initiated by your education and support – we welcome your encouragement to move our service beyond its current delivery.'*

Encouragement from the University Vice Chancellor, the Consulate General of 60 India in Birmingham and the British High Commissioner in Hyderabad has enabled inclusion, enrichment and sharing of best practice in diabetes care.

The human lived experience of diabetes balanced with the science of medical management lifted our approach with the students and their programme. We promote person-centred care by sharing perspectives coupled with multidisciplinary team experiences with people with diabetes, to maintain inclusivity and outreach.

Feedback from a student articulates this:

> *'What a truly exciting experience to see a full 360° effect of diabetes and translate this to our own patient populations – this has opened my eyes and I will refine my person- centred approaches going forwards.'*

The national need in diabetes care across India, great social challenges, vulnerable populations and a shortage of medical practitioners in-country is being responded to. Echoing the World Health Organization's theme of 'Universal Health Coverage for All' (2018), the situation across India within diabetes care has brought this into sharp focus.

Reciprocal knowledge gain

It could be considered that a Western cultural approach and UK ideals of diabetes care delivery fall short of the real experience of providing diabetes care within India. Our diverse international team worked with community leaders and students to ensure our educational approaches are inspiring, appropriate and responsive to local communities and traditional ways of delivery of diabetes care. This has been valued by all the medical doctors, as articulated in this feedback:

> *'Western and Eastern ideas can complement each other and taking the best from both does inform us both – this has been a truly inspiring educational experience for me – the best of my career to date to be honest.'*

As students are all sponsored and come from every region across India, their cohesiveness in their learning about advancing diabetes care has been nurtured. They are mutually supportive of each other and reach out to share best practice. Peer working by students on regional projects across India demonstrates this impact. This has been facilitated in terms of policy redesign and outreach at conferences and meetings. This has also led to students being offered and undertaking prestigious roles and awards in national diabetes services as shown in Table 8.1.

2020	Young Diabetologist in India Award
2021	Chairperson at the Conference of American College of Physicians – India Chapter
2021	Fellowship of the Uttar Pradesh Diabetes Association
2021	Speakers at the Indian Specific Congress of Hypertension
2021	Fellow of the Indian Society of Hypertension
2021	Research Society for the Study of Diabetes in India Award for Best Innovation in Diabetes Care in Challenging Circumstances
2022	Governing Council Member of the Research Society for the Study of Diabetes in India
2022	Fellow of the Indian Society of Hypertension
2022	Research society for the Study of Diabetes in India Care Award for Excellence, Commitment and Dedication for People with Diabetes in Challenging Situations during Covid-19.

Table 8.1: Student achievements

Measurable impact is also demonstrated by the students' individual publications (Mukherjee, 2021; Datta and Mohan, 2022) during and since their programme and in the transformation of their diabetes services in the country.

Summary and reflections

To celebrate India at 75, we harnessed the power of multi-dimensional online learning by connecting and reducing perceived distance in transformative education. By driving diabetes care developments and enhancements at the local point of delivery, we have capitalised on delivery of nurturing education in diabetes care and achievable sustainable outreach across India through these doctors and their successes. Indeed, this impact would simply not have been possible without the continual engagement of our students, all full-time practising medical doctors, and commitment of our collaborative partners across India and the UK.

References

Arokiasamy, P. (2018) India's escalating burden of non-communicable disease, The Lancet Global Health, https://www.thelancet.com/journals/langlo/article/PIIS2214-109X(18)30448-0/fulltext.

Arnold, D. (2009) 'Diabetes in the Tropics: Race, Place and Class', Social History of Medicine, 22, pp. 245–261

Bose, J. (1924) 'On the Potency of Insulin in the Tropics', Indian Medical Gazette, 59(3), pp. 132–133, PMID: 29007387; PMCID: PMC5172754

Chow, C., Ramasundarahettige, C., Hu, W., AlHabib, K., Avezum, A., Cheng, X., Chifamba, J., et al. (2018) 'Availability and affordability of essential medicines for diabetes across high-income, middle-income, and low-income countries: a prospective epidemiological study', Lancet Diabetes Endocrinol, 6, pp. 798–808, DOI: 10.1016/S2213-8587(18)30233-X

Datta, S. and Mohan, V. Ed (2022) 'Advances in Statin Therapy in Diabetes, with and without co-morbidities', chapter 97 in Advances in Statin Therapy & Beyond in CVD: A Textbook of Cardiology, Jaypee Brothers, pp. 527-532. ISBN 9789354653933

Diabesties Foundation http://diabesties.foundation/

Fralick, M., Jenkins, A.J., Khunti, K., Mbanya, J., Mohan, V., Schmidt, M., (2022) 'Global accessibility of therapeutics for diabetes mellitus', Nature Reviews Endocrinology, 18, 199-204, https://doi.org/10.1038/s41574-021-00621-y

Kasthuri, A. (2018) 'Challenges to Healthcare in India – The Five A's', Indian Journal Of Community Medicine: Official Publication of Indian Association of Preventive & Social Medicine, 43(3), pp. 141–143, https://www.ncbi.nlm.nih.gov/pmc/articles/ PMC6166510/

International Diabetes Federation (2021) Diabetes Atlas, 10th Edition, https:// diabetesatlas.org/atlas/tenth-edition/

Mukherjee, S. (2021) 'Candid and Equitable Diabetes Care: Beyond the Bounds of Possibility?' Medicine Update, 31, 55, ISBN-978-81-948742-8-7, Evangel Publishing Pvt. Ltd

Sharma, S., Thakur, K., Kant, R. and Kalra, S. (2020) 'Nurse-led diabetes clinics in Southeast Asia: scope, feasibility, challenges and facilitators', Journal of Diabetes, Metabolic Disorders & Control, 7, 2, pp. 47–51

Vijayakumar, M., Balakundi, M. and Metri, K. (2019) 'Challenges faced in diabetes risk prediction among an indigenous South Asian Population using the Indian Diabetes Risk Score', Public Health, 176, pp. 114–117, doi.org/10.1016/j.puhe.2018.09.012

Wells, J., Pomeroy, E., Walimbe, S., Popkin, B. and Yajnik, C. (2016) 'The Elevated susceptibility to Diabetes in India: An Evolutionary Process', Frontiers in Public Health, 4, 145, https://doi.org/10.3389/fpubh.2016.00145

World Health Organisation (2018) World Health Day - Universal Health Coverage: For Everyone, Everywhere, https://www.who.int/news-room/events/detail/2018/04/07/ default-calendar/world-health-day-2018

About the contributors

Anne Phillips, Professor in Advancing Diabetes Care, BCU, is a Queen's Nurse and a National Teaching Fellow with the Higher Education Academy. After a career in specialist and community diabetes nursing in London and Yorkshire, Anne came to BCU to lead the MSc in Advancing Diabetes Care. The majority of students in the MSc are medical doctors working across all regions of India in rural, community, urban and inner-city diabetes services. Anne was born in Kolkata (formally Calcutta until 2001) and grew up in Assam living on the Tea Gardens, where her father was a Tea Garden Manager working for Assam Team Company.

Wasim Hanif is Visiting Professor, BCU, and Consultant Physical and Head of Service in Diabetes at Birmingham NHS Foundation Trust, is a Professor of Diabetes & Endocrinology, Consultant Physician, and Head of Service in Diabetes at University Hospital Birmingham. Wasim is a Board Member of the Centre for Diabetes Endocrine & Metabolism, University of Birmingham, and Clinical Advisory Group Lead for Research in Diabetes and Endocrinology at the Institute of Translation Medicine, Birmingham. Wasim is Medical Director for the MSc in Advancing Diabetes Care.

Martha Stewart is a diabetes specialist nurse at University Hospitals Birmingham and a senior lecturer on the MSc in Advancing Diabetes Care programme at BCU. Martha began her career as a secondary school teacher in Zimbabwe where she was born. She came to the UK in 1999 and trained as a nurse in Nottingham. Martha developed the role of diabetes education at her NHS Trust, winning awards for this inaugural work.

Jayne Robbie is a diabetes specialist podiatrist at University Hospitals Birmingham and a senior lecturer on the MSc in Advancing Diabetes Care programme. She is course lead for the MSc in Advancing Practice in Peripheral Vascular Disease at BCU as well as a Diabetes UK Clinical Champion and NICE committee member.

Theresa Smyth, Honorary Visiting Professor in Advancing Diabetes Care and Nurse Consultant in Diabetes at University Hospitals Birmingham NHS Foundation Trust University.

Chapter 9

Learning from each other: the partnership between Royal Birmingham Conservatoire and the A R Rahman Foundation

Louise Lansdown, Lamberto Coccioli and James Bunch

Summary

Since 2018, the Royal Birmingham Conservatoire (RBC), the A R Rahman Foundation and the KM Music Conservatory in Chennai have been working together to offer members of the Sunshine Orchestra access to transformative online music education. We retrace the steps of this unique collaboration between two very different musical worlds.

Introduction: the sounds of Chennai

To a firangi (foreigner) visiting India for the first time, Chennai – the capital city of the Tamil Nadu state – is a loud, colourful and boisterous place. The perpetual sounding of car and motorcycle horns ('Horn OK Please!') is punctuated by the elaborate, melodious trumpeting of large lorries and buses crowding the streets. The early morning call of the muezzin mixes with the bells of the nearby Hindu temple. Sacred songs are juxtaposed with the calls of wandering vegetable cart or chai sellers, or by Sachin Sundar's catchy new 'garbage anthem' 'Namma Ooru, Semma Joru' wailing from loudspeakers attached to the garbage collectors' vehicles.

Local festival and election seasons see the lampposts and fences of neighbourhoods festooned with rented loudspeakers broadcasting old Kollywood tunes of M.G. Ramachandran or Jayalalithaa, both former film actors and former Chief Ministers of Tamil Nadu. Daily life in the city is, in short, experienced as a total immersion in music and sound. Alongside its pervasive ambient sonic fabric, the city of Chennai is home to a profusion of public performance traditions that span categories: folk and vernacular, South Indian classical music (i.e. Carnatic), film music, rock, electronic dance music, and Western classical music.

Chennai's most prestigious music festival, the Margazhi Music Month, foregrounds Carnatic classical music, for which the city is renowned.[2] Taking place from late November to mid-January each year, the music season sees over 1,000 concerts organised by members of the Federation of City Sabhas (music societies), the Madras Music Academy, and other venues. Away from these more privileged environs, singer T.M. Krishna's Urur-Olcott Kuppam Margazhi Vizha brings the season's wealth of Carnatic music and Bharatanatyam dance to the fishing villages skirting Chennai's upscale Besant Nagar neighbourhood. The festival mixes these classical forms together with 'folk' forms (Kattaikkuttu, Villu Pattu and Parai Attam) aiming, in the words of T.M. Krishna, to 'break the socially conditioned class- and caste-based bubble'.

A.R. Rahman

Since the 1950s, film has been India's most prominent public-facing art form. From early on, Indian film producers placed music and dance in much more prominent positions than their Western counterparts. Early film composers tended to draw their inspiration, instrumentation and practical framework from Carnatic music. But by the 1970s, composers like M.S. Viswanathan, T.K. Ramamurthy and Ilaiyaraaja were moving away from the elevated Carnatic roots of film music and incorporating more folk and international influences. Ilaiyaraaja is known for introducing elements of Western classical and popular music into his sound, in some ways prefiguring and leading towards the work of one of his regular young collaborators, A.R. Rahman.

Figure 9.1: A R Rahman

Rahman, whose father R.K. Shekhar was also a film composer, has for at least a decade been the most recognisable name in Indian film music, gaining international prominence in 2008 with the success of his soundtrack for director Danny Boyle's Slumdog Millionaire.

Though his music maintains a connection with Indian classical and folk music, its more striking features

2 'Margazhi' is the Tamizh calendar month corresponding to December.

are an intrinsic sense of global stylistic fusion and openness to technological experimentation.

Like many Western film studios, personnel at Rahman's Chennai-based Panchathan Record Inn and AM Studios are organised into highly segmented and specialised roles, in a collaborative environment supervised by the composer. The work carried out in the studios incorporates recorded improvisation sessions, experimental sound design (using modular and software synthesisers, MIDI control devices and the Kyma sound design environment), and cues orchestrated using conventional music notation. Many of the young musicians and engineers working in Rahman's studios come from the music school he founded in 2008, the KM Music Conservatory.

The KM Music Conservatory

Rahman created the KM Music Conservatory (KMMC) to offer students a new model of music education that was largely unavailable throughout the country, giving them the opportunity to gain skills in high demand in the Indian film industry. The other prominent arts education institutions in Chennai – Madras University, Madras Music Academy and the Kalakshetra Foundation – focus their activities around Carnatic classical music and dance. KMMC is unique in its context for the diversity of its provision, embracing Western classical and popular music, Carnatic and Hindustani classical music, and audio engineering. Since its inception, KMMC has exposed students to a variety of disciplines and practices. Together with standard Western conservatoire-type music education, the curriculum offers courses in electronic music production and Indian classical music, where students explore elements of both Carnatic and Hindustani traditions and folk music.

KMMC hosts regular student and faculty concerts, and yearly events such as opera scenes, the KM Classical Guitar Festival, and the 'KM Day', with performances ranging throughout the school from preparatory division to third-year students and ensembles.

Ensemble concerts at the school include choral groups, Qawwali ensembles, Hindustani ensembles, rock bands, musical theatre productions, percussion ensembles, and a contemporary music 'scratch orchestra'[3].

All concerts at KMMC are open to the public and free of charge. Many of the concerts are filmed and most are streamed live on the school's social media.

Several notable guest artists have visited KMMC throughout the years, including the BBC Scottish Symphony Orchestra, the German National Youth Orchestra, composer James MacMillan, violinist Nicola Benedetti, WDR Jazzpreis winners Ramesh Shotham and Roger Hanschel, Deutscher Jazzpreis nominee Sebastian Gramss, and Welsh baritone Jeremy Huw Williams, who gave the world premiere of Param Vir's song cycle A Kinsman to Danger in 2018 with pianist Paula Fan.

Alumni of the school have gone on to further musical study at institutions like the Middlesex University, Queensland University of Technology, the Royal Conservatoire of Scotland, Leeds University, the University of Edinburgh, University of Southern California, UC-Irvine, California Institute of the Arts, McGill University, the University of Ottawa, and many others. Alumni have been featured in Wire magazine, performed at London's Café OTO and won Mirchi Music Awards for film soundtracks. Many work successfully in recording studios throughout India.

The Sunshine Orchestra

Founded in 2008, the Sunshine Orchestra is a charitable initiative that offers musical training and career opportunities to underprivileged children in Chennai. Generously supported by the A R Rahman Foundation, the Sunshine Orchestra is its flagship project and an Indian Symphony Orchestra in the making. Once students of the orchestra complete their high school degree, they gain free entrance to full- time courses at KMMC at foundation and diploma level, corresponding to Rahman's commitment to nurturing and empowering their talent through the most vital stages of their education.

3 The scratch orchestra Hundredfoot Road has performed repertoires by Cage, Glass, Eastman, Dolphy and Messiaen, and has been the primary vehicle for the performance of new student works. The orchestra has presented improvisatory musical games, live film music performance, open instrumentation pieces, electronic dance music, conceptual and theatrical works, field recording and sound art.

There are currently 13 string players in the orchestra, all highly skilled young musicians in their 20s who, considering their background, are following an entirely unique and unusual career trajectory.

RBC's String Department meets the Sunshine Orchestra

In late 2018, thanks to the existing connection between RBC's Principal Julian Lloyd Webber and A.R. Rahman, RBC's Associate Principal Lamberto Coccioli travelled to Chennai to visit KMMC, where he met with Fathima Rafiq (Executive Director of KMMC), Adam Greig (Academic Coordinator) and Srinivasa Murthy, the Director of the Sunshine Orchestra, who invited Lamberto to attend the orchestra's rehearsals. Impressed and persuaded by what he saw, on his return to the UK, Lamberto discussed with Louise Lansdown, Head of Strings, the possibility to develop a collaborative programme with KMMC and the Sunshine Orchestra.

All this became reality the following year, when Louise travelled to Chennai with her colleague Anthony Alcock (Section Leader Double Bass, City of Birmingham Symphony Orchestra and visiting tutor at RBC) and a recent RBC graduate, violist Emily Bogjiatis, who was passionate about Indian film music and played it regularly. The visit was very successful, as shown by the enthusiasm and excitement of Louise's initial reaction:

> *It was a whirlwind week in Chennai! Primarily working with the members of the Sunshine Orchestra, rehearsing, talking about the Western classical repertoire and specific technical issues relating to playing, but also listening to the orchestra play their own music and demonstrate the techniques that they use in Indian music: the scales and the incredible Bollywood style of playing. It became clear during this time that the orchestra had developed as players and musicians primarily in the group, with some individual lessons scattered over the years. Their schedule was fascinating, often with six hours of rehearsals seven days a week, all together. And on top of that travelling, concerts and recordings.*

It was a delight on the first day in Chennai to meet with Srinivasa Murthy, the Sunshine Orchestra mentor, conductor and trainer, a Bollywood violinist who proudly introduced us to the orchestra and presented a programme consisting of a mixture of Bollywood and Western classical music. It was clear from talking with him how much expertise and love he had showered on the Orchestra over many years. He has since retired, and I know they are ultimately looking for someone who might replace him – not easy shoes to fill!

Among the highlights of the work carried out in Chennai by Louise, Anthony and Emily was an afternoon spent dividing the then 14-piece string orchestra into quartets and quintets, shining a spotlight on the quality of each player's individual sounds, revealing their ability to blend and their listening skills. In brief, enjoying the autonomy of chamber music after the relative anonymity of the orchestral section. Individual characters were allowed to shine through, and there was a clear sense that players owned the musical line in a different and more compelling way.

At the end of the week, the Sunshine Orchestra strings performed as part of an informal concert at KMMC to showcase the work done together with the guests from RBC, resulting in a thrilling finale as they revelled in a newfound freedom and flexibility playing Mozart and Elgar. In a short meeting just before heading back to the airport, Louise proposed to Adam Greig a potential ARCO project to continue the collaboration with RBC.

Figure 9.2: Anthony Alcock and Srinivasa Murthy during rehearsals of the Sunshine Orchestra. © A R Rahman Foundation.

Figure 9.3: Louise Lansdown coaching the Sunshine Orchestra's string players. © A R Rahman Foundation.

Figure 9.4: Anthony Alcock coaching the Sunshine Orchestra's string players. © A R Rahman Foundation

What is ARCO?

In 2015, along with viola students and colleagues at RBC, Louise Lansdown founded ARCO South Africa. ARCO was born initially as an online distance learning scheme to provide teaching of violin, viola, cello and double bass delivered by RBC strings students and staff to students at the Morris Isaacson Centre for Music, in Soweto, South Africa. ARCO now includes student teachers from RBC's woodwind, brass and vocal departments. The concept behind ARCO is very simple: young students in Soweto receive lessons from RBC students, while RBC students gain experience and receive teacher training. This simple concept has produced astounding results so far, and following the enormous success of the Soweto partnership, Louise and RBC colleagues decided to found ARCO India in February 2021.

ARCO in India

The Covid pandemic inconveniently delayed the start of the collaboration until February 2021, but the lockdown seemed the perfect time for the ARCO team to extend connections with individual members of the Sunshine Orchestra while they were shut away from society, unable to rehearse and perform together as a group. After meeting with Adam Greig and Khatija Rahman, Director of Outreach Programmes and Global Initiatives at the A R Rahman Foundation in January 2021, a call was put out to interested RBC students to take part in the ARCO India initiative. After the selection process a planning meeting took place on Zoom, involving the students and the staff who were going to mentor them.

Weekly individual teaching began towards the end of February 2021 with RBC student teachers each assigned to a different member of the Sunshine Orchestra. The members of the orchestra are all over 18, and most in their 20s. An unusual age dynamic is evident, as in many cases RBC student teachers are younger than the orchestra members they are teaching. In many ways, this makes the relationship a more equal one, and one that needs very special care and context. Both student teachers and Sunshine Orchestra players value the mutual learning and opportunity to share musical and cultural traditions. Even in this relatively short time, their work together has led to immense development for everyone. Personalities were matched together where possible and from the start every RBC student was asked to teach similar material - scales, studies, repertoire –to try and find a baseline and understand what areas needed focusing on. With individual lessons around 14 months in, and during some of the toughest lockdown periods in India, the RBC student teachers were in some cases the only musical contact and tuition that Sunshine Orchestra members received in their isolation.

Teacher training sessions for RBC student teachers were conducted online twice monthly, and separate sessions for violin, viola, cello and double bass were held, often with one or all of the players of each Sunshine Orchestra section present and performing 'live'. Alternative discussions and top-tip meetings were also held in response to those 'live' online teaching sessions, often pinpointing pitfalls associated with teaching spiccato, vibrato, shifting and other complex technical skills online.

Conclusions

Real life has resumed for the Sunshine Orchestra and from October 2021 to March 2022 they were the resident orchestra in Bangalore for a TV talent show on the Zee Kannada channel called Sa Re Ga Ma Pa. In late March 2022, the orchestra was in Dhaka, Bangladesh, performing on A.R. Rahman's live show. Amid the orchestra busy recording times in January 2022, Louise and Adam conducted the first ever assessments with each member preparing scales, studies and repertoire, and Adam accompanying on the piano where needed. This was a first in so many respects for the orchestra members: playing with piano accompaniment and being assessed on their solo playing with a mixture of technical and repertoire-based material. The performance marking criteria for RBC's Bachelor of Music Year 1 were used for the assessment, and an informal conversation concluded the process. The day was truly memorable, with many positive surprises and remarkable progress and artistic development from each of the players. Future assessments are on the horizon in 2022 and beyond. Weekly classes with Adam have commenced at KMMC to practise rehearsing and performing with the piano. With great support and nurture, the hope is that this collaboration will grow and expand over the coming years, with a live visit from the Sunshine Orchestra to Birmingham and with RBC student teachers being finally able to visit Chennai.

About the contributors

Dr Louise Lansdown

Violist and South African Louise Lansdown has been Head of Strings at RBC since 2012. Louise, along with her RBC students and colleagues, is the founder of ARCO, a major distance learning education project that

RBC runs in collaboration with the Morris Isaacson Centre for Music in Soweto, South Africa. The project was nominated for the Guardian Internationalisation Award in 2018.

Louise is the founder of the Cecil Aronowitz International Viola Competition and Festival, launched at RBC in October 2014, as well as the founder and President of the British Viola Society. Louise plays on a French Viola c.1750 and 1890 Sartory bow, both previously belonging to the South African violist Cecil Aronowitz. A keen Hindemith scholar, Louise was awarded a PhD from the University of Manchester in 2008 for her research on The Young Paul Hindemith: Life, Works, Influences and Music Activities until 1922. She is a member of the South African Ubuntu Ensemble and is preparing a CD of South African solo viola music by John Joubert, Hendrik Hofmeyr, Monthati Masebe and others.

Professor Lamberto Coccioli

In a career spanning over 30 years, Lamberto Coccioli has lectured and performed all over the world in his different roles as composer, researcher, performer and academic leader. After working for five years with composer Luciano Berio in Italy, he moved to the UK to become Head of Music Technology at RBC where he directed the €3.1m EU-funded Integra - Fusing Music and Technology project to develop composition and performance of music with live electronics (2005-2012). As a spin-off of the project in 2009, Lamberto co-founded with Jamie Bullock Integra Lab, the music interaction design research centre based at RBC.

Since 2012 he has been RBC's Associate Principal, playing a key role in the development of RBC's international strategy and in the design and construction of the new RBC building with its innovative digital infrastructure.

Dr James Bunch

James Bunch is a composer and music educator living and working in Chennai, India. Since 2014 he has been a lecturer in music composition at the KMMC, assuming the role of the diploma programme leader in 2016. His music has been performed throughout North and South America, Europe, and Asia. His DMA comes from the University of Illinois, where he was a student of Keeril Makan, Erik Lund, Philipp Blume, Steven Andrew Taylor and Zack Browning. His research interests include intertextuality in the music of Salvatore Sciarrino and, more broadly, experimental music, sound art and transnational education.

Chapter 10

Celebrating the multilingual poetry of India and its diaspora at 75 years of independence

Vivek Sachdeva and Gregory Leadbetter

Summary

In 2021, colleagues at Guru Gobind Singh Indraprastha University and BCU came together to curate a series of three online events celebrating the multilingual poetry of India and its diaspora (September 2021–August 2022) in commemoration of the country's 75th anniversary of independence in 2022. In light of these events, this chapter briefly reflects on the ongoing history of India's extraordinarily rich poetic heritage.

A brief history of Indian poetry

India's poetry tradition is vast, rich and diverse. Discussing its every aspect in a short chapter is an impossible task. Here, therefore, we offer just a glimpse of the immensity of Indian poetry, which encompasses poetry written in all Indian languages in and outside India. We deliberately avoid categorising language by 'standard form' and its dialects, as the classification and segregation of languages in this way is a colonial construct and hegemonic in nature. Prof. G.N. Devy argues that in precolonial times language diversity was an accepted phenomenon and languages were not categorised in terms of standard form and deviations from that form.

India is a home to many languages. The known history of poetry writing in India dates back to the Vedic age. Distinguishing the performed or theatrical elements of poetry from the oral, Lienhard (1984) divides the oral tradition into two categories: Mahakavya (epic) and Laghukavya (minor form). The Ramayana and the Mahabharata are two famous ancient Indian epics, which traversed from the oral tradition to the written. Besides Sanskrit, in ancient times poetry was also written in other languages such as Pali, Prakrit, Tamil and Odia.

Figure 10.1: World Poetry Day Celebrations (2018) in Ravindra Bharathi.

During the medieval period, many new poetic traditions flourished. The influence of the Bhakti movement and Sufism enriched India in intellectual, cultural and poetic terms. In Telugu, a new tradition began with translation of the Mahabharata by Nanniah in the 11th century (Chenchiah and Bahadur); in Malayalam, with Ramacharitam (12th or early 13th century); Baba Farid or Sheikh Farid (12th to 13th century) wrote Sufi poetry in Punjabi; Akka Mahadevi (12th century) was a female poet from Kannada; Namdev or Namdeo (13th century) wrote poetry in Marathi; and Lal Ded (1320–1392) was a Kashmiri female mystic poet. Kabir (1398–1518) and Ravidas (15th–16th century) at Kashi or Varanasi, Guru Nanak (1469–1539) in Punjab, and Mirabai (16th century) in present-day Rajasthan wrote poetry in their regional languages. The poetry written during this period was devotional in nature, mystical in thought and questioning in spirit. Their poetry stridently criticised orthodoxy, dogmatism, casteism and other socio-religious evils in society. Gurmat Kaav,[4] Punjabi Sufi poetry and Punjabi Qisse[5] were dominant forms of poetry in the medieval Punjab. Baba Farid, Shah Hussain (1538–1599), Sultan Bahu (1630–1691) and Bulleh Shah (1680–1757) are famous Sufi poets, while Hazrat Peelu (1580–1675), Waris Shah (1722–1798) and Hashim Shah (1735–1843) are famous poets of Punjabi Qisse.

4 *Gurmat Kaav* is the devotional poetry written by Sikh Gurus. Their poetry is compiled in the holy book of the Sikhs, Sri Guru Granth Sahib.

5 Qissa (Qisse for plural) is Punjabi for narrative or legend. It is a genre of Punjabi poetry. A Qissa is a long narrative in verse.

During the medieval period, Amir Khusrau (1235–1325) enriched Indian poetry, music and culture by laying down the foundation of syncretic culture in India. Indian languages (khari boli) around Delhi were mixed with Persian and Turkish giving birth to a new culture and language. Malik Mohammad Jayasi (1477–1542) wrote in Awadhi and Persian script, and Abdul Rahim Khan-i-Khanan (1556–1627) wrote Hindi couplets. During the 18th century, there was a phenomenal rise in the popularity of Urdu. The baton of Urdu poetry was carried forward by Mir Taqi Mir (1723–1810), Mirza Ghalib, Muhammad Ibrahim Zauq (1790–1854) and the Mughal king, Bahadur Shah Zafar (1775–1862). Along with the themes of physical love, spiritual love and philosophical contemplation on life, Urdu poetry reflected on social and political turbulence of the times. Profound thought, love and mystical ideas were expressed in a strict metrical form called ghazal.

In the 19th century, every regional language of India had its 'patriarchal pantheon represented by specific concerns, conventions and form' (Sachidanandan, 2001, p. vii), contributing to the formation of linguistic identities in colonial India. The tradition of Indian English poetry also began during this period. Henry Louis Vivian Derozio (1809–1831), an Anglo-Indian poet, was the 'first Indian nationalist poet of any language' (Paranjape, 2001, p. 127). Michael Madhusudan Dutt (1824–1873) followed in the footsteps of Derozio to introduce a recognisable modernity into Indian English poetry. Toru Dutt (1856–1877) wrote on Indian themes in the English language and Sarojini Naidu (1879–1949) wrote about common people of India, while Rabindranath Tagore (1861–1941) translated his Bangla poetry into English. It can be said that in their hands, the English language became a potent medium to express Indian thought and sensibility.

The colonial period also marked the rise of revolutionary poetry. Besides Punjabi Ghadar Poetry, Urdu poets often blended the idea of romance with revolution. Some of them continued to write in post-colonial times as well. Faiz Ahmed Faiz (1911–1984),[6] Majaz (1911–1955), Sahir Ludhianvi (1921–1980) and Kaifi Azmi (1919–2002) in Urdu; Nagarjun (1911–1998), Muktibodh (1917–1964), Raghuvir Sahay (1929–1990) and Manglesh Dabral (1948–2020) in Hindi; and Sant Ram Udasi (1939–1986) and Pash (1950–1988) in Punjabi are some important poets who wrote the poetry of dissent.

6 A member of the Progressive Writers' Movement, Faiz Ahmed Faiz was born in the district of Narowal (now in Pakistan), undivided India. He continued to live in Pakistan after partition.

However, Indian English poetry took a different trajectory during the same period. Some of these poets carried forward the aesthetics of the previous age, combining it with modern concerns, while other poets were influenced by ideas of poetry emerging in different parts of the world. 'The inwardness of Dom Moraes, R. Parthasarathy and Kamala Das is closer to the nineteenth century Romantic tradition,' writes Sarang, while 'Kolatkar, Mehrotra and Mahapatra bear the heritage of French Symbolism and Surrealism' (2007, p. 5). Modern Indian English poets wrote on identity, language and culture, thereby writing the new nation in their poetry. 'Idealism, mysticism, and the beauties of nature are replaced by skepticism, secularism, and the searing city scape' (Paranjape, 2001, p. 142) in much modern Indian English poetry. Instead of spiritual and metaphysical issues, immediate material reality became the subject of their poetry. Nissim Ezekiel (1924–2004), A.K. Ramanujan (1929–1993), Jayant Mahapatra (b.1928), Arun Kolatkar (1932–2004), Kamala Das, later Kamala Surayya (1934–2009), Keki N. Daruwalla (b.1934), Eunice de Souza (1940–2017) and others took Indian English poetry in bold new directions.

Similarly, poetry in other Indian languages also blossomed in the 20th century. Indian poets wrote on issues of gender, caste and women's rights. Mahadevi Verma (1907–1987), Amrita Pritam (1919–2005), Kamala Surayya, Eunice de Souza, Indira Goswami (1942–2011) and Meena Kandasamy (b.1984) are prominent women poets across languages whose poetry shakes conventional notions of femininity in India. Paul Kaur (b.1956), Anamika (b.1961), Neetu Arora (b.1978) and Arundhathi Subramaniam (b.1973) are contemporary women poets continuing this tradition in India. Namdeo Dhasal (1949–2014) and Lal Singh Dil (1943–2007) were and Sharankumar Limbale (b.1956) and Sukirtharani (b.1973) are some eminent male and female Dalit voices in poetry. Indian diaspora poets such as Agha Shahid Ali (1949–2001), Meena Alexander (1951–2018), Chitra Banerjee Divakaruni (b.1956), Ajmer Rode (b.1940), Amarjit Chandan (b.1946) and Rupi Kaur (b.1992) have added new dimensions to Indian poetry and its heritage.

Indian poetry has varied hues and complexions: it includes epics, devotional poetry, love poetry, erotic poetry, romanticism, and poetry of resistance and protest. This is a space wherein poets have expressed the concerns of men, women, sexualities, caste, class, modernity and postmodernity. Through Indian poetry, linguistic identities are negotiated, nation is mapped, dissent is expressed and culture is rewritten.

On the occasion of the 75th year of India's independence, colleagues at BCU in the UK and Guru Gobind Singh Indraprastha University, New Delhi, conceived a joint initiative to celebrate the vast range and diverse tradition of Indian poetry in a series of three online poetry events, held in September 2021, April 2022 and July 2022.

Figure 10.2: Harmeet Vidyarthi

The invited poets represent the regional, linguistic and gender diversity of India and the Indian diaspora in the UK. Some of the invited poets are bilingual, writing in their first language as well as in English, while others write only in their first language.

We regret that we could not include poets from all Indian languages in these poetry events, nor is it possible to sum up more than 3,000 years of poetry writing in India in this short essay. There are so many languages such as Santhali, Kashmiri, Assamese, Meitei, Gujarati, Rajasthani or Chhattisgarhi that could not be discussed in detail. We can only offer our sincere apologies for not being able to include these poetic traditions, despite our best intentions. We understand that the tradition of Indian poetry is too vast and the space available to us too small. But such is India!

'What each of our events revealed, however, is a taste of the wonderful vigour, range, ambition and vitality of Indian poetry today. The series included Anvar Ali, Sanjeev Kaushal, Rati Agnihotri, Neetu Arora, Rekha Moothedath, Mussavir, Roshan Bral, Harmeet Vidyarthi, Arundhathi Subramaniam, Gagandeep Sharma, and Subodh Sarkar from India, and Rupinder Kaur and Jessica Mookherjee from the UK.' The poets, both reading from their work and in conversation, have been at once serious and playful, spirited and grounded, acutely aware of what is at stake in our societies and how we live, and the powerful intervention that poetry – in its fine attention to language, and hence to all in which language participates – has made and continues to make in our humanity. These occasions have been a celebration not only of a recognised history, but of possibility.

Multilingual diversity brings new horizons for 'When you've been too long in the rooms of English', in the words of a poem by Jeet Thayil (2008, p. 228) – but it also creates new rooms within English, too (for 'English' here we could substitute any language). Language nourishes language. Poetry, as language, wants to travel, to connect, to cross and defy borders – both to sow and to assume new life, through contact and translation – to open up, as its history shows it can, new worlds of thought and feeling far beyond where it is first spoken or written. Among its numberless pleasures and its revitalising powers, poetry brings with it the seeds and possibilities of new cultural bonds and partnerships both within and between countries and peoples – and that is something we should go on celebrating.

References

Grover, N., Bhattacharya, T. and Randhawa, S., eds. (2013) The People's Linguistic Survey of India: Sign Language, series ed. G.N. Devy, Orient Blackswan, 2013

Kumar, A. (2009) Poetry, Culture and Politics: Essays on Indian Texts and Contexts. Routledge

Lienhard, S. (1984) A History of Indian Literature: A History of Classical Poetry Sanskrit – Pali – Prakrit, Vol. III, series ed. Jan Gonda. Ottoharrassowitz

Paranjape, M. (2001) 'Reflections on the Changing Identity of Indian English Verse', Indian Poetry: Modernism and After – A Seminar, ed. K. Sachidanandan, Sahitya Akademi, pp. 122–152

P. Chenchiah, M.L. and Raja M. Bhujanga Rao Bahadur. A History of Telugu Literature. The Association Press, Calcutta: https://archive.org/stream/history oftelugul00chenuoft/historyoftelugul00chenuoft_djvu.txt

Sachidanandan, K. (2001) 'Introduction.' Indian Poetry: Modernism and After – A Seminar, ed. K. Sachidanandan. Sahitya Akademi

Sarang, V., ed. (2007) Indian English Poetry Since 1950: An Anthology, Disha Books, Orient Longman

About the contributors

Gregory Leadbetter is Professor of Poetry at BCU. His research focuses on Romantic poetry and thought, the traditions to which these relate, and the history and practice of poetry more generally. His books of poetry include Balanuve (with photographs by Phil Thomson) (Broken Sleep, 2021), Maskwork (Nine Arches Press, 2020; longlisted for the Laurel Prize 2021), The Fetch (Nine Arches Press, 2016) and the pamphlet The

Body in the Well (HappenStance Press, 2007). His book Coleridge and the Daemonic Imagination (Palgrave Macmillan, 2011) won the University English Book Prize 2012.

Vivek Sachdeva is an academic, creative writer and translator. He is Professor of English at Guru Gobind Singh Indraprastha University, New Delhi. His research focuses on film adaptation and Indian cinema. His critical work includes Fiction to Film: Ruth Prawer Jhabvala's The Householder and Heat and Dust (Orient Blackswan, 2017) and Shyam Benegal's India: Alternative Images (Routledge, 2020). The Biryani Shop and Other Stories (Hawakal Publishers, 2022) is his collection of short stories. He translates from Punjabi to English. He also learns Indian classical vocal music.

Chapter 11

A personal reflection on India's growth in its private higher education provision since independence

Panchalingam Suntharalingam

Summary

Since independence in 1947, India has seen abundant growth in private higher education provision, predominantly since the beginning of the 1990s. This chapter is an overview of the prolific growth of private higher education provision which is over twice the size of the public sector. The growth of these institutions in all sectors such as the arts, science, technology, medicine, business, and law has not emerged as a result of planning either by state governments or the central government, but by the political, social, and economic changes that have been demanded by existing and emerging industries across the whole country. The result of this expansion has seen many of these institutions seeking a UK memorandum of understanding (MoU) as a means of providing international recognition of its home provision courses using its locally trained graduates in providing internationally recognised degrees in key subjects as listed above.

Introduction

Before and just after independence, it was mainly the upper castes (Brahmans and Kayasthas) who took advantage of the limited state higher education provision and secured employment in government or private service or took up independent professions and improved their economic status. The 'lower' castes recognised, particularly after independence, that higher education was the means to achieve a better economic status. A higher education degree empowered them to exert political pressure on state governments to consider the opening of new universities or permitting the affiliation of colleges in small towns.

Pre-1990s

According to Karve and Shah (1964, p379) in the 1960s, when the educated people of the advanced castes spoke out against the lowering of standards in higher education or affiliated colleges due to a rate of expansion of educational opportunities greater than the availability of qualified lecturers and corresponding resource provision of that establishment, there was a general outrage against the attempts 'to perpetuate the present imbalance in Indian society and to keep down the backward castes in a permanently backward condition'.

As more members of the lower castes gained education and became more affluent and held positions of authority, there were more exertions on state governments to fast-track legislature to establish new higher education provisions or to exercise its executive authority to affiliate a new college to an existing university. This created a problem that still exists today that does not necessarily mean that suitably qualified teachers are available or that library or laboratory facilities or student accommodation or sports fields, etc., are included in the resources provided. The fast-tracking of the provision has been at the expense of due diligence where local politicians or leaders with influence with government officials have been able to persuade state governments to agree to expand the provision to the rapidly increasing population.

The aspiring and growing population of India regarded universities mainly as examining and degree-granting bodies. However, it was emerging that only the degrees of governing bodies established by statute had general recognition for purposes of employment.

The Gillard, (1963) Robbins Report on Higher Education in India had an enormously enthusiastic reception in the UK. The government welcomed it and ministers commended it as "The most important social document to be produced since the Beveridge Report (1942)". Gupta (1964), who had suggested opening more technical and vocational schools to reduce the number of high school graduates demanding admission into colleges and universities, is still valid today. However, it was clear that unless reasonably numerous and attractive avenues of employment were available to these graduates, these institutions were not going to attract many high school graduates. The evidence is clear even today as shown in the employment statistics (AISHE 2019–20). The country was seeing a rapidly increasing number of high school graduates who were competing to secure admission to institutions of higher education that had limited spaces. No state government was in a position to advocate or encourage a policy of granting admission only based on merit, with the number of places available causing an outcry from the underprivileged castes.

The author's observation, and that of Tilak (2004), shows that the expansion of private higher education was an unavoidable issue based on the opportunities available to the rapidly expanding population. The importance of knowledge in securing a better future was an extremely important theme for equity and democratic rights irrespective of caste and affordability. The newly formed private higher education institutions impinge on these aspects significantly.

Higher education teaching proficiency

With the increasing demand for lecturers and technicians to provide education to the new cohorts, the quality of provision and standards for benchmarking were overlooked by most private providers. There was no central body such as the Quality Assurance Agency (QAA) in the UK to oversee standards. Compared to UK higher education institutions, Indian postgraduate teaching qualifications, teaching, and research experience with suitable resources were not considered essential requirements of a private university provision.

The expansion of higher education institutions in India emerged not through planning either by state governments or the central government, but through the political, social, and economic changes that have taken place. The data collection and research processes to estimate how many university-trained persons in arts, science, technology, medicine, law, etc. will be required to cater for the rate of expansion and how many institutions delivering these courses and the resources, such as accommodation and necessary facilities, were not accurately calculated.

Post-1990s

From the early 1990s, anecdotal evidence shows that the governments in the various states and the central government in India were not in favour of private education. However, from 1990 to 2020, some government policies were formulated and adopted out of compulsion and some through conviction. With this new private university provision set to continue growing, there is practically no desire for the central government to set up new universities. There is also the availability of real estate and no real need for yet another university, given that there are many private universities in existence. Instead, the focus of the government should be to ensure that the existing (private) universities work within good regulatory and enabling frameworks for all state and private universities. This is key to maintaining benchmark standards akin to the QAA in the UK for internationalisation and recognition.

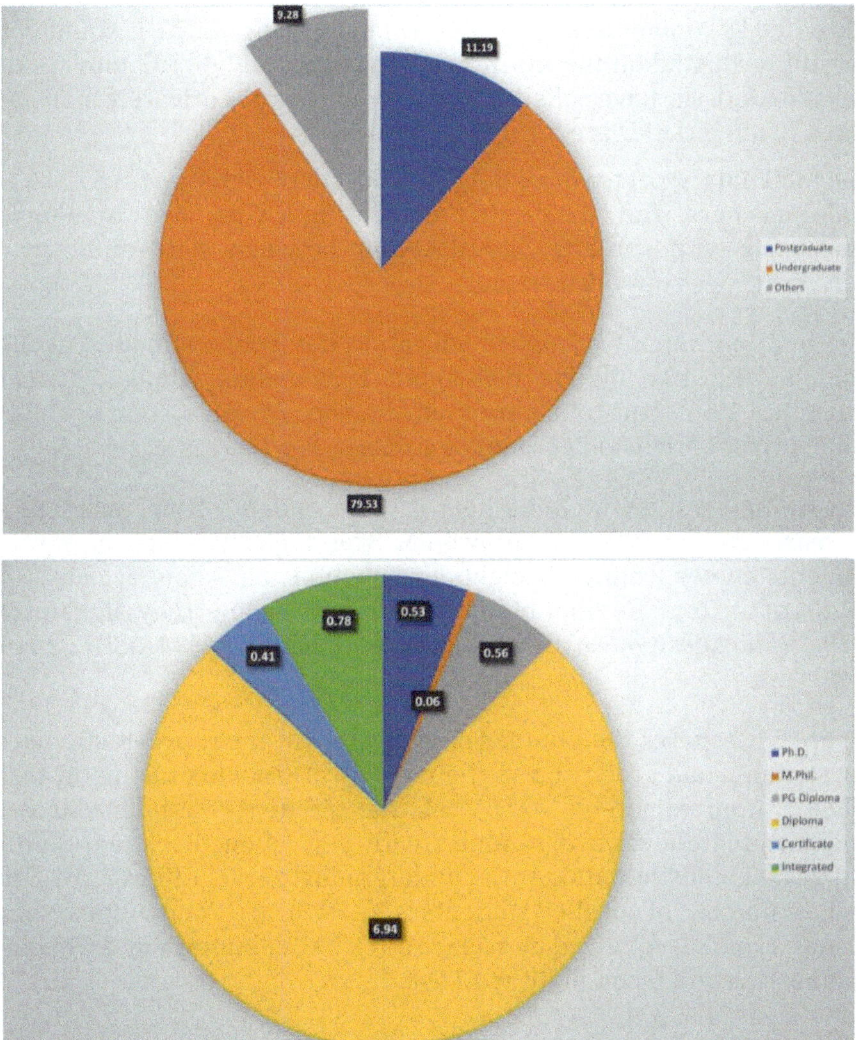

Figure 11.1: Percentage of student enrolment by levels (AISHE, 2019–20).

There are several claimed advantages of this rapid private higher education expansion, and this draws attention to the dangers involved in a high degree of graduate dependence on the private sector and the subsequent international recognition of its provision in India.

The current status of state and private higher education provisions in India

At the time of writing this chapter, AISHE (2019–20) reported that there were 1,043 universities, 42,343 colleges, and 11,779 standalone institutions listed on the AISHE web portal. A total of 307 universities are affiliated, i.e., have colleges, 396 universities are privately managed, and 420 universities are located in rural areas.

The total number of teachers is 1,503,156, out of which about 57.5% are male teachers and 42.5% are female teachers. The breakdown associated with subjects and the split between state and private universities has not been stated.

The total enrolment in higher education has been estimated at 38.5 million, with 19.6 million males and 18.9 million females. Females constitute 49% of the total enrolment. State provision accounts for 34% while private provision accounts for 66%.

Private universities in India also recruit students from overseas to increase their international profile. The highest share of foreign students comes from the neighbouring countries: Nepal accounts for 28.1% of the total number of foreign students, followed by Afghanistan 9.1%, Bangladesh 4.6%, Bhutan 3.8%, and Sudan 3.6% (AISHE, 2019–20).

Figure 11.2 shows the number of institutes (orange) providing places for students and green shows the number of students taking up these places. Approximately 79.5% of the students are enrolled in undergraduate-level programmes, with only about 0.5% enrolled in PhDs (202,550 students). At the undergraduate level (30,647,287), the highest number of enrolled students is 32.7% in arts/humanities/social sciences courses followed by science at 16.0%, commerce at 14.9%, and engineering and technology at 12.6%.

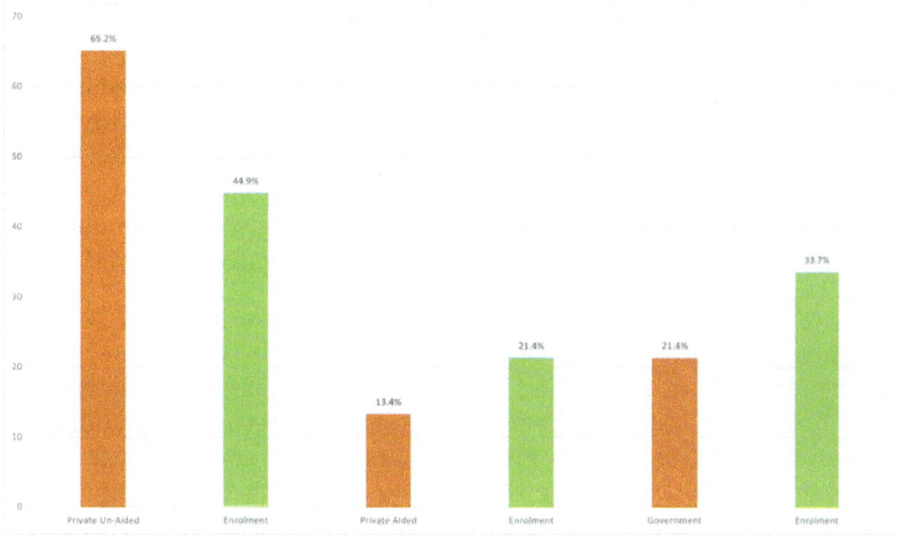

Figure 11.2: Percentage enrolment in private and state higher education (AISHE, 2019-20).

More than 78.6% of India's universities/colleges operate in the private sector, aided and unaided taken together, but these only cater for 66.3% of the total enrolment. Enrolment in private and government universities/colleges is shown in Figure 11.3.

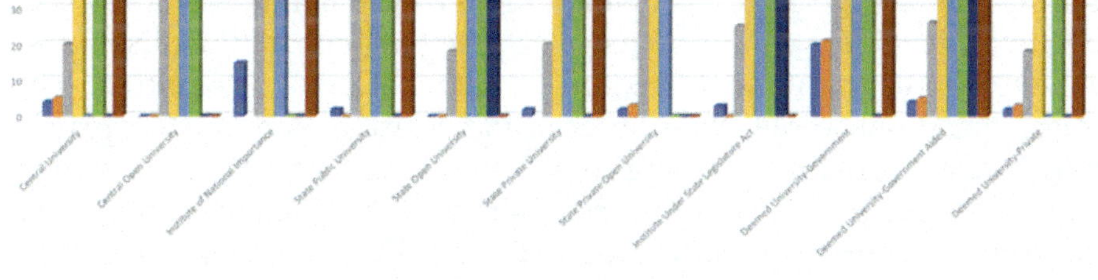

Figure 11.3: Enrolment by level in different types of universities (AISHE 2019-20).

Enrolment in different types of universities

There are at present 13 State Open Universities set up by different state grants. These State Open Universities are single-mode institutions, which means they provide education only in the distance mode. These universities cater to students who are unable to pursue regular courses due to various reasons. These Universities are also instrumental in shaping the career growth of learners who are already employed.

The total number of students enrolled at all Universities is 81,380,000 for undergraduate students (AISHE, 2019–20) of which the largest number of students is 1,397,527 in state public universities followed by state open universities which account for 922,944. The number of female students is lowest for institutes under state private open universities (2,499) followed by institutes under the State Legislature Act (3,702) whereas the share is highest in the state public universities. The share of female students is lowest for institutes of national importance (24.7%) followed by government universities (33.4%) and state private universities (34.7%), whereas the share of female students for institutes under the State Legislative Act is 61.2%. The share of female students in state public universities is 50.1% and in central universities, it is 48.1%.

Location of the private universities/colleges

Bangalore, an urban district in India tops the number of universities/colleges with 1,009 colleges followed by Jaipur with 606 colleges. The top 50 districts have about 32% of colleges (AISHE, 2019–20).

International partnerships

During the past decade, a growing number of Indian universities have begun to develop a comprehensive strategy for internationalisation as a key component in their vision for international recognition. This raises questions about what 'internationalisation' is and what private universities in India are doing to achieve it, and why they consider it worth committing the time, effort, and resources. The answers to these questions process have implications for the UK host university and the overseas partner University in India.

The need for universities in India to embark on internationalisation has been a result of responding directly to the complex range of phenomena such as 'globalisation', ranking and seeking to prepare Indian students for success in the globally integrated economic environment. Many private higher education providers in India are moving decisively to internationalise their curricula, promote cross-cultural understanding, and provide opportunities for the development of foreign-language skills. At the same time, international partnerships represent a valuable source of income and knowledge exchange for universities in countries such as the UK. It also makes it possible for UK university staff to work and engage with other young learners from diverse backgrounds on the Indian subcontinent.

Figure 11.4: Convocation graduates and course team at iCAT, Chennai, India

The provision of local university degrees in the private higher education sector has seen many of these universities seeking a UK MoU, UK articulation, or franchise course partnerships as a means of providing international recognition of its home provision of degree courses. Degrees delivered by a private local University would otherwise raise scepticism from local applicants if its degrees are not internationally recognised especially in the UK. Figure 11.4 shows an example of graduates from Birmingham City University's articulated three-year undergraduate degree delivered in Bangalore and Chennai with quality assurance standards administered by BCU, UK.

Summary

The author has been involved in the overseas recruitment of students and academic partnerships since the 1990s. Since then, the author has witnessed a prolific growth of these private higher education institutions seeking affiliations with overseas providers in all sectors such as the arts, science, technology, medicine, business, and law, particularly in undergraduate courses. These undergraduates on completion of their franchised or articulated degrees with a UK University then go on to seek a Master's degree in an overseas country that recognises their locally obtained undergraduate qualifications affiliated with a UK university.

References

All India Survey on Higher Education (AISHE) 2019-2020. Government of India, Ministry of Education, Department of Higher Education Planning, Monitoring and Statistics Division, New Delhi. https://www.education.gov.in/en

Beveridge W. Social insurance and allied services 1942. Bull World Health Organ. 2000;78(6):847-55. PMID: 10916922; PMCID: PMC2560775. (n.d.).

Gillard, D. (n.d.) Robbins Report (1963). Available at: http://www.educationengland.org.uk/documents/robbins/robbins1963.html (Accessed: 17 October 2022).

Gupta, A. K. D. (1964). REFLECTIONS ON HIGHER EDUCATION IN INDIA IN THE LIGHT OF THE ROBBINS REPORT. Minerva, 2(2), 160–168. http://www.jstor. org/stable/41822006

Karve, D. D., & Shah, A. B. (1964). HIGHER EDUCATION IN INDIA. Minerva, 2(3), 379–382. http://www.jstor.org/stable/41821626

The Quality Assurance Agency for Higher Education (2022). Available at: https:// www.qaa.ac.uk/ (Accessed: 17 October 2023).

Tilak, J. B. G. (2014). Private Higher Education in India. Economic and Political Weekly, 49(40), 32–38. http://www.jstor.org/stable/24480821

About the contributor

Dr Panchalingam Suntharalingam is an Associate Professor and College Academic Lead for Distance and Transnational Education for the Birmingham School of Architecture, BCU. He is also the Course Director for MA Design and Visualisation at BCU. Dr Suntharalingam has developed partnerships worldwide and teaches and recruits students on undergraduate and postgraduate courses in Design and Visualisation, Product Design, Interior Architecture, and Design in the UK, India, Hong Kong, and China. Dr Suntharalingam's areas of expertise and interests include design and visualisation, engineering product design, industrial design, knowledge transfer partnership (KTP) programmes, software programming, enterprise development, medical product design, interior products, applied research, rapid prototyping, and computer-aided design. Dr Suntharalingam has extensive design and scientific knowledge in interdisciplinary fields and holds a patent for a medical product that has sold over 50,000 products in the USA and over 8,000 products in the UK.

Dr Suntharalingam has published numerous international papers on medical products; he has also designed opening title sequences featured on the BBC and ITV networks, including for well-known programmes such as Top Gear. His wealth of experience with the manufacturing industry includes 19 KTPs, with companies such as AGA Rangemaster, gaining four 'Outstanding' Innovate UK awards for achievement in innovation. In 2020, one of his KTPs was shortlisted for the Best of the Best KTPs in the UK. He is also an external examiner at various national and international universities for undergraduate, postgraduate, and PhD courses.

Chapter 12

Radio in India

Sam Coley, Arul Aram and Lavanya Rajendran

Summary

This chapter explores the last 75 years of Indian radio and considers the medium's relevance in an increasingly post-digital world. We investigate the rise of community broadcasting and reflect on a collaborative radio training partnership, funded by the British Council, which took place in early 2022 and 2023 between BCU and Anna University.

Introduction

At Indian independence in 1947, the country had only six radio stations. Today, All India Radio (AIR), the country's public broadcasting service, has a network of 479 radio stations, while there are 388 commercial FM stations and 454 community radio (FM) stations. AIR, started in 1936, was renamed Akashvani in 1956. This chapter considers the growth and evolution of radio in India and its pathway to becoming one of the country's most cherished and valuable mass mediums. We focus on the rise of community radio, particularly Anna Community Radio, in Chennai, the capital of the Tamil Nadu State, India.

In the beginning

The innate human need to communicate can be traced back to our earliest ancestors. While the origin of language is hard to determine, Armstrong (1999) believes humans first used gestures to help explain our thoughts and feelings. We then progressed to the vocalisations of speech and used cave paintings and smoke signals to transmit ideas across time and distance. Tomasello (2008) claims human communication is essentially a cooperative enterprise, which came from a need to coordinate collaborative activities efficiently. The invention of radio in the late 19th century was a logical extension of this innate desire to communicate and coordinate. By enabling voices to be heard across vast distances, radio became the first electronic mass media and was quickly embraced around the world.

In June 1923, the Radio Club of Bombay broadcast India's first official radio programme. Four years later, All India Radio (AIR) became the country's first organised station. The first Controller of Broadcasting in India was Lionel Fielden, a senior BBC producer, who helped guide the station until it came under government control in 1936. The growth of radio in India was a relatively slow process. By the time India gained independence, there were still only 18 transmitters covering 2.5% of the country and reaching just 11% of the population. In comparison, today AIR is one of the world's largest media organisations, broadcasting to 92% of India, in 23 languages and 179 dialects. This impressive transformation took time and was hampered by the arrival of competition from visual entertainment such as films, television, and other subsequent technologies. Yet radio remained remarkably resilient. The medium was revitalised in India by the introduction of Frequency Modulation (FM) technology, which began broadcasting in 1977, and led to early experimentation with private FM broadcasting.

Mass appeal

Radio in India has enjoyed broad appeal to mass audiences. One of its key strengths is its immediacy. Unlike early written forms of communication, listeners could hear the latest news, often as it occurred, and illiteracy was not a barrier. Radio was often employed by the government and various civil society organisations to aid development programmes, such as AIR's support of the Green Revolution in the late 1960s and the early 1970s. This project was so successful that hybrid varieties of rice promoted in various parts of the country came to be popularly known as 'radio rice'. The medium was also harnessed to enhance teaching and learning. Various educational programmes were broadcast in different cities by Gyan Vani FM radio under the umbrella of Indira Gandhi National Open University from 2001, with each station reaching out to a 75 km radius. The success of these initiatives, among others, helped to demonstrate radio's ability to provide vast audiences with tangible, 'real world' benefits and paved the way for the establishment of community radio in India.

Community radio in India

Community radio officially came to India following the Supreme Court's 1995 declaration that the Indian airwaves or frequencies were a public property, and their use had to be controlled and regulated by a public authority in the interests of the public and to prevent the invasion of their rights. Following this ruling, a community radio policy came into being in 2002 to start community radio stations in educational institutions. Then, in 2006, another policy extended community radio to civil society organisations. At this point, educational institutions and civil society organisations were able to procure licences to run community radio stations. Unlike commercial radio, the focus of community radio was centred on catering to the needs and concerns of local communities, using 50-Watt transmitters which could reach a radius of 15 km, unless they were prevented by obstructions such as tall concrete buildings, particularly in urban landscape. Today, the government of India is likely to permit community radio stations to use more powerful 100-Watt transmitters.

Figure 13.1: Anna Community Radio Signage (photograph courtesy: S. Coley).

The power of community

In the context of radio, the word 'community' refers to anyone who is listening to the station and/or whoever comes within its range. It is a decentralised form of communication, more akin to narrowcasting rather than broadcasting. Community radio is a medium of communication used by people living in close proximity who share a socio-cultural heritage and speak one language or dialect. It is a fascinating oral medium which can reach out effectively to people at the grassroots with its community-first approach. More than the power of technology, it is the people's participation that enables community radio to create positive change in society. It breaks media stereotypes with its inclusive nature. It is a powerful yet inexpensive medium which can reach out to the poor and needy.

Figure 12.1: Community members during programme production (photograph courtesy: Anna Community Radio).

Community radio stations in India have been conducting community-centric programmes on a broad range of topics such as HIV/AIDS and tuberculosis awareness, the empowerment of women, environmental issues, climate change mitigation and adaptation, health and nutrition, child marriage, disaster management, and career guidance. While community radio stations have not been given permission to gather and broadcast news, they are allowed to rebroadcast AIR news bulletins. The surrounding community can interact with the respective radio station by writing letters, sending SMS texts, using social media and making phone calls about various programmes. Live phone-in programmes are also carried out to promote community participation. Rather than having professional radio jockeys, community radio stations take volunteers from the community, who are then trained to create innovative programmes by going out into their community to look for stories, interview people, and to prioritise the issues they feel are important. The focus is on community action and community mobilisation, with people from the community producing programmes, and helping their community to take action. Baseline surveys are conducted with the community to identify their needs. Community volunteers are given hands-on training, such as how to work together in groups, write scripts, offer constructive feedback, practise, record, and improve their work. This training is ideally presented in accessible, innovative ways which engage and motivate community members and students as well where the radio station is located in an educational institution. These radio presenters/producers then go back to their community and involve many others in looking for stories and interviewing people to help make a positive change.

Anna Community Radio

Following the freeing up of the Indian airwaves, Anna Community Radio was started on 1 February 2004, becoming the country's first community radio station. Pavarala and Malik (2007) refer to community radio as the 'third tier' of Indian broadcasting, designed to redefine notions of democracy and development in the move towards a more egalitarian and equitable society. Anna Community Radio has always reflected this ideal, with its focus on serving poor communities, particularly women, who live around the campus in low-income localities. Interestingly, the station departed from the concept of campus radio and plunged into communication for development even at its inception under the leadership of R. Sreedher.

The station was initially based on AIR's local radio experiments and on narrowcasting audio initiatives run by civil society organisations such as Voices and Drishti Media. However, the establishment of Anna Community Radio finally provided a more consistent and powerful advocate for its audience of underrepresented listeners. Anna Community Radio refrains from broadcasting film songs but takes special care to produce and broadcast folk songs which are original creations. It should be noted that many other community-based radio stations have taken to populism by airing film songs to attract and hold listeners.

Over the years, Anna Community Radio has grown from strength to strength, serving as both a trusted media outlet, and as a training facility for students and community members to gain valuable broadcasting experience. Alongside its radio transmissions, the station's content is simultaneously delivered through the internet as well. Like many community stations, Anna Community Radio undertakes a range of offline activities too, and frequently conducts training workshops for members of its community and the wider radio fraternity. The station has adopted eight communities in its coverage zone, particularly poor households, and slum clearance tenements, with the primary target group being poor women in those communities. During the 2004 tsunami, Anna Community Radio provided relief and rehabilitation activities as well as broadcasting relevant disaster relief content. The station also held a pioneering international conference on community radio supported by the Commonwealth of Learning and the UNESCO in December 2004. The government of India was very appreciative of the station's efforts and replicated the experiment in remote places in the Andaman and Nicobar Islands. Anna Community Radio also served the community during the 2015 floods that devastated Chennai. Then, during the 2020–2021 Covid-19 lockdown period, when educational institutions were shut, Anna Community Radio broadcast educational content, particularly spoken English, so children isolated at home could benefit and feel a sense of connection.

In 2022 the station was recognised by the Indian government as one of the leading examples of the community radio movement. Anna Community Radio has also received several national awards for best community radio practices. At the National Community Radio Awards function, held in New Delhi on the 16th of March 2015, Jamila, the first radio jockey from the community, was a special invitee. When the then Information and Broadcasting Minister asked her what difference community radio made to the lives of its listeners, she replied: 'Before I joined as a volunteer in the community radio, I used to be ill-treated by my drunken husband who often disrupted the children's education too. Now I am an empowered woman, and come what may, I shall not allow any force to disrupt the education of my children and other children in my community.'

An international partnership

In late 2021, a partnership was re-established between Anna University and BCU, which drew on earlier research and Study Abroad initiatives between the two institutions. A collaborative media training initiative, funded by the British Council, took place in early 2022 to share best practices in community radio broadcasting, while encouraging students from the UK and India to create content for their respective student stations, Scratch Radio in Birmingham and Anna Community Radio in Chennai. This ten-week capacity-building programme trained undergraduate students from Anna University and BCU alongside some students from the target community to produce radio content. The project was called 'Samugam', the word for community in the Tamil language. Over 40 students successfully took part in a series of online classes and heard from a range of experts from the field of radio production and community broadcasting from both the UK and India. Class attendance for the sessions was very good and student feedback was enthusiastic. Furthermore, the participants' content creation activities continued after the project had come to its official conclusion. Based on this initial success, we put in place a long-term transnational education collaboration, strengthening the links between the two institutions. In 2023, a follow-up British Council-funded 'Live Project' module was delivered remotely, with 10 students from Anna University completing a Birmingham City University class online.

Conclusion

While community radio in India had a slow start, it gradually gained momentum to reach today's impressive figure of 454 stations. More opportunities for future growth lie ahead. As the medium has continued to evolve and adapt to new technologies, community radio in India has been quick to embrace the use of social media, on-demand audio, streaming, podcasting, etc. But while delivery platforms may have changed with radio stations taking to internet radio too, the central principles of community broadcasting in India remain the same. Stations such as Anna Community Radio stand as an example of radio's ongoing impact and its importance in the everyday lives of its listeners.

References

Armstrong, D. (1999) Original Signs, Galludet University Press.

Pavarala, V. and Malik, K. (2007) Other Voices: The Struggle for Community Radio in India, Sage.

Supreme Court of India (1995) Judgment of a case of the Secretary, Ministry of Information and Broadcasting vs. the Cricket Association of Bengal & ANR on 9 February, AIR 1236, 1995 SCC (2) 161, https://indiankanoon.org/doc/539407/

Tomasello, M. (2008) Origins of Human Communication, MIT Press.

About the contributors

Dr Sam Coley is an Associate Professor for the Faculty of Arts, Design and Media at BCU, UK, where he teaches a range of audio production modules. Coley is a member of the Birmingham Centre for Media and Cultural Research's Media and Place and Popular Music Studies research clusters, with an interest in the field of radio documentary production. He continues to work as a freelance radio documentary producer and has served as a Grand Jury member of the New York Radio Festival since 2012.

Dr I. Arul Aram is Professor and former Head of the Department of Media Sciences, Anna University, Chennai. He was Director of the University Grants Commission's Educational Multimedia Research Centre during 2010-11. He also headed Anna Community Radio, India's first community radio station. Under his leadership, Anna Community Radio received a national award for Best Communication Practices. He served as the Vice-President (South) of the Community Radio Association. He was Additional Director at Anna University's Centre for Faculty Development in 2019–20. His areas of specialisation and research interests include environmental communication, peace journalism, community media, and climate change communication. He coordinated the first UKIERI project of Anna University.

Dr Lavanya Rajendran is Associate Professor at Anna University and has extensive and diverse experience in teaching. She also serves as the Deputy Controller of Examinations of Anna University. Her areas of interest include community media, web design, graphics, animation, game development, media research, video production and cloud computing. She was awarded the Royal Dutch Fellowship for Training the Trainers programme in 2012. She was the co-coordinator of the first British-funded UK-India Education and Research Initiative (UKIERI) project, awarded for technology-related research to Anna University and visited BCU as part of this project.

Chapter 13

Memories of academic international engagement; cross-cultural knowledge sharing and future possibilities in a post-pandemic world

Jacqueline Norton

Summary

This chapter reflects upon the development of international partnerships in the current climate and associated relationships with colleagues from higher education international institutions. It includes reference to interviews with colleagues based in the Tamil Nadu region, collective memories, and mutual future insights into the creative sector and partnership engagement.

Introduction

In recent years international partnership development for UK higher education institutions has faced a number of challenges. On 31 January 2020 Britain left the European Union after a majority democratic vote to leave on 23 June 2016. Less than three months later, on 23 March 2020, the UK entered its first lockdown after a global pandemic, Covid-19, had been rapidly spreading around the world. There have also been significant contributors that are serving to impact on the international educational landscape and the development of institute strategies including recent geopolitical shifts around the world, as well as the potential global impact of the current situation unfolding in Eastern Europe.

Pre- and post-pandemic, there's been a heightened global awareness of the impact of climate change brought to the fore by the United Nations, the 2030 Agenda, the Sustainable Development Goals and their impact on the international educational environment. The recent UN Climate Change Conference (COP26) (Design Council,2021) hosted by the UK in Glasgow in 2021 (UK Government, 2021), reinforced the importance of these goals. Ongoing developments in bilateral agreements and policy updates (British High Commission New Delhi, 2021), such as the release of the National Education Policy in July 2020 including further recent updates (DigitalLEARNING, 2021, Heneghan, 2022, Sahay, 2022) approved by the University Grants Commission serve to provide government support related to internationalising education and strategic agendas (Government of India, 2020).

Working in a creative educational environment, international partnerships are often developed and sustained through mutual respect and understanding among academics, reinforced by a passion to support global citizenship and internationalisation opportunities for those we teach and those involved in the teaching and delivery of the curriculum.

This chapter will refer to the generosity and importance of knowledge sharing in a post-colonial educational environment, demonstrated by colleagues and students, and the kindness and respect I have experienced as a national and international design academic and now as a senior international faculty member of staff, both in receiving colleagues from India and visiting our partner institutes overseas. Whether partnerships are formed through an initial MoU or the establishment of a transnational education partnership arrangement as the collaboration develops, the intent remains the same. While the international education environment continues to evolve, these partnerships demonstrate a willingness to work together towards supporting a common academic goal in bringing together both staff and students, thus forming professional partnerships, trust and friendships through international communities of practice despite the challenges of the present climate and in recent years.

Developing international communities of practice in a pre- and post-pandemic world

The first time I went to India was almost ten years ago in the summer of 2012, by invitation from a previous Associate Dean in my faculty, Professor Derek Cassidy. I was Subject Leader for Design in my university at the time, with the responsibility of Programme Director for multiple undergraduate courses taught at BCU and at our overseas partner institutes in Hong Kong and later India. One of these courses was being launched at two new transnational partner institutes in Maharashtra and the Tamil Nadu region, with campuses in Mumbai, Chennai, Hyderabad and Bangalore. In the lead-up to the visit, I contributed to the advance preparation of documentation and consultation on the partnership approval, led by a team of staff within the university. I was accompanied on my visit by two senior fellow academics, the late Professor Richard Snell and Associate Professor Marlene Little, to provide in-country staff development, training, cross-cultural knowledge sharing in relation to the curriculum and briefings in advance of the simultaneous partnership launch at both institutes.

Figure 13.1: Memories of Mumbai, India [photograph] (India own private collection, J. Norton, 2012).

To this day I hold fond memories of working with my colleagues overseas in providing valuable subject expertise to staff and students to support the new partnership launches. This was compounded by the opportunity of being afforded a valuable interactive immersive cultural experience through transnational education (Fernandez and Sigona 2020), getting to know colleagues, the incoming students, the cultural context and the institutional environment. I especially remember Mumbai being a city like no other: the vibrant colours, hustle and bustle and sounds, the benefits of observing first-hand the practice and innovation of local craft and the openness from our newfound colleagues including their willingness to share best practice within a welcoming educational environment. Visiting Chennai holds similar memories, a city I have been able to visit on multiple occasions in my current role.

On accepting the invitation to contribute to this publication I approached three colleagues, Chowdhury, Nagpal and Swaminathan (2022), whom I have previously worked with in India, in order to receive their reflections on working with BCU and their thoughts on the impact of the pandemic and recent government policy updates (see Appendix 1 at the end of this chapter).

Figure 13.2: More memories of Mumbai, India [photograph] (India own private collection, J. Norton, 2012).

I first met Chowdhury (2022) in 2012 while I was the previous Subject Leader for Design, and she was appointed as Head of Academics at one of our Indian transnational education institutes. Chowdhury has been happy to share her previous experience of working with ADM and the current challenges and opportunities of working in the creative private sector including connecting in a physical versus virtual environment (February 2022).

Virtual mode definitely enhances the accessibility of talents that is available in any corner of the world. It also opens up the possibility of extended accessibility of information (provided adequate infrastructure is set) and scope of improved transferable skill in terms of communication competency & digital communication skill. The usual challenges that are faced in the virtual/remote mode are the real-life experience of being together, the scope of learning from each other, lack of face-to- face supervision, social isolation that we are not used to. (Chowdhury, 2022)

Chowdhury introduced me to Swaminathan when SASI Creative Colleges, based in Coimbatore, were looking to expand their existing portfolio beyond their established architectural five-year accredited undergraduate award into further design disciplines. Chowdhury had previously completed a SEDA-accredited staff development course with BCU and provided consultation while SASI were setting up their design curriculum framework.

I invited them to visit BCU in April 2019 and received a reciprocal follow-up invitation to visit the SASI campus in Coimbatore in July 2019, while I was visiting the Tamil Nadu region on other university business. An MoU was later signed with SASI in January 2020 during a student and staff mobility visit by invitation from ADM to attend the in-person fourth annual Building Information Modelling (BIM) 2020 event hosted by BSoAD.

Figure 13.3: Memories of Chennai, India [photograph] (India own private collection, J. Norton, 2018).

As Mr Swaminathan recounts:

> *'We connected with Jackie Norton and Marlene Little in 2019 and we were very impressed with the proactive approach taken by them to collaborate. Our students were absolutely impressed with their visit to BCU campus in January 2020 and had a great learning experience in the BIM conclave... We were humbled with the kind hospitality shown by all the staff of BCU to us and we are awaiting our turn to host BCU members and students at our campus in India.'* (Swaminathan, 2022).

Nagpal is now working as a practising artist and educator in the private sector, having previously worked in senior academic roles for two of our transnational education institutes. She referred to the impact of the phenomenal growth in cross- cultural knowledge sharing since the opening up of air travel over 50 years ago as well as the changes she has witnessed in her lifetime, increasing opportunities for accessibility with each technological advancement (February 2022). In her current practice, the shift to the virtual world, accelerated during the pandemic, posed its challenges; however, Nagpal recognises the need to be able to adapt to the changing trends in order to enjoy 'the journey of our educational life'.

Figure 13.4: Memories of Coimbatore, India: visit to SASI Creative Colleges [photograph] (India own private collection, J., Norton, 2019). Pictured left to right: Prof Mohammed Ali Sharieff, Principal/ Director, SCSA; Shaswati Choudhury, SASI Academic Consultant; Dr Baskaralingam Vaseeharan, Director - Collaborative Programmes, Alagappa University, Karaikudi (visiting external adviser); Jackie Norton, Associate Professor International and Deputy Director of International Partnerships (ADM); Marlene Little, Associate Professor and Link Tutor; Mr Rajdeepan Swaminathan, Managing Trustee SASI Creative Colleges.

She reflected on the cultural benefits and knowledge sharing of academic engagement and her visits to BCU and her enthusiasm for the recent policy updates:

> *The NEP will bolster our education system and will go a long way in transforming India into a global education hub. It will accelerate digital learning and increase focus on the skill improvement and competency development of the students. In the field of art and designing I see a bigger revolutionary change. We all have rich heritage and culture and have been trying to preserve it. International partnership working with UK universities will give a momentum to our efforts. Students passionate with art and designing will get an opportunity to learn from mentors at a global level. (Nagpal, 2022)*

Additional extracts from the interviews with Chowdhury, Nagpal and Swaminathan are included in Appendix 2.

Conclusion – the international partnership evolution: co-creators and changemakers

Chowdhury, Nagpal and Swaminathan (2022) agreed with me on the revolutionary change occurring in the educational and creative sectors post the launch of NEP 2020 and post-pandemic, communicating that working with UK universities will provide an opportunity to accelerate digital learning and increase the focus on improving skills and international competency of students. Changes in BCU policy and curriculum development relating to equality, diversity and inclusion and decolonising of the curriculum for example all support the India education agenda and the diversity of its demographic (Trines, 2018). Since the launch of NEP 2020 and its strategic development, UK policy updates serve to reinforce the commitment and importance of UK universities continuing to engage and develop higher education institution alliances, building upon and sharing best practice.

Reimagining our post-pandemic world and the state of flux within the international educational paradigm means higher education institutions and academics are reflecting on what we did well in recent years and what we need to do better to survive the international education evolution and ever-changing factors including the geopolitical landscape. The digital and new technologies revolution aligned to increasing education-related agendas (Jisc, 2019; UN, 2018; UK Government/UN 2021) highlights the need to empower staff, students and alumni as co-creators related to the future of international curriculum and partnership development.

Alongside the necessary due diligence in an increasingly risk-averse environment, added opportunities and the benefits of exploring research collaborations, joint funding bids and allocated grants (British Council India, 2021). Universities continue to explore models and modes of delivery whether this is through exploring micro credentials, hybrid or flex models. on delivering the design curriculum is focusing more on creativity, value added opportunities and the benefits of exploring research collaborations, joint funding bids and allocated grants (British Council India, 2021). Universities continue to explore models and modes of delivery whether this is through exploring micro credentials, hybrid or flex models.

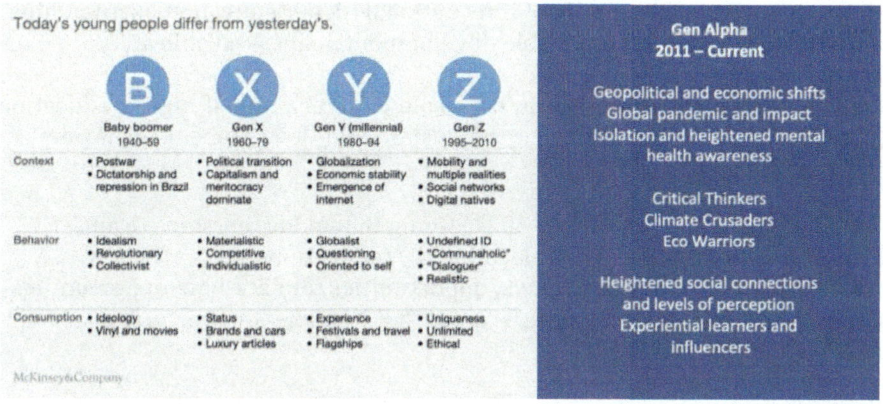

Figure 13.5: Defining generations (Francis and Hoefel, 2018). academic perspective

The recent student and alumni '10k Indian Voices' report (Sannam S4, 2021) highlighted the importance of how higher education institutions look for guidance and advice from external as well as internal stakeholders. It refers to the importance of how UK higher education institutions listen and work with our GenZ (see Figure 13.5) international student demographic, in better understanding the student journey and their experiences. I recently highlighted the evolution of the student experience in an evaluative paper I presented at an international conference (Norton, 2021) and referred to the current Gen Z digital natives (Dorn et al., 2021), compared to the future preparation higher education institutions need to consider for Gen Alphas.

Academics and students as contributors, co-creators and changemakers in support of sustaining the evolution of the international agenda in universities is a current topic. The current BCU India Group has enabled colleagues to have 'a seat at the table' and share ongoing best practice and knowledge sharing with our colleagues at home and overseas.

References

Birmingham School of Architecture and Design, BCU (2022) BIM in Birmingham (20 April 2022). Available at https://www.bcu.ac.uk/architecture-and-design/ working-with-industry/bim-in-birmingham [Accessed 27 April 2022]

British Council in partnership with the Association of British Commonwealth Universities (July 2021) Role of International higher education partnerships in contributing to the sustainable development goals. Available at https://www.britishcouncil.org/sites/default/files/role_of_international_higher_education_partnerships_in_contributing_to_the_sustainable_development_goals.pdf [Accessed: 19 February 2022]

British Council (17 September 2021) Going Global Partnerships Grant – Opportunities in India. Available at https://education-services.britishcouncil.org/ news/opportunities/update-new-opportunities-added-going-global-partnerships- grant-%E2%80%93-opportunities [Accessed 20 April 2022]

British High Commission New Delhi (published 4 May 2021) UK and India

announce new era in bilateral relationship. Available at https://www.gov.uk/government/news/uk-and-india-announce-new-era-in-bilateral-relationship [Accessed 2 February 2022]

Chowdhury, S. (2022) Virtual Interview with J. Norton. 15 February, Microsoft Teams

Das, A., Jabin, N. and Wohra, S. (February 2022) Education in India and the Post-Colonial Perspective: An Analysis. In book: Contemporary India: Society, Economy and Policy (pp. 487–498). Available at https://www.researchgate.net/publication/358635467_Education_in_India_and_the_Post-_Colonial_Perspective_ An_Analysis [Accessed 27 April 2022]

Design Council (Uploaded 11 November 2021) Design for Planet – COP26 Blue Zone. Available at https://www.youtube.com/watch?v=MGTQ0ObF-4A [Accessed 16/02/2022]

DigitalLEARNING (27 September 2021) National Education Policy 2020: Reforms in Higher Education. Available at https://digitallearning.eletsonline.com/2021/09/national-education-policy-2020-reforms-in-higher-education/ [Accessed 27 April 2022]

Dorn E., Hancock B., Sarakatsannis, J. and Viruleg, E. (McKinsey & Company) (July 27 2021), COVID-19 and education: The lingering effects of unfinished learning. Available at: https://www.mckinsey.com/industries/public-and-social-sector/our- insights/covid-19-and-education-the-lingering-effects-of-unfinished-learning [Accessed 08/09/2021]

Fernandez, A. and Sigona, M. (January 2020), Cross-Cultural Experiences in Transnational Education; Preservice Teachers and Global Perspectives. In book: The 11th International Conference on European Transnational Educational (ICEUTE 2020). Available at:
https://www.researchgate.net/publication/343677232_Cross-Cultural_Experiences_in_Transnational_Education_Preservice_Teachers_and_Global_Perspectives [Accessed 29 April 2022]

Francis, T. and Hoefel, F. (McKinsey & Company) (2018), True Gen: Generation Z and its implications for companies. Available at:
https://www.mckinsey.com/~/media/
mckinsey/industries/consumer%20packaged%20goods/our%20insights/true%20
gen%20generation%20z%20and%20its%20implications%20for%20companies/ generation-z-and-its-implication-for-companies.pdf?shouldIndex=false [Accessed 08/10/2021]

Government of India, Ministry of Human Resource Development (2020) National Education Policy 2020. Available at
https://ncert.nic.in/pdf/nep//NEP_2020.pdf [Accessed February 2021]

Heneghan, D. (April 2022) India University collaborations: What the latest UGC announcement means. Available at https://sannams4.com/india-university- collaborations-what-the-latest-ugc-announcement-means/ [Accessed 27 April 2022]

Jisc (uploaded 16 April 2019) Education 4.0 – transforming the future of education (through advanced technology). Available at
https://www.youtube.com/ watch?app=desktop&v=aVWHp8FsV1w [Accessed: 18/02/2022]

Nagpal, J. (2022) Virtual Interview responses with J. Norton. 15 February, Microsoft Teams

Norton, J. (2021) COVID-19 and its impact on Transnational Education Partnership Student and Staff Experience. In: Proceedings of the SUIC's 6th

International Conference New Challenges for Art, Design, and Business Management. Bangkok, Thailand, 26 November 2021. Book version ISBN: 978-974-641-798-3, Silpakorn University International College, pp. 72–85

Sahay, S. (21 April 2022) Simplified procedures for academic collaboration between Indian and foreign HEIs for dual, joint degree and twinning programmes. In British Council bi-weekly Digest (15 April 2022 – 29 April 2022). Available at https://education-services.britishcouncil.org/news/market-news/simplified- procedures-academic-collaboration-between-indian-and-foreign-heis-dual [Accessed 29th April 2022]

Sannam S4 (October 2021) 10K Indian Voices; Your Voice Matters, Decoding 10K Indian students' influences and higher education aspirations. Available at https:// insights.sannams4.com/2021/10k-indian-voices [Accessed 11 April 2022]

Swaminathan, R. (2022) Virtual Interview with J. Norton. 8 February, Microsoft Teams

Trines, S. (2018) Education in India, In Education Systems Profiles, World Education News and Reviews (13 September 2018). Available at https://wenr.wes.org/2018/09/ education-in-india [Accessed 22 April 2018]

United Nations: Department of Economic and Social Affairs Sustainable Development (2015) The 17 Goals. Available at https://sdgs.un.org/goals [Accessed 19/02/2022]

UK Government (2021) 'UN Climate Change Conference UK 2021, Delivering the Glasgow Climate Pact. Available at https://ukcop26.org/ [Accessed 23 February 2022]

About the contributor

Jacqueline Norton is an Associate Professor with international specialist expertise in transnational education and strategic partnership development, management and operations. She is the Deputy Director of International Partnerships for the Faculty of Arts, Design and Media at BCU, UK. Jacqueline is a Senior Fellow of the Higher Education Academy and a Fellow of the Royal Society of the Arts. She has 25 years' experience working in design practice, related to the automotive, hospitality and retail sectors. With 18 years' academic experience, she has previously held senior positions including Director of Academic Partnerships, International Coordinator for the School of

Architecture and Design, Subject Leader for Design, and Programme Director for courses taught at institutes in India and Hong Kong. She applies her entrepreneurial leadership skills to her current role growing international external networks both nationally and internationally, including working with in-country senior representatives from the British Council and the Department of International Trade.

Acknowledgements

I would like to thank my colleagues and friends Mr Rajdeepan Swaminathan, Mrs Shaswati Chowdhury and Mrs Juhi Nagpal for their generosity in sharing their time and responses following my invitation to contribute to this chapter.

Appendix 1: Interviewee short biographies (context)

Mr Rajdeepan Swaminathan is Managing Trustee of Swaminathan Rajalakshmi Educational and Charitable Trust established in 2009 including the SASI Creative Colleges, located in Coimbatore, Tamil Nadu, India, comprising the SASI Creative School of Architecture, established in 2009 and SASI Creative College of Design, established in 2019. Mr Rajdeepan Swaminathan is also the Managing Director of SASI Advertising Pvt Ltd (established in 1979), one of the largest pan-Indian advertising agencies in South India.

Mrs Shaswati Chowdhury holds a senior position in BOT VFX (India), a creative company based in Chennai, Tamil Nadu. The private limited company aims at 'serving the post-production needs of the film and television industry globally' with a 500-strong workforce. She is the previous academic consultant for SASI Creative School of Architecture, Coimbatore, from January 2019 to January 2020, and Head of Academics at the Department at the Innovative Centre for Advanced Technologies, Design and Media College (Chennai, Bengaluru and Hyderabad), from November 2010 to February 2018.

Mrs Juhi Nagpal is a Principal Artist at BAFA (By Artist for Artist) Bengaluru, Karnataka, India, from January 2019 to the present day. She is the previous Interior Design Discipline Leader and Faculty of the Interior Design Department at ITM, Institute of Fashion, Design and Technology, Mumbai, from September 2014 to December 2016 and later the Head of Interior Design Department at the Innovative Centre for Advanced Technologies' Design and Media College (Chennai, Bangalore and Hyderabad), from December 2016 to March 2018.

Appendix 2: Selected interviewee extracts

The following extracts refer to the interviewees' pre- and post-pandemic observations and considerations about future scoping opportunities as a consequence of the NEP 2020 roadmap.

Swaminathan, R. 2022 Extracts from virtual interview responses with J. Norton. 8 February 2022, Microsoft Teams

Topic: NEP 2020 future opportunities

For the first time in nearly two decades, we have a policy that is comprehensive and establishes a policy that brings the various norms of the different regulatory bodies such as the Medical Council, Architecture Council, and others into a single board bringing more transparency and fairness.... As an institution, we aspire to be the very best place for creative studies. One of the initiatives in improving our quality of education is to collaborate with other leading institutions in the world on research and academics.

India currently has over 37.4 million students studying across 993 universities, 39,931 colleges and 10,725 standalone institutions. The Gross Enrolment Ratio (GER) in higher education still stands only at 26% in 2020. The National Education Policy 2020 has fixed a target of 50% by 2030. Developed nations like Germany have a GER of 70%. The number of Indian students opting for higher education abroad grew from 440,000 in 2016 to 770,000 in 2019 and is set to grow further to roughly 1.8 million by 2024.

These demographic factors present a large scope of growth for higher education abroad and foreign university collaborations in India. Another dynamic is the large rise of International Baccalaureate (IB) programmes at the school level. Students pursuing IB programmes are accustomed to international education patterns and style of education. Their choice for higher education would be to continue in the IB format abroad. With NEP, the student now gets the opportunity to pursue foreign collaborated programmes in India which would match the format of their IB school programme. This clearly is a win-win for all stakeholders in the education system. This presents a huge market opportunity for foreign institutions to collaborate with higher education institutions in India.

Nagpal, J. 2022. Extracts from virtual interview responses with J. Norton. 15 February 2022, Microsoft Teams

Topic: The continuing impact of the technical revolution

The evolution of technology has not only made the globe a smaller place but an open learning classroom for all. I have witnessed this transition of the planet from a newborn to the present day, technologically developed world. It has been absolutely phenomenal to see cross-cultural knowledge sharing. It has widened the scope of opportunities for all of us and the present young students to learn and evolve. We all are uniquely talented and so we all have something special to contribute to the world. With each advancement, the opportunity to share the knowledge has grown and become easily accessible.

Topic: The BCU environment

I was awestruck with the infrastructure. The ambience of the building made me feel out of this world. From natural serene beauty that surrounded the concrete structure to the library that held all the world's knowledge, everything was mesmerising.

Chowdhury, S. 2022. Extracts from virtual interview responses with J. Norton. 15 February 2022, Microsoft Teams

Topic: Academic creative endeavours

Ancient Indian literary works such as Banabhatta's Kadambari described a good education as knowledge of the 64 Kalas (arts). The very idea that all branches of creative human endeavour, including mathematics, science, vocational subjects, professional subjects, and soft skills should be considered 'arts' has distinctly Indian origins. This notion of a 'knowledge of many arts' or what in modern times is often called the 'liberal arts' (i.e., a liberal notion of the arts) must be brought back to Indian education, progressing towards meeting the requirement for the 21st century. Effective learning requires a comprehensive approach that involves appropriate curriculum, engaging pedagogy, continuous formative assessment, and adequate student support. The curriculum must be interesting and relevant, and updated regularly to align with the latest knowledge requirements and to meet specified learning outcomes. Thus, curriculum, pedagogy, continuous assessment and student support are the cornerstones for quality learning. Expertise on technology-based programmes can be shared with the other countries and lack of adequate expertise in art and design and adapting the teaching and learning methodology can be obtained to support this reformation.

Topic: NEP 2020 future focus

Association with universities in the UK possessing expertise to deal with foreign partners will expedite the process of transformation and could lead to better course design, training programmes, pedagogy, research and innovation, and development of an entrepreneurial mindset among students. The teaching fraternity too can highly benefit from the available teachers' training facility in practice which can easily encompass India's current requirement and future development strategy.

Part Three

Personal reflections on India at 75

Chapter 14

Reminiscing about Indian film in Birmingham

Dharmesh Rajput

Summary

This chapter is a nostalgic reflection of growing up as a second-generation British Asian in Birmingham and the impact of Indian cinema and British Asian television from the 1960s to present day on cultural identity.

Introduction

Watching films is a big part of all our lives and the experience has evolved so much over the years, from the big screen to home entertainment and now streaming on the move. I was lucky enough to grow up seeing films across two cultures: the West and East, the latter famously referred to as Bollywood. Birmingham has several connections with film: Birmingham-born Alexander Parkes invented celluloid (UK Patent Office, 1857); Oscar Deutsch opened the first Odeon-branded cinema in Perry Barr in 1930 (Glancey, 2002) not far from where I live; and the city is also home to The Electric, originally built in 1909, the UK's oldest working cinema (Vernalls, 2022), a cinema where I spent much of my time when I should have been at college in the late 1980s and early 1990s. I also spent a lot of 'study time' developing a love for world film at other independent cinemas such as the long-gone Aston Triangle and the Midlands Art Centre, which to this day often feels like a second home. The city boasted nearly 100 cinemas in the first half of the 1900s (Richards, 2015), and later the UK South Asian cinema scene was launched here. It's the city where I was born and grew up and helped me develop a passion for film.

Many movies and television shows have been filmed in Birmingham, including Bollywood films such as *Tezz* (2012) and *Yamla Pagla Deewana* (2011), Hollywood films such as *Ready Player One* (2018), *Kingsman: The Golden Circle* (2017) and the soon to release, eighth instalment of *Mission Impossible* (2023), as well as Punjabi films such as *Chal Mera Putt* (2019). The city was home to the BBC Asian Programmes

Unit (1965–2008) which produced all the early programmes for the South Asian community in the UK, mostly made at the iconic Pebble Mill, where I was privileged to eventually work.

In this chapter I present a brief history of Bollywood and Indian cinema in Birmingham using personal nostalgic anecdotes of growing up and seeing Indian films on the screens of the UK's second city, from beautiful old cinemas such as the Grand Palace and Elite, to the small screens at home in the age of VHS and DVD, moving on to the present-day plethora of opportunities to see Bollywood films and beyond at multiplexes, independent cinemas, streaming platforms and film festivals.

Bollywood arrives in Birmingham

The UK was physically devastated by World War 2 and needed to rebuild itself but faced a significant shortage of labour. Immigration was seen as a solution and the British Nationality Act of 1948 (11 & 12 Geo. 6 c56) gave Commonwealth citizens free access to Britain. Thousands of people arrived from India, Pakistan, and the West Indies through the 1950s, for short-term work and many stayed permanently. My parents arrived much later in the cold October of 1966, just a few months after England's victory over Germany in the FIFA World Cup. They adjusted to British life, working Monday to Friday, sometimes with overtime at the weekends, fish and chips, pub culture and day trips to the seaside, but like many others missed news from back home and culture including film and music.

Jaswant Singh Sidhu and Avtar Singh Randhawa and their families had pioneered bringing Indian films to the UK earlier in the 1950s (BBC News, 2013) as a way of staying in touch with their homeland and offering those who had arrived in Britain a social life that they were more attuned to. Between them, they leased and bought several cinemas across the Midlands and set up the Eastern Film Society showing Bollywood films such as *Mahal* (1949), *Ladki* (1953) and *Do Bigha Zameen* (1953) (Birth of Bollywood UK, 2016).

With the films came the stars, who often stayed at the Sidhu and Randhawa residences, as Jaswant's son, Amarjit Sidhu of 1980s Bhangra band, Chirag Pehchan recalled when I spoke to him. Film stars such as Nargis and others would stay with the Sidhu family without the airs and graces you would normally associate with high profile celebrities. They were always very humble and down to earth.

A staple for me, growing up in the 1970s and 1980s, was seeing these big Bollywood names, singers, producers, and directors on Asian programmes on the BBC, early on a Sunday morning. The programmes, all made in Birmingham at the Pebble Mill studios, included *Naya Zindagi, Naya Jeevan* [New Way, New Life] (BBC1, 1968– 1982) which followed on from the earlier *Apna Hi Ghar Samjiye* [Make Yourselves at Home] (BBC1, 1966–1968). These shows were the only time we would get to see Asian people on TV, and they helped the South Asian community stay in touch with news and culture from the Indian subcontinent.

The programme evolved as *Asian Magazine* (BBC1, 1982–1987) and then *Network East* (BBC1 & BBC2, 1987–2003), which I was proud to eventually work on as a researcher from the late 1990s.

I remember vividly how we used to sit as a family with our breakfast of steaming hot cups of chai, masala omelette sandwiched between hot buttered toast, watching Mahendra Kaul, Saleem Shahed, Ashok Rampal and other presenters interview the likes of Amitabh and Jaya Bachchan, Raj Kapoor and Rekha and see performances from legends such as Lata Mangeshkar, Kishore Kumar, Noor Jahan and more. It was an exciting moment, calling the family into the living room when the theme tune came on – an absolute appointment to view to get a weekly fix of South Asian culture on television. I have fond memories of seeing British pop sensation Nazia Hasan as she debuted as a playback singer for the Bollywood film *Qurbani* (1980) performing her disco hit 'Aap Jaisa Koi' [Someone Like You] live on TV. The music often led to mum reminiscing, evoked by songs, and interviews we'd heard. I recall a particularly joyous moment with my mum, watching a joyous interview with music director and playback singer C. Ramchandra interviewed by Mahendra Kaul in his calm, assured style arousing memories for the viewers. As it was a Sunday, there was no way he was going to let C. Ramchandra off the hook without singing the catchy 'Aana Meri Jaan Sunday Ke Sunday' from the 1947 film *Shehnai.* It was a song she had loved, and it had made her very happy to see the interview and hear the song.

1970s on the silver screen

Several cinemas were showing Indian Bollywood films and Pakistani films, as existing cinemas continued to be taken over by Asian entrepreneurs excited by film. The Waldorf in Walford Road, Sparkbrook, in the 1970s, was run by Avtar Singh Randhawa. It closed in the 1980s and was converted into a Hindu temple (Richards, 2015).

The Carlton in Balsall Heath, Piccadilly Cinema on Stratford Road, Sparkbrook, also known for a time as Dreamland Cinema, and Imperial Cinema, Moseley, were all hugely popular. The cinemas I was familiar with and visited most often were the Grand Palace and Elite on Soho Road, Handsworth.

Figure 14.1: BBC Pebble Mill, Birmingham.

Figure 14.2: Waldorf Cinema.

Sundays often took some planning between a few families as the newest Bollywood release hit the cinemas. We would all dress in our best clothes and meet at someone's house or at the bus stop. If the bus took too long, we would walk, an entourage of old and young; some armed with homemade snacks and tea in Thermos flasks would set off to escape for three hours ofaction-packed, romance-filled, music, dance and drama. It was always an exciting experience, getting to the cinema, buying the tickets, seeing the colourful posters and lobby cards,picking up flyers of forthcoming movies. Then, getting to the seats, working out who was going to sit where, and the trailers would start. It was always colourful and big and, in your face; the words 'Action', 'Romance' or 'Drama' would fly across the screen against a backdrop of hit music from the films, high-impact dialogue and the best of the action sequences battling against the noise and chatter of the audience. Lights down, the audience quietens, and the film starts – everybody is engrossed, some vocally respond to the characters on screen, there are moments of delight, thrill, and tension; tears when the audience's favourite actor's character dies and I would wait anxiously for the light in the kiosk to come on as the smell of hot popcorn and samosas filled the cinema. You could tell it was nearly time for the intermission before the words shouted out from the screen at a critical moment of the film. The shutter in the kiosk was down, but you could see the light in the gap around the kiosk window and hear and smell the preparation for the interval snacks. The shutter would open, and a rush of people would clamour for a fix of crisp, golden samosas with a spicy potato filling and chutney, hot spiced popcorn, and the obligatory ice cream tubs. One of the things I remember with joy and frustration was the glass bottles of Coke that I looked forward to, but the paper straw would disintegrate while you were drinking and by that time the film would have started again so there was no alternative but to drink straight from the bottle.

One of my favourite memories was of seeing the 1979 superhit action-comedy *Mr Natwarlal* – doubly funny as the uncle who we went to see the film with had the same name. We went to a late-night showing, walking from Lozells to Soho Road to see the super hit film starring Amitabh Bachchan and Rekha, which has a fantastic soundtrack including a children's number sung by the 'Big B' himself, a rare occurrence in Bollywood movies, where songs are normally performed by playback singers. We got to the cinema early, and I sneaked in to see the end of the film and exited with the leaving audience only to go back in with my family and my cousin's family to proudly sit and watch the film from the start. It was a thrill for an eight-year-old boy to stay out so late, and an added adventure to be able to visit the cinema auditorium on my own without any supervision!

Figure 14.3: Bobby film poster.

Video killed the cinema screen

The 1980s saw the war between Betamax and VHS tape formats, with VHS winning as the preferred home video system (Knight, 2015), and due to the increase in films available on tape, there was a decline in cinema-going and many Asian cinemas shut down. We didn't buy a video player straight away; Friday nights hailed the arrival of Bollywood weekend as a big, strong, Punjabi man delivered the massive top-loading Ferguson video player with the chunky keys effortlessly carried under his arm like a newspaper. My job was to run to Sid's Newsagents to hire the films, 50p each or £1 for three old titles for the weekend, or £1.00 to £1.50 for the latest release which you could only have for 24 hours. You had to make sure he was giving you the original print and not a pirate copy and invariably some sweets were bought and consumed before I ran back home ready to watch. All meals that weekend would be consumed in front of the TV with the human remote control, that's me, pressing pause or stop when we had to clear plates away or if someone needed a toilet break. I remember fondly seeing classics such as *Prem Rog* (1982), *Kudrat* (1981), *Naseeb* (1981) and *Anand* (1971) as well as old favourites like *Saraswatichandra* (1968) and Gujarati films including *Mangal Fera* (1949), *Maa Baap* (1987), *Mehndi Rang Lagyo* (1960) and more. My dad used to keep a book listing all the films we saw, and my sister used to record songs by placing a tape recorder in front of the television to record our favourite tracks from the film, which involved much forwarding and rewinding of the video tape. We eventually bought our own Hitachi VHS player with a remote control that had to be connected to the player by a long wire trailing across the room. My position was elevated to now being in charge of the remote control. Slowly my own collection of Bollywood movies started, many taped off the TV when BBC and Channel 4 showed films in early morning or late-night slots, more family moments taking us away from *Dallas* and *Coronation Street* to watch classic Bollywood films such as *Bobby* (1973), *Sholay* (1975) and *Amar Akbar Anthony* (1977).

The beginning of the cinema revival

DVDs didn't play as significant a part in my cinema history as VHS did, maybe due to cost and because Asian satellite channels had emerged, and they were showing Bollywood films. The 1990s was not as big an era for me as far as Bollywood was concerned as I had started university and was building my career, but there were some films that cut through and Madhuri Dixit's 'Choli Ke Peeche' track had everyone talking, so the film *Khalnayak* (1993) became a 'must-see' movie. The only way to see the film was to pay above normal ticket price of £10 at a special screening at Odeon New Street. Cinemas weren't yet showing Bollywood movies in the way they do now. There was a definite buzz in the cinema as crowds of people flocked to see Sanjay Dutt as the antihero, and lead actress Madhuri Dixit as a female undercover police officer delighting the crowds with her acting and dance moves.

From the 1990s onwards, we were lucky in Birmingham to have several cinemas showing Indian films and the variety extended beyond Bollywood with a growth in the number of South Indian movies being shown. In 2013, I worked with Sampad South Asian Arts & Heritage to celebrate 100 years of Bollywood in Birmingham, with film screenings, a poster exhibition, variety shows, and a gala dinner attended by legendary actress, Zeenat Aman and actor and producer Abhay Deol, celebrated as a champion of independent Indian cinema and known for his unconventional roles.

India ranks among the most prolific in terms of annual film output and the range of films including mainstream Hindi movies known as Bollywood, as well as films in a variety of regional languages, with Tamil and Telegu specifically doing very well. The advent of over-the-top streaming platforms has enabled wider audiences to see films as they are presented with different language options and subtitles and there has been an increase in these platforms creating their own content that bypasses the big screen.

I used to love the Birmingham International Film and Television Festival which ran in the 1980s and 1990s and always had a South Asian element. I saw *Bandit Queen* (1994), *1942 A Love Story* (1994) and conversations with Shekhar Kapur, Dev Anand, and Amitabh Bachchan. There was nothing of the same calibre to replace it so when the London Indian Film Festival expanded to Birmingham in 2015, I jumped at the chance to work on it. Supported by BCU as a sponsor and students who work on the festival as volunteers, shooting video and taking photos, the festival is now a mainstay of the Birmingham cultural calendar. As Deputy Director now across the festival brands in London, Birmingham, and Manchester, we have a yearly supply of the best independent South Asian films available with talent such as Anurag Kashyap, Buddhadeb Dasgupta, Leena Yadav, Anubhav Sinha, Mrunal Thakur, Aparna Sen, Konkana Sen Sharma, Taapsee Pannu and Pan Nalin, director of Chhello

Show (Last Film Show), India's entry to the Oscars 2022, having visited the city and talked to Brummie film fans! It's wonderful and a privilege to be able to continue the legacy of Indian film in Birmingham.

References

Birth of Bollywood UK, (2016), Iconic Productions https://www.youtube.com/ watch?v=xxEgDZWm8qY

Blakemore, M. Waldorf Cinema in Birmingham, GB, Cinema Treasures http://cinematreasures.org/theaters/37418

BBC (2013), How did Bollywood reach Birmingham? https://www.bbc.co.uk/news/ uk-england-birmingham-23080887

Glancey, J. (2002) 'The mogul's monuments. How Oscar Deutsch's Odeon cinemas taught Britain to love modern architecture', The Guardian, https://www.theguardian. com/arts/critic/feature/0,1169,717532,00.html

Halifax, J. (2016) 'Look at Birmingham's fondly remembered cinemas', Birmingham Mail https://www.birminghammail.co.uk/news/nostalgia/look-birminghams-fondly- remembered-cinemas-11077582

Knight, S. (2015) 'Sony finally decides it's time to kill Betamax', TechSpot, https:// www.techspot.com/news/62733-sony-finally-decides-time-kill-betamax.html

Richards, A. (2015), Old Birmingham cinemas remembered, Birmingham Mail https://www.birminghammail.co.uk/news/nostalgia/old-birmingham-cinemas- remembered-8503764

Vernalls, R. (2022) 'UK's oldest working cinema to reopen after pandemic forced its closure', The Independent, https://www.independent.co.uk/news/uk/birmingham- people-charlie-chaplin-east-sussex-government-b1995461.html

Filmography

Tezz [feature film] Directed by Priyadarshan. United 7 Entertainment, India, 2012. 121 mins.

Ready Player One [feature film] Directed by Steven Spielberg. Warner Bros./ Amblin Entertainment/Village Roadshow Pictures/Dune Entertainment/Amblin Entertainment/De Line Pictures/Farah Films & Management/Reliance Entertainment, USA, 2018. 140 mins

Kingsman: The Golden Circle [feature film] Directed by Matthew Vaughn. Twentieth Century Fox/Marv Films/Cloudy Productions/TSG Entertainment/Shangri-La Entertainment, UK/USA, 2017. 141 mins

Mission: Impossible – Dead Reckoning – Part One [feature film] Directed by Christopher McQuarrie. Paramount Pictures/Skydance Media/New Republic Pictures/TC Productions/Bad Robot, USA, 2023

Chal Mera Putt [feature film] Directed by Janjot Singh. Rhythm Boyz Entertainment, India, 2019. 124 mins

Mahal [feature film] Directed by Kamal Amrohi. Dube Industries/The Bombay Talkies Ltd/The Bombay Talkies Studios, India, 1949. 165 mins

Ladki [feature film] Directed by M V Raman. A.V.M. Productions, India, 1953. 161 mins.

Do Bigha Zamin[feature film] Directed by Bimal Roy. Bimal Roy Productions, India, 2012. 121 mins

Qurbani [feature film] Directed by Feroz Khan. F K International, India, 1980. 157 mins

Shehnai [feature film] Directed by P L Santoshi. Filmistan, India, 1947. 133 mins

Mr Natwarlal [feature film] Directed by Rakesh Kumar, Navjeevan Productions, India, 1979. 148 mins

Prem Rog [feature film] Directed by Raj Kapoor. K.R. Films Pvt. Ltd, India, 1982. 183 mins

Kudrat [feature film] Directed by Chetan Anand. Trishakti Productions, India, 1981. 164 mins

Naseeb [feature film] Directed by Priyadarshan. Aasia Films Pvt. Ltd/M.K.D. Films Combine, India, 1981. 197 mins

Anand [feature film] Directed by Hrishikesh Mukherjee. Rupam Chitra, India, 1971. 122 mins

Saraswatichandra [feature film] Directed by Govind Saraiya. Sarvodaya Pictures, India, 1968. 156 mins

Mangal Fera [feature film] Directed by Ratilal Hemchand Punatar. India, 1949. 139 mins

Maa Baap [feature film] Directed by Kishor Vyas. Vijay Films International, India, 1977. 121 mins

Mehndi Rang Lagyo [feature film] Directed by Manhar Raskapur. India, 1960. 151 mins

Bobby [feature film] Directed by Raj Kapoor. R K Films Ltd, India, 1973. 168 mins

Sholay [feature film] Directed by Ramesh Sippy. NH Studioz, Sippy Films, India, 1975. 204 mins

Amar Akbar Anthony [feature film] Directed by Manmohan Desai. Hirawat Jain and Company/M.K.D. Films Combine/Manmohan Films, India, 1977. 184 mins

Khalnayak [feature film] Directed by Subhash Ghai. Venus Records & Tapes/United 7 Entertainment, India, 1993. 190 mins

Bandit Queen [feature film] Directed by Shekhar Kapur. Channel Four Films/NH Studioz/Narendra Hirawat & Co, India, 1994. 119 mins

1942 A Love Story [feature film] Directed by Vidhu Vinod Chopra. Vinod Chopra Productions, India, 1994. 157 mins.

About the contributor

Dharmesh Rajput is a former BBC Producer and Digital Producer at FutureLearn. He is now Lecturer and Course Director for the BA Media Production at the Institute of Media and English at BCU. He teaches television production to undergraduates and works to develop opportunities for students with arts organisations. Outside of university, Dharmesh is the Deputy Director for the London, Birmingham and Manchester Indian Film Festivals and works on a variety of arts and film initiatives developing and building community relationships.

Chapter 15

The modernisation of India and its impact on fashion

Jasbir Kaur

Summary

The Indian fashion system that exists today doesn't even begin to resemble that of my youth. In fact, you could say fashion as we understand it from a 'Western' perspective was pretty non-existent as recently as 30 years ago in India. This writing, although presented in an academic context, is very much based on autobiographical reflections exploring the way in which fashion can transform clothing and connect individuals with their heritage.

Introduction

As a child of immigrant parents who travelled from India to settle in the UK in the 1960s, I have recollections of a sometimes-cconfused youth, growing up rejecting the traditional dress of my heritage, hand-stitched and worn by my mother and aunts, as something alien and strange, in favour of skinny jeans and T-shirts that fitted in with my 'Western life' and school friends. Little did I know that I would end up embracing the once shunned traditional clothing as it morphed into 'fashion' within a few short years.

Born in England, and not actually visiting India until I was in my early 30s, most of my insight into my culture and identity through dress was informed by exposure to traditions and festivals kept alive by my extended family, and the sights and sounds of Bollywood through the screen. These reference points provided the most obvious expressions of culture through differences in the way we chose to dress.

This personal journey tracking the development of the clothing of my heritage not only ignited a curiosity in fashion more generally but has also led to observations spanning decades that have formed a framework of scholarly activity in the subject.

Context

The interesting thing about India is the particular way that modernisation and professionalisation has taken place in relation to fashion. There has been continuity of a traditional form running alongside classic modern international fashion, which many commentators in Asia call 'Western fashion'. India and the Indian diaspora have moved from a 'hand-stitched at home' model to a 'ready-to-wear' one. First- generation Indians will recall growing up with the familiar hum of the domestic sewing machine where their mothers and aunts stitched salwar kameez at home.

In addition, India has gone from having no big retail culture, little fashion media output, and no celebrity designer culture to something resembling a complete model of a fashion industry in a relatively short span of time. The significant factor that makes the development of Indian fashion particularly interesting in relation to other systems of fashion developing globally is the fact that Indian fashion designers have largely retained and modernised traditional Indian dress forms such as the sari and the salwar kameez, as opposed to adopting Western dress.

My natural curiosity of changes in attitudes to what is essentially modernised traditional dress has led me to attempt to uncover the motives that have led to this phenomenon. Personal observations and reportage suggest that Indian fashion has recently and is still undergoing transition into a modern world. Also, the way in which Indian fashion has developed around the world is significant as motivations for growth vary greatly from place to place. In India the fashion industry has been subject to government initiatives that have stimulated expansion and professionalised the industry (Nagrath, 2002; Sengupta, 2005), whereas in the West the Indian diaspora has developed the industry through female entrepreneurship (Bhachu, 2003). Both methods have been successful, and it would be useful to understand the conditions present in different parts of the world that have caused this phenomenon.

The motivation to critically evaluate the sequencing of events that took place in various parts of the world where this activity was occurring is to establish what the significant points of development were and whether the transcultural communications between India and the Indian diaspora were central to the emergence of Indian fashion.

Figure 15.1: Sikh woman wearing a turban and salwaar kameez.

And further to this there is an investigation of the relationship between the media representation of fashion and the selling of clothes, which is a kind of watershed change in any fashion industry. An initial survey of this developing relationship through the screen, magazines, the media and promotion companies would gather views from two perspectives, either from the point of view of the fashion industry promoting itself through FDCI (The Fashion Design Council India), or from the view of marketing companies like the International Media Group which promotes 'Lakmé India Fashion Week', and see fashion as media entertainment and so, a saleable item.

Modern marketing techniques have evolved the relationship between media personalities and fashion through the formation of India's Fashion Weeks showcasing India's rising fashion stars. In this case, the relationship has been between the creative people, the business world and government bodies. Profiling individuals and key organisations instrumental in its evolution leads to various lines of enquiry: How and why was it started? Who was supporting it and setting it up and what was their vision? Who was providing funds to leverage that kind of event? And who was directing it?

A definition of Indian fashion

The focus here is the evolution that has led to a contemporary Indian fashion system. It is generally agreed that the roots of this phenomena are embedded in the late 1980s and 1990s (Sengupta, 2005; Rocca, 2009; Piyush et al., 2012) when India's fashion system started to become systematised, when the communication systems became developed around it, and when it became part of popular culture. Other than the long-standing key text that debates the nature of Indian identity through dress (Tarlo, 1996), publications specifically about Indian fashion are scarce. Tarlo focuses on the way in which people dress in India from a historical and cultural perspective, and not in terms of fashion consumption.

It was not until 2005 that there was any sort of comprehensive documentation of India's fashion industry. Indian Fashion (Sengupta, 2005) could easily claim to be the first ultimate guide to Indian fashion. This was followed a few years later by Sengupta's second publication Ramp Up in 2009, which explored the Indian fashion industry from a business perspective, and how it fares on an international fashion stage. In the same year another Indian fashion primer, Contemporary Indian Fashion (Rocca, 2009), was published. Indian Fashion (Sengupta, 2005) and Contemporary Indian Fashion (Rocca, 2009) are the only encyclopaedic texts that provide an ample account of who's who in Indian fashion. And that is really where the similarity ends, perhaps due to the credentials of the authors.

Sengupta provides a complete account of what Indian fashion represents, inclusive of the key bodies that were instrumental in its professionalisation. India's National Institute of Fashion Technology and FDCI are both given special mention, whereas Rocca omits them. The fact that Rocca also asks whether an Indian designer will ever dress

Western women suggests that the content is defined in terms of the West, as a year before the publication of his book Victoria Beckham appeared on the cover of Vogue India dressed in a Tarun Tahiliani sari.

The modernisation of India

Prior to India's independence, the nation's identity was in a state of confusion. It was an era where the urban elite wore Western clothing, 'in fact Western clothes were seen as status symbols' (Piyush et al., 2012). This remained the case until Gandhi's adoption of Indian clothing inspired the middle and upper classes to abandon the Western dress that had signified their social status (Dwyer, 2000; Tarlo, 1996). Following India's independence, many of its prime ministers, both male and female, have worn traditional dress, communicating nationalism through their clothing (Tarlo, 1996).

Figure 15.2: Vaani Kapoor walked the ramp at the Lakme Fashion Week 2018.

Figure 15.3: Rituparna Sengupta – Kolkata.

Figure 15.4: Alia Bhatt graces Vogue India's Fashion's Night Out.

In 2001 the then chairman of Goldman Sachs Asset Management, Jim O'Neill (now Baron O'Neill of Gatley), named India as one of the four BRIC countries: Brazil, Russia, India and China, the biggest and fastest-growing emerging markets. Since this time India has been rising as an economic force globally: 'in 1990, economic liberalization of the Indian economy took place, which also propelled the fashion industry' Welters and Lillethun (2011, p. 551). Online. news agency, FashionUnited.in, credit the growth in India's fashion industry to 'higher disposable incomes, emergence of mall culture, changing sense of style, dressing and growing fashion consciousness among urban Indians' (www.FashionUnited.in 2012).

It is hard to ignore the political, economic and social development of India as it is all entwined with the emergence of a fashion system that mirrors those of the West. As Western societies have seen patterns of modern consumption develop, and the notion of social status groups emerge throughout the 20th century (Bocock and Thompson, 1992), these phenomena have been analysed by various social and economic theorists such as Veblen, Simmel and Barthes writing after the 1950s. Although the period of transition to economic growth and social development is much faster than that which has occurred in the West, it may be possible to map some of these theories onto India's development in order to attempt to understand the motives and dynamics that have caused Indian fashion to evolve.

The professionalisation of the Indian fashion industry

The greatest motivation to modernise Indian fashion in areas of the West was to transform the 'hand-stitched at home' garment into a 'ready-to-wear' piece to buy 'off the shelf' (Bhachu, 2003; Puwar and Raghuram, 2003). Both texts refer to extensive fieldwork carried out in the UK, but Puwar and Raghuram's focus is broader than that of Bhachu. They present perspectives on gender and the South Asian diaspora, and they use a biographical approach to understand the historical and geographical complexities of making and selling clothes in the South Asian diaspora. Although this makes interesting reading, Bhachu specifically investigates the role of the Indian fashion entrepreneur and gleans data from in-depth interviews with designers and boutique owners. This provides more relevant and detailed material for the reader about the motivations leading to change in Indian fashion. Bhachu refers to these Asian women as 'cultural and commodity brokers' (2003, p. 140), and suggests they are modern pioneers; she says their activities 'are transforming and defining new global economic and cultural realms' (2003, p. 144).

In those parts of the world where Indian communities have migrated, female entrepreneurship has fuelled the formation of an Indian fashion design industry and the development of an Indian boutique culture (Bhachu, 2003; Puwar and Raghuram, 2003; Rajagoplan and Heitmeyer, 2005). While in India, journalists (Ahmed, 2011; Dutt, 2013; Papnai, 2010) and a few seminal texts (Sengupta, 2005, 2009; Rocca, 2009) suggest the development of fashion in India is largely a result of government interventions, and in contrast to the modernisation of Indian fashion in the West, the development of India's fashion industry is very much to do with receiving recognition from the West for its arrival on the international fashion stage. (Nagrath, 2002).

Conclusion

It is clear that some exchange of ideas happened from East to West and West to East over a period of 25 to 30 years. These are yet to be linked so as to present a historical chronology of the various activities that transpired simultaneously, creating the catalyst that caused a rapid evolution to occur in Indian fashion. These special circumstances in Indian society have allowed traditional dress forms to become 'fashionalized' (Polhemus and Procter, 1978) and not 'alien', as experienced during my youth. It would seem that now might be the right time to plot a timeline of the sequence of events that eventually formed the Indian fashion industry.

Indian clothing is ordinary clothing as worn daily by my mother's generation, but it jumped the gap from pre-industrial to post-industrial Indian society, and interestingly it remains ethnically identifiable. And whereas ethnic dress is usually worn by members of the same group, 'This is clearly not the case with fashionable Indian dress, which carries the hallmarks of its traditional form but is contextualised in fashion terms through it being worn by celebrities' (Eicher, J and Sumberg, B, 1995, p. 304). Perhaps this is part of the allure for my own teenage daughters as they continue the appreciation of this fashionable yet traditional dress form, wearing it with pride and allowing it to remain intact.

References

Ahmed, I., (2011) The Fashion Trail, Modern Mumbai and Lakme Fashion Week. Available at: http://www.businessoffashion.com/2011/03/the-fashion-trail- modern-mumbai-and-lakme-fashion-week/ (Accessed 03 04 2022)

Barthes, R., Stafford, A. and Carter, M. (2006). The Language of Fashion, Oxford; Berg.

Bhachu, P. (2003). in 'Designing Diasporic Markets: Asian Fashion Entrepreneurs in London' in S. Niessen,. A.M., Leshkowich, and C. Jones, (eds), Re-Orienting Fashion: The Globalization of Asian Dress, Oxford: Berg, pp. 118-139.

Bocock, R. (ed), (1992). The Social and Cultural Forms of Modernity: Understanding Modern Societies, Book III. Cambridge: Polity Press.

Craik, J., (1993). The Face of Fashion, Cultural Studies in Fashion. London: Routledge

Dutt, Y. (2013) 'Indian fashion's greatest hits' in Hindustan Times. Available at: https://www.hindustantimes.com/brunch/indian-fashion-s-greatest-hits/story-EvKhsaYo2LArj6uBioFqsM.html (Accessed 03 04 2022).

Dwyer, R.. (2000). 'Bombay Ishtyle' in S. Bruzzi., & P. Church-Gibson, (eds). Fashion Cultures: Theories, Explorations and Analysis, London: Routledge, pp 178-190.

Eicher, J.B. & Sumberg, B. (1995). 'World fashion, ethnic, and national dress'. In J.B. Eicher (Ed.),.Dress and Ethnicity: Change Across Space and Time. Oxford: Berg, pp 295-306.

Eicher, J.B. (1995). Dress and Ethnicity: Change Across Space and Time. Oxford: Berg.

FashionUnited, (2012). 'Designer Wear: Affordability, corporatisation success mantra'. Available at: https://fashionunited.in/v1/fashion/designer-wear-affordability-corporatisation-success-mantra/201203289417 (Accessed 03 04 2022)

IANS (2013) Luxury India, Ritu Beri on the Potential of a Billion Buyers Available at: https://www.idiva.com/fashion/how-to/luxury-india-ritu-beri-on-the-potential-of-a-billion-buyers/20086 (Accessed 03 04 2022)

Nagrath, S. (2003). '(En)countering Orientalism in High Fashion: A Review of India Fashion Week 2002', in Fashion Theory, volume 7, (3-4), pp. 361-376. London: Routledge

Nazareth, S. (2013) 'The Couple Who Took Fashion off the Street', . Available at: https://www.business-standard.com/article/specials/the-couple-who-took-fashion-off-the-street-197101801010_1.html (Accessed 03 04 2022)

Papnai, C. (2010). 'Lord of the ramp'. Available at: https://www.telegraphindia.com/culture/lord-of-the-ramp/cid/460637 (Accessed 03 04 2022)

Polhemus, T. and Procter, L. (1978). Fashion and Anti-fashion: Anthropology of Clothing and Adornment, London: Thames and Hudson.

Puwar, N. and Raghuram, P. (2003). South Asian Women in the Diaspora, London: Routledge.

Rajagoplan, R. and Heitmeyer, J. (2005.) 'Ethnicity and consumer choice: A study of consumer levels of involvement in Indian ethnic apparel and contemporary American clothing', in Journal of Fashion Marketing and Management, An International Journal of Fashion Marketing and Management, Volume 9 (1), pp. 83-105. Emerald Group Publishing: Bingley.

Rocca, F. (2009). Contemporary Indian Fashion. Bologna: Damiani.

Sengupta, H. (2005). Indian Fashion, India: Pearson Education.

Sengupta, H. (2009). Ramp Up: The Business. Of Indian Fashion. India: Pearson Education.

Tarlo, E. (1996). Clothing Matters: Dress and Identity in India. University of Chicago Press.

Times of India. (2012). 'Retail sector in India growing at phenomenal pace.' Available at: http://timesofindia.indiatimes.com/home/education/news/Retail- sector-in-India-growing-at-phenomenal-pace/articleshow/14381624.cms (Accessed 03 04 2022)

Welters, L. and Lillethun, A., (2011) The Fashion Reader, 2nd Edition. Oxford: Berg.

About the contributor

Jasbir Kaur is Director of Postgraduate Studies in Fashion and Textiles. Following initial studies in textile and fashion design, Jasbir transitioned to fashion research. The early phase of her career has equipped her with extensive experience in commercial textile design and fashion research and she now shares a breadth of knowledge and expertise with students and research communities. With over 20 years' experience as an academic, she is an internationally published author in the area of textiles and the interrelationship between that and fashion.

Jasbir has been exploring the modernisation and professionalisation of the Indian fashion industry in India and among the Indian diaspora in the West. Her research findings are rooted in first-hand experiences and observations of the way Indian fashion has evolved over past decades. Indian fashion has swiftly come of age, it now mirrors the activities of modern fashion systems from around the world that have taken much longer to mature. Today, it carries all the components required to engage the modern consumer in India and overseas. Jasbir has spoken nationally and internationally about the motivations leading to the evolution of modern Indian fashion.

Chapter 16

Women in India at 75 – a contemporary examination of women in India from the perspective of the British Indian diaspora

Beverley Nielsen

Introduction – setting the scene

Having worked with Professor Lord Kumar Bhattacharyya at the renowned Warwick Manufacturing Group at the University of Warwick in the early 2000s, his dedication to excellence and personal improvement couldn't be missed by anyone employed there. The Professor's contribution to manufacturing was recognised across the globe, in India in particular, through the award of the Padma Bhushan in 2002. At his memorial service in March 2019, his eldest daughter, Anita, spoke of the texts he used to send to his three daughters every morning. These messages always concluded with the same advice, 'don't forget to always do what your mother tells you', reflecting the esteemed position of mothers in Indian families.

President Bill Clinton's visit to Warwick University in 2000, in dwelling on the opportunities for a 'global Third Way', also struck me as especially significant in highlighting the role of women:

> *...the education of girls is especially critical. Studies show that literate girls have significantly smaller and healthier families [....] That can make a huge difference... If all children on every continent had the tools to fulfil their God-given potential, the prospect for peace, prosperity and freedom in the developing world would be far greater.*
>
> (Clinton White House Archives, 2000)

In his latest book, The Journey of Humanity: The Origins of Wealth and Inequality (2022), economist Oded Galor notes that as more women work and families become smaller and better educated, wealth per capita rises: 'History is very important, but if we understand it, we can design our futures.' As this trend has developed, he explains, there's been a 14-fold increase in prosperity since the 19th century. The Indian government has incorporated equality into its constitution with each citizen guaranteed this right in articles 14 to 18. There's been an equal commitment to education for all over the past 30 years. The rate of literacy in post-Independence India has improved for both males and females. While in 1991, fewer than 40% of the 330 million women aged seven and over were literate (US Census Bureau, 1998), by 2021 the National Statistics Office found countrywide female literacy stood at 70.3%, although male literacy was 84.7%. Kerala topped the list with the highest female literacy rate at 95.2% and Rajasthan was ranked the worst-performing state with just 57.6% female literacy levels (Business Insider India Bureau, 2021).

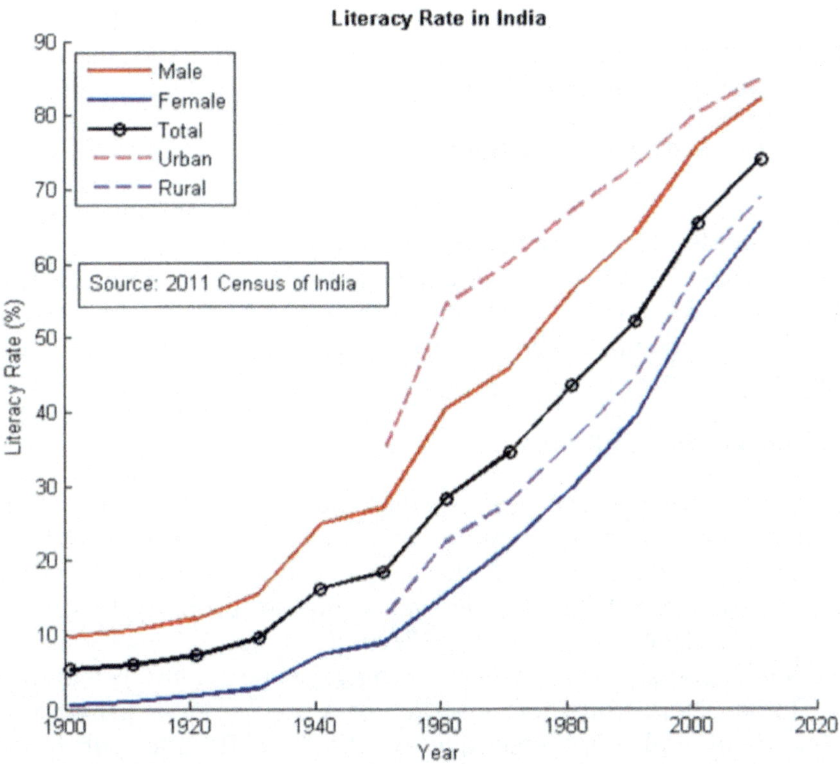

Figure 16.1: Census of India 2021.

Female enrolment in education has made significant progress. The 2019 UN Population Fund showed that girls' enrolment was higher than boys' in Indian schools at both primary and secondary level. Overall, 98% of primary school-age girls were enrolled, compared to 97% of boys. Worldwide, this compares with 90% female enrolment and 92% male enrolment. However, at secondary level, India's enrolment rates were lower than worldwide, at 66% for both genders (The Indian Express, 2019).

According to the 2017–18 All India Survey of Higher Education, 27.4% of all 18- to 23-year-olds were enrolled in college or higher education during 2017–18 (Sharma, 2020). The same survey in 2019–20 indicated women's enrolment was 27.3% compared to 26.9% for men. While the percentage of women students at state universities was 50.1% and 48.1% for central universities, it was lowest for institutes of national importance at 27.4%, followed by government (33.4%) and state private universities (34.7%) (Gohain, 2021). Women appear to be doing well at Master's level and on medical sciences programmes, but less so in professional and technical courses.

Meeting the British Indian diaspora

In preparing this chapter, women from the British Indian diaspora, primarily within the West Midlands, were interviewed to elicit their views on women's chances of personal and professional empowerment. This enabled me to garner insights on their perspectives of women in India at 75. It's with sincere gratitude that a range of their views are included.

What does India at 75 mean?

Everyone interviewed was impressed by India at 75. All remain deeply loyal to the country of their families' origin while being proudly British. Most, having been born in Britain, are second-generation Indians. However, two were born in India. All wanted to do more to support India, visiting frequently and considering it a 'second home'. As MP Preet Gill explained, 'There is something very special and remarkable about India. There's nowhere else like it in the world.' Lakshmi Kaul, former Head and Representative of the Confederation of Indian Industry (CII) UK, observed:

> *'India at 75 is an amazing story of resilience. India remains among the top inward investors into the UK with 900 Indian companies creating*

141,005 local jobs in the UK. Interestingly, the average percentage of women on boards is higher for Indian companies; 26% of Indian companies have at least one woman on their board compared to 17% of Nifty500 companies (CII and Grant Thornton, 2022). These statistics demonstrate the progress of India, abroad, a reflection of its attitude to economic growth and success across the spectrum.'

India's strong ties continue with records showing its position as a top-20 ultimate inward investor into the UK in 2020, accounting for over £12 billion of inward foreign direct investment into the UK (Jowett, 2022).

'India is feeling bullish at present,' noted Anita Bhalla. 'After Brexit, it can shop around. Numbers of professionals can go to England because they want to, rather than because they need to,' adding that, in the week that the then British Prime Minister Boris Johnson, visited India to meet with Indian Prime Minister Modi with the purpose to discussing a free trade agreement, 'India doesn't need to trade with the UK. Brexit has probably helped India to say to the UK, "you need us more than we need you".'

Those interviewed felt the Modi government had done much to tackle gender inequality. However, as Suki Pantal noted, 'Whilst there is a national government in India, each state has its own administration. They aren't all dictated to by national government, with each having a bigger impact on their own population.'

Culture and place

There was awareness that the caste system still played a significant role in Indian society in setting expectations. This culture is changing. Preet Gill explained,

'There are huge challenges in India as elsewhere. Gender equality challenges are no different there than anywhere else. In India they're not just facing policy issues but those of religion and faith. Do women hold temple roles? It's a patriarchal system. Men are making the decisions. It's much tougher if women are in poverty in India.'

Rosie Ginday's reference to her own family was illuminating.

'My gran got married when she was 9 years old. She lived with my grandad from when she was 12. But the ceremony was held when she

was just 9. Mum was married at 18. My cousins have married at between 21–25 years old and my sister-in-law was married when she was 28.'

Those interviewed were forthright in stating that the status of Indian women is 'no longer about getting married and having kids' as one interviewee explained, and that children of both sexes are expected to study and gain qualifications and careers before marrying. Nonetheless, cultural attitudes still require reform. Preet Gill explained her experience, 'Men, without thinking about it, can make comments which make a lot of judgements about you. Women are still shut down all the time. Respect is the key thing.' Baljit Dhadda also noted the need to 'engage with male attitudes and misogyny, continuing to raise the importance of education and providing support networks for women who become independent as there can be a lot of social stigma'.

These concerns were echoed in a recent interview with Indian historian Romila Thapar, speaking about her own experience of abuse:

The trolls started with attacking the history we are writing, then at some point it became sexist. And there I was as the only woman in the galaxy of historians... And that continues to this day. It's tough being a woman historian in this country.

(Parkin, 2022)

Education and future prospects

A number of interviewees made suggestions as to ways that young Indian women could be encouraged and given assistance in developing professional careers. All recognised that in India childcare and domestic responsibilities still tend to be regarded as women's roles. However, because many young women now leave home, parental support was often no longer available. This, it was indicated, emphasised how essential childcare support is. Some expressed frustration at the pace of change in India for women. Anita Bhalla noted, 'A lot more women are going to universities but political change in India can be slow. The ripple impact of progress has to speed up, move deeper through society and into disadvantaged and rural areas to deliver more enhanced progress.'

Jas Rohel was typical in stressing the vital importance of education:

'Give free education, laptops, bring coding languages and work skills into villages and follow young girls on their journeys and if you can educate one young woman, they can get a whole village out of poverty.'

Lakshmi Kaul emphasised:

'The importance of educating mothers via a prominent programme I was associated with during my days in India, called the "Mother Teachers", made mothers the epicentre of all educational and community activity thereby ensuring the entire family and neighbourhood was educated in the process. Education in this context was not only literacy and numeracy but also awareness of rights, holistic development, bringing about parity in healthcare access and other social development opportunities.'

These actions are amply illustrated by the statement: 'take one mum and educate them and you can educate a community' (Parkin, 2022).

Creating opportunities available at school level rather than waiting until college was considered crucial. Baljit Dhadda noted the huge potential offered by technology, especially as women don't have to travel to learn and skills development can be achieved where they live: 'There's a chance through open education for women to source education freely. It's making a link between what will be accredited and work afterwards. Girls are burdened by other responsibilities so need reasons to spend that time "out".'

Figure 16.2: Smriti Irani, Minister of Women and Child Development, addressing people at the launch of the National Web Portal for Apprenticeship Training Scheme, implemented by the Ministry of Human Resource Development through Boards of Apprenticeship Practical Training, in New Delhi.

Lakshmi Kaul was clear that more self-help groups and avenues for microfinance were important. As she explained:

> *'Women need to help more women. Incentivisation of bank accounts is important, assisted by digital empowerment. The Prime Minister's flagship programme, Digital India, has been instrumental in ensuring financial inclusion of all. There are many "SHEroes" in India who have constructed their own "empowerment ecosystem", by being harbingers of change within themselves and the society they live in. It is important to take responsibility for failure and success but also to encourage and support others on their own journeys of self-realisation. Having good role models and surrounding yourself with people of aspiration is critical and not always easily possible for women both in India and UK.*
>
> *'It is pertinent to note though that a conducive environment of parity has not been a luxury women have enjoyed the world over. Women are still fighting many battles everywhere, including that of equal pay, equal opportunities and career progression. As a woman entrepreneur it is still not as easy to navigate the male dominant environment across industry. An environment of learning and sensitivity is imperative for all genders. Diversity cannot be a token face in a photograph for promotional purposes; it ought to be delivered on the ground, every single day.'*

The benefits of 'blind' job applications, role models and mentors were acknowledged to be a critical component of success. Baljit Dhadda added that job selection panels should be inclusive, drawing upon approaches informed by 'lived experience'. Suki Pantal specifically cited the potential for more role models of independent professional women to be portrayed on the TV channels watched so avidly in India. She also pointed to the need for stronger school peer networks. Jas Rohel believed increased links were essential between business and universities, supplemented with practice-based curriculum to assist the transition to work.

Anita Bhalla added that more rural apprenticeships were important, asking, 'How do you convince elders that digital education can help?' Dipika Mistry noted:

'Education is given much respect and held in very high esteem in India and it's pretty critical if you have ambitions. Young women need to be supported with careers advice, women's entrepreneurial networks, teaching and mentoring. You still have to be quite courageous as a young woman to say no to the cultural demands of getting married and having a family. You need to break through the constraints of these bonds if want to have your own independence.'

Preet Gill stressed how strong-minded Indian women are and the importance of discipline:

'When people leave school there is a level of clarity on where you want to go and it's very different to what you see here. They just go for it. Maybe it's because of poverty. People feel it's achievable and are very hard working. Academia is not only about teaching you to learn, but about who you are as a citizen. More girls are getting jobs and not getting married as quickly. The opportunities for jobs are limited in certain states so they will have to leave home. It's important to have policies, quotas, to make sure women are advancing. Equality Impact Assessments matter.'

Legal protections

Legal protections were regarded as insufficient given the challenges facing women. While there was much optimism regarding cultural change, more protection was needed. Baljit Dhadda noted, 'Property transmission laws have changed for women, but to live freely is very difficult. Education is part of the answer, but there are legal, religious and cultural issues. Property is passed through male lines – a patrilineal system. This weakens women.' This theme was taken up in a report by the University of Manchester Global Development Institute:

Notwithstanding the 2005 Hindu Succession Amendment Act which granted equal inheritance rights to sons and daughters in joint family property[...]barely 16% of women in rural landowning households own land, constituting only 14% of all landowners and owning 11% of the land.... Accuracy in estimating this key gender gap in women's economic status is imperative, as is implementing laws to ensure the claims of all women to this vital resource. (Agarwal et al., 2020)

Lakshmi Kaul added that while there were regressive policies against women in the West, India was perhaps the only nation that banned triple talaak, ensuring that minority women are protected from the whims of their male partners. Ms Kaul pointed to India's written constitution guaranteeing fundamental rights to all its citizens, something, she noted, many progressive Western nations were still struggling with: 'USA, for example, does not have maternity leave policy for new parents; this directly pushes women into poverty as many are forced to discontinue work if they wish to prioritise family and children.'

Anita Bhalla cited the importance of infrastructure to women in providing 'clean water, lighting, toilets and sanitary provision, safe transport as a human right for young girls wherever they live'. The theme of personal safety for females of all ages in India was universally seen as an issue requiring radical improvements to be achieved with urgency. The ability to move safely to and from work was a priority with all-women buses and female crews suggested. Some interviewees considered police authorities had not demonstrated sufficient willingness to punish the perpetrators of misogyny, noting links between the reduction in female power and repressive cultural attitudes to female sexuality.

One aspect of Indian culture considered problematical was the media. Some interviewees suggested that coverage of dreadful violence against women in India is not adequately condemnatory. Equally, the Indian judicial system was thought to be too 'lengthy and laborious', with 'shame' remaining a major issue for violated women. As one told me, 'Who's going to marry them?' Overall, it's believed, the entire Indian societal system should be reformed to ensure it puts the rights of women and girls at the heart of the process.

Conclusion

All those interviewed for this chapter passionately stressed the fact that Indian women have achieved success. Notable examples cited include dotcom entrepreneur Kiran Mazumdar-Shaw, founder and executive chair of Biocon, Sharmistha Dubey, CEO of Match Group and known as the 'boss of romance', Sonia Syngal, CEO of Gap Inc, one of a few female CEOs on the Fortune 500, as well as multi-millionaire actress and former Miss World, Priyanka Chopra. One of those interviewed, Rosie Ginday, was featured in Indian Vogue. These prominent examples and success stories apart, there are numerous examples of successful women in India in everyday life and across career streams, emphasised Lakshmi Kaul. Examples shared by her included Bhavna Kant, one of the first three Indian woman fighter pilots; Kanchan Chaudhary Bhattacharya, the first female Director General of Police; Justice M. Fathima Beevi, the first female judge to be appointed to the Supreme Court of India; Kalpana Chawla, the first Indian woman to go into space; Tessy Thomas, Director General of Aeronautical Systems and the first woman scientist to head a missile project in India; Surekha Yadav, the first woman train driver; Karnam Malleswari, the first Indian woman to win an Olympic medal; and Arunima Sinha, the first female amputee ever to climb Mount Everest. More recently, India appointed its second female President of India, Mrs Droupadi Murmu, the first tribal person to become the Head of State. 'This list of firsts and success stories in India goes on and on; something not many other countries could yet boast of,' said Ms Kaul. The importance of role models was essential and should be vigorously supported and promoted through increased investment. Baljit Dhadda echoed this by stressing that 'More direct resourcing is needed if more women are to be successful in future.'

As the views of all interviewees emphatically demonstrate, India is brimming with female talent. Nonetheless, all agreed, nurturing young women to fulfil their potential while reforming the cultural, societal and legal system remains key to success. For Indian historian Romila Thapar, it is important their shared history of fluid identities and inspiring diversity, blossoming in an open, liberal society, is acclaimed, not checked; where 'asking[...]questions freely and exploring the answers to those questions in a free manner' remains encouraged (Parkin, 2022). This will be critical in ensuring India develops both as a modern society and effective economy in this century and beyond.

Acknowledgements

This chapter includes interview contributions and personal reflections on the position of women in India at 75 from Anita Bhalla OBE DL, Chair, Birmingham City University; Baljit Dhadda, Director Education, Green Park Executive Search; Preet Kaur Gill, MP for Birmingham Edgbaston, Shadow Minister for Primary Care and Public Health; Rosie Ginday, MBE, Founder and CEO, Miss Macaroon; Lakshmi Kaul, Former Head and Representative, CII, UK; Dipika Mistry, Corporate Finance Manager, EY; Suki Pantal, Founder and Owner, Suki's Curries and Spices; and Jas Rohel, CEO, Education Awards.

References

Agarwal, B., Anthwal, R. and Malvika, M. (2020) Which women own land in India? Between divergent data sets, measures and laws. GDI Working Paper 2020-043. Manchester: The University of Manchester

Business Insider India Bureau (2021) These are the Indian states with the lowest female literacy rate, Confederation of Indian Industry, Grant Thornton (2022) India meets Britain Tracker, The latest trends in Indian Investment in the UK, (grantthornton. co.uk)

Clinton White House Archives (2000) The President's Trip to Ireland and the United Kingdom,
https://clintonwhitehouse4.archives.gov/WH/New/december2000/speech12_14a.html

Gohain, M.P. (2021) '18% more women in higher education in five years', The Times of India,

Galor, O. (2022) The Journey of Humanity: The Origins of Wealth and Inequality, Bodley Head

Jowett, A. (2022) Foreign Direct investment by ultimate controlling economy, UK trends and analysis, July 2022, data and analysis from Census 2021, Office for National Statistics

Parkin, B. (2022) 'Nationalists have one kind of history, we have another', FT Weekend, 23/24 April 2022

Sharma, K. (2020) 'Study Shows how India's Higher Education enrolment can jump to 65% from 27%', The Print

The Indian Express (2019) Telling numbers: Indian girls have higher school enrolment rate than boys, says report | Explained News

US Census Bureau (1998) Women's Education in India (census.gov)

Chapter 17

Indian Muslims: A Personal Reflection

Imran Mogra

Summary

In this chapter, I celebrate the loyalty and some of the major contributions of a few prominent Indian Muslims. The personalities have been chosen to represent a range of disciplines with a focus on revealing key information about them while also reflecting the diverse nature of India itself. I end with a reflection on the Muslim community post-independence.

Introduction

In August 1947, the British were forced to abdicate Hindustan swiftly through an ill-thought and messy political strategy under the supervision of the inexperienced Viceroy, Louis Mountbatten. The borders established by a barrister who had never travelled beyond Paris to the East were presented to the nation two days after partition, subsequently bringing an end to hundreds of years of brutality, extraction of resources and usurping of enormous wealth. At that point India and Pakistan were crafted as independent nations, and this resulted in the largest human dispersion witnessed in history. Sadly, the bloodbath resulted in over a million deaths, and many continue to suffer, personally and communally to this day. As for the British, their exit plan was secure because they had only a handful of casualties.

In 1700, Hindustan's share of the world economy was 24% (Maddison, 2003). The current combined population of Bangladesh, India and Pakistan is approximately 1.8 billion, and as such could have become a superpower, economically and politically. The Sikh community would not have to cross the border to pay homage to their Guru. Its military budget would probably be less, and it had the potential to have been a formidable nuclear power. Bangladesh perhaps would not have been heard of. That said, the reality is as it is. In this chapter, I begin with a Muslim who envisioned a united Hindustan, and, thereafter, celebrate some Indian Muslims who have made major contributions to its rich cultural life.

Maulana Husain Ahmad Madani (1879–1957)

A prominent luminary in the history of modern Islam, Maulana Husain Ahmad Madani was a scholar par excellence, patriot, political activist and spiritual mentor who made significant sacrifices for the achievement of independence. The literature about the political theories and practical ideas of Maulana Husain Ahmad Madani is plentiful.

Figure 17.1: Husain Ahmad Madani 2012 stamp of India

However, its popularity is limited beyond his native Urdu. Goyal (2004) laments the absence of the role of Muslim scholars (Ulamā) in general, as it was their fraternity which first warned against the threat of India's political power and cultural life from the British who became rulers of this vast and wealthy country. Such Muslim scholars also inspired the First War of Independence in 1857.

Granted that not all scholars and the elite among the Muslim communities were in favour of a united India. Generally speaking, academic work on the contributions of Muslim scholars is yet to fully acknowledge their political thoughts, practices and contributions in pre- and post-independent India. These were individuals who were at the forefront of the struggle and participated shoulder-to-shoulder with and propelled the likes of Gandhi, Nehru and others. They collaborated with the Hindu and Sikh Nationalist-led Ghadar Party, which was active in India, Europe and the USA (Hasan, 2015). In other words, the widespread notion of the Ulamā being 'obscurantist' and hostile to Nationalism is challenged (Mian, 2004).

In the city of the Prophet

Maulana Husain Ahmad Madani hailed from Uttar Pradesh. However, after his family migrated to Madinah, he continued teaching for approximately 18 years in the mosque of the Prophet. His study circle, which included an international audience, expanded over time. However, even though he was passionately engrossed in teaching the Hadith of the Prophet, exegesis of the Qur'ān and jurisprudence, he was not aloof from the political and economic state of the Muslims. The city of Madinah provided an opportunity to study political developments in the world and to be acquainted with the latest trends in political thought (Goyal, 2004). He advised his students to serve their country and people, rather than seek personal salvation. He gained first-hand knowledge about the plunder of colonial powers that not only exploited the colonies politically and economically, but also sought to destroy their religion, culture and ethical norms (Goyal, 2004).

The prisoner of Malta

Like many of his comrades, Maulana Husain Ahmad Madani endured life in prison. He was incarcerated from 1917 until 1920 for condemning the brutality of the British (Mian, 2005). In Malta, there were approximately 3,000 individuals of different races, regions and religions including Muslims, Christians, Jews, Europeans, Turks, Arabs, Africans, blacks and whites imprisoned for their opposition of British policies. It was all humanity in miniature (Goyal, 2004). Interacting with these people widened Madani's political horizons and deepened his resolve to liberate his homeland from the shackles of the occupiers as he heard first-hand accounts of the havoc in their respective countries. It also sculpted and refined his vision of the India he wanted after independence. After his release, Madani became actively involved in India's self-rule movement (Goyal, 2004).

Nature of politics

Although Maulana Husain Ahmad Madani had entered the field of politics through his teacher after the failed Silk Letter Movement, his politics were unemotional. Indeed, Goyal (2004) asserts that an intellectual approach to the problems of society and state is amply evidenced within Madani's writings on Indian politics, economics and international affairs. He abandoned the idea of returning to Madinah, a cherished desire of many a Muslim, for liberating his country and fellow humans.

He assumed the leadership of Jamiat Ulema-i-Hind and supported the Khilafat Movement and the Non-Cooperation Movement. He also supported Gandhi in connection with the Quit India Movement. He reacted to his captives and adversaries in a humane manner (Madani, n.d.). Nevertheless, Madani was uncompromising with those who had usurped his Motherland. To this end, he was fiercely dedicated to liberation, favoured democracy and inter-religious peace, and fought relentlessly for what he believed in. From 1916, he was arrested once every ten years until independence, spending over seven years in British detention (Metcalf, 2009).

Composite Nationalism

Over time, two main models emerged for the future of India. Goyal (2004) maintains that the word 'secular' did not appear until the 1930s when Gandhi and then Nehru began to stress it as a separation of religion from politics. However, neither of them propounded a theory of Nationalism; it was left only to Maulana Husain Ahmad Madani to purport theories promoting the idea of United Nationalism. Maulana Husain Ahmad Madani penned a booklet *Muttahida Qaumiyat Aur Islam* (Islam and Composite Nationalism) making a theological case in favour of composite Nationalism, and envisaged a multi-cultural, -racial and -religious state.

Thus, the concept of Secular Nationalism is the combined legacy of Gandhi, Azad, Nehru and Maulana Madani (Goyal, 2004). The latter has almost been kept out of the limelight; although the political role of Abul Kalam Azad has been appreciated, Maulana Madani's political role has not received its due acclaim. The two do, however, share in common that their theoretical assumptions have been neglected. Gandhi revered Madani and Nehru held him in high esteem (Hasan, 2015). Curiously, Goyal (2004) laments that there is hardly any mention of Maulana Madani in the writings of Gandhi and Nehru, although he had spent as much time in British jails as any of them. He travelled throughout India calling for self-determination. He had formulated clear political ideas, which had matured in Malta with prisoners from different nationalities. On the ground, this meant total freedom, and its success depended on the cooperation of all communities (Goyal, 2004).

Sincerity

In later years, Madani was honoured with the title of Shaykh al-Islam in recognition of his eminence in scholarship. Maulana Husain Ahmad Madani viewed independence as his sole goal. Thus, once freedom had been established, life moved on and he took a step back from political life. When the time came to honour key players in the liberation struggle by the Nehru-led government, it is well known that he was bestowed the highest civilian honour of the Padma Vibhushan. However, he politely declined this, stating concerns that the award would indebt him to the government (Hasan, 2015). This speaks volumes of his sincerity to God and his commitment to his birthplace.

Figure 17.2: Amjad Khan

Independence was not an individual effort. Nevertheless, the selfless sacrifice, determination and freedom achieved by Maulana Madani was a blueprint for the liberation of all colonised people across the world afterwards. He enjoyed equal respect among both Muslims and non-Muslims (Nisar, 2012). After accomplishing his goal, he withdrew into a life of spirituality and teaching. The India that he envisaged was a pluralistic India that had positive relations within itself and with the communities and the countries in its neighbourhood.

Khans of Bollywood

Films influenced the state formulation of India during the anti-colonial and post-independence periods. In 1957, the producer-director Mehboob Khan's Mother India contributed hugely to shaping India's national identity in its formative years and conveyed a sense of Indian Nationalism to urban and rural citizens alike (Schulze, 2002). Muhammad Yusuf Khan, of Peshawar, is considered one of the greatest actors in Indian cinema. With the screen name Dilip Kumar (1922–2021), he starred in some of the biggest commercially successful films in the period 1949– 1961; as such, he co-leads the record for the greatest number of Filmfare Awards won.

Prior to the 1990s there were numerous successful Khans. The famous Gabbar Singh, the character played by Amjad Khan (1940–1992) made him the most famous villain in Bollywood history. However, the term Khans, refers to four Khans who ruled the cinematic world thereafter.

Aamir Khan captured the Indian and Chinese film markets. He was awarded the third-highest civilian honour of Padma Bhushan. Abdur Rehman 'Shah Rukh' Khan (dubbed the King of Bollywood) grew up in Bangalore. As an actor, film producer, entrepreneur and television personality, he won abundant awards and is a heartthrob who was recognised as one of Time Magazine's 20 Asian Heroes under 40. Salman Khan, born to a Hindu mother and a Muslim father, was brought up in both faiths. As part of his philanthropic services, he initiated a NGO called 'Being Human' which supports the underprivileged. Salman Khan self-identifies as both Hindu and Muslim. Saif Ali Khan grew up a Muslim but is more inclined towards spiritualism than organised religion. He was one of the highest-paid actors and is considered among the most high-profile celebrities in India. Saif descends from a line of Nawabs (Princes/Governors) and inherited the title when his father passed away (Wiki 2022).

Music

The moment I heard about the passing of Mohammed Rafi (1924–1980) remains etched in my memory. I had bought my snacks for *iftār* from a shop near our local mosque. Beyond that, Rafi, as he was dearly known, was a household name. An Indian playback singer and musician hailing from contemporary Amritsar, he was one of the greatest and most influential singers. For his services, he was awarded the fourth-highest civilian award. Rafi recorded approximately 7,000 songs in a wide range of genres and was acknowledged as one of the 'Best 50 Indians' ever born (Korti and Jain, 2016). What might surprise readers is that these were in many Indian languages, dialects and some foreign languages. The government of India announced two days of public mourning in his honour. Outside the studio, Rafi was a philanthropic artist. 'The Man with a Golden Voice' also had a golden heart. He was humble and self-effacing in his charitable giving, especially his *zakāt*. In the summer of 2008, the City of Birmingham Symphony Orchestra released 16 songs as a double CD titled Rafi Resurrected. Birmingham is also said to be home to a shrine dedicated to Rafi on Fazeley Street.[7] Relatives of his wife were killed during the partition, so she decided to migrate to Pakistan.

However, Rafi desired to remain in India, and so their love had to part. He penned a song at the assassination of Gandhi. Prime Minister Nehru personally invited Rafi to his residence to sing the song. The rendition moved Nehru to tears (Dev, 2015).

7 I unsuccessfully searched for it on 27 March 2022; part of the street is cordoned off for construction.

Sports

Part of Indian culture is having a love affair with cricket. Mohammad Azharuddin (now an Indian politician) was a former captain of the national team. Hailing from a Hyderabadi Muslim family, he led the Indian team in 47 Test matches and 174 one-day internationals, with victories in 90 of the latter. He was known for his attacking brand of cricket and strong slip catching. Lingering on the theme of sport, Sania Mirza, also from Hyderabad, is India's tennis queen par excellence, who lifted the racket at six. She single-handedly placed Indian women's tennis and the tricolour on the global stage. A former Wimbledon doubles champion, multiple Asian Games and Commonwealth Games medal winner, and former world Number One in doubles, Mirza reached a career-high singles ranking of 27. She is married to former Pakistan cricket captain Shoaib Malik.

Politics

Before considering Science, it is important to recognise that, on the political front, there have been three Muslim presidents Zakir Husain (1897-1969), Fakhruddin Ali Ahmed (1905-1977) and Professor Abdul Kalam (1931–2015).

Science

Professor Abdul Kalam (1931–2015), born in present-day Tamil Nadu and whose father was said to be an Imam, is India's best-known nuclear scientist and its 11th President, nicknamed the People's President (Gandhi, 2017). He developed a low-cost coronary stent with colleagues and headed several successful missiles programmes including the 'Agni'.

Figure 17.3: The President, Dr. A.P.J. Abdul Kalam addressing the nation on the eve of 58th Republic Day, in New Delhi on January 25, 2007

He lived a modest and generous life. Religion and spirituality were very important to him. As a proud and practising Muslim, his father impressed upon him the value of interfaith. Later in life, Kalam proposed that the answers to India's issues lay in dialogue and cooperation among its religious, social and political leaders. He embodied syncretism by appreciating various elements of the diverse spiritual and cultural traditions of India. Alongside Qur'ān and Islamic practices, he was also versed in Hindu traditions, Sanskrit, and lived a vegetarian life (Gandhi, 2017). He wrote poetry, played instruments, and enjoyed a daily diet of devotional music.

Present day India

Fast-forward 75 years and the effects of partition have endured a rivalry between the peoples of the countries of South Asia, their leaders, their nuclear arms race, and sports. Some might argue that the current climate for minorities within India is less than reassuring. Others might well disagree. The increased violence against religious and other minorities is alleged to be fuelled by New Delhi's current Nationalist ideology. There are serious concerns among those advocating human rights who are being silenced because they are perceived to be upsetting the status quo (Brader, 2021). The fear among many Indian Muslims is that in a growing right-wing fundamentalist political and cultural atmosphere, perpetrators of violence can walk away freely (Khan and Lutful, 2021). They feel their choice to be loyal Indians and to rightfully live in their Motherland remains insufficient to warrant state protection in the context of and within a government that is hard-line and right wing. Their economic well-being, rituals and sacred spaces, and, for some, their very identity are being assaulted (Khan, 2020).

Contemporary geopolitical, cultural and ethnoreligious problems are also rooted in the historical consciousness of the peoples of Hindustan. Similarly, it is undeniable that elements of Hindu and Muslim cultures influenced one another and infused each other's lifestyles. Even today, one can still see examples of both communities together at holy shrines. Nevertheless, based on the past of all Hindustani communities, the evolution and creation of modern Indian identities have foreseen the emergence of tensions, a phenomenon found in other parts of the world where diverse people and nations live harmoniously. At the same time, Indian Muslims observe examples of unity, harmony and co-existence. This behoves the current democratically elected leaders and their citizens to become beacons of a state where all people regardless of religion, ethnicity, language or region can live together as the chronicles of history bear witness.

Conclusion

Celebratory events tend to begin with anthems. However, I would like to end with the national anthem as it has fascinating revelations. It was penned in 1904 by Allamah Sir Muhammad Iqbal (1877–1938), poet-philosopher, political-ideologue, and later pro-partition. It is one of the enduring patriotic poems composed originally for children in the ghazal style of Urdu poetry, celebrating Hindustan's greatness as a civilisation (Jamal, 2011). It quickly became an anthem of opposition to British rule. Entitled *Tarāna-e-Hindi* (Anthem of the People of Hindustan), the first verse of the ode says:

Sāre jahān se aachā Hindustān hamārā

The best of all lands is our Hindustan

Reference

Brader, C. (2021) Human rights concerns in India. [Online] https://lordslibrary. parliament.uk/human-rights-concerns-in-india/ (Accessed 06 June 2022)

Dev, S. (2015) Mohammed Rafi: Golden Voice of the Silver Screen. New Delhi: Om Books International

Gandhi, A.K. (2017) Dr. A.P.J. Abdul Kalam: Biography of A Saintly Scientist. New Delhi: Prabhat Book

Goyal, D.R. (2004) Maulana Husain Ahmad Madni: A Biographical Study. New Delhi: Anamika Publishers & Distributors

Hasan, T. (2015) Colonialism and the Call to Jihad in British India. New Delhi: SAGE

Jamal, N. (2011) Iqbal Hamara. Lahore: Beacon Books

Khan, S. (2020) 'Social Exclusion of Muslims in India and Britain', Journal of Social Inclusion Studies, 6, 1. pp. 56–77

Khan, M.A.M. and Lutful, R. (2021) 'Emerging Hindu Rashtra and Its Impact on Indian Muslims', Religions. Special Issue on Religion and International Relations: What do we know and how do we know it? 12, 9, p. 693 [Online] https://doi. org/10.3390/rel12090693 (Accessed 06 June 2022)

Korti, R. and Jain, D. (2016) Mohammed Rafi: God's Own Voice. New Delhi: Niyogi Books

Maddison, A. (2003) Development Centre Studies The World Economy: Historical Statistics. Paris: OECD

Madani, H.A. (n.d.) Autobiography (Naqsh-i-Hayāt). Karachi: Darul Ishaat
Metcalf, B.D. (2009) Husain Ahmad Madani. London: Oneworld Publications

Mian, S.M. (2005) The Prisoners of Malta (Asiran-i Malta). New Delhi: Jamiat Ulama- i-Hind and Manak Publications. Tr. M.A. Husain and H. Imam

Nisar, R. (2012) 'Maulana Husain Ahmad Madani and Composite Nationalism', Insight Islamicus, 12, pp. 149–161

Schulze, B. (2002) 'The Cinematic "Discovery of India": Mehboob's Re-Invention of the Nation in Mother India', Social Scientist, 30, 9/10, pp. 72–87

Wiki (2022) Khans of Bollywood [Online] https://en.wikipedia.org/wiki/Khans_of_ Bollywood (Accessed 17/10/2022).

About the contributor

Imran Mogra has authored Jumpstart RE! (Routledge, 2018), Islam: A Guide for Teachers (SAGE, 2020) and Religious Education 5-11: A Guide for Teachers (Routledge, 2023). His recent publications include Fundamental British values: Are they fundamental? and Social justice and care for the world – adopting a critical view in religious education.

Imran is a senior lecturer in professional studies and religious education in several programmes in the Department of Early Years and Primary Education, Birmingham City University, England.

Part Four

India's economic evolution

Chapter 18

What is this India business? Influences and competitive advantage

Paul Davies and Steven McCabe

Summary

This chapter provides reflection on what being engaged in business in India means. Using experience gained by one of the authors, the intention is to examine how business in India has evolved in recent decades and the lessons that may be learnt.

Personal statement by Paul Davies

Having been the managing director of an international, US IT company's subsidiary in India, I fell instantly in love with India and Indian business. My Indian colleagues, clients and customers never ceased to amaze me with their own unique take on life and business. I owe them a debt of gratitude for the different perspectives they brought to life and business. If I am at all critical of Indian business today, it is always with an underlying admiration, sometimes a great deal of frustration, and then a sense of the pure pleasure any engagement with Indian businesspeople brings.

Introduction

In August 1947, when independence and partition arrived, there was communal violence, disruption to ordinary life and a very real sense that India would not survive, something people forget now. It was touch and go whether the indomitable spirit of Indians would manage to come through. As we now know, it did and, crucially, success followed. This was celebrated with the publication of a book on Indian business, What's This India Business? (Davies, 2004). What follows is a distillation of what 'doing' business in India involves and why, almost two decades after the publication of this book, this country maintains distinct advantages (Harris et al., 2020).

What does business in India mean?

In understanding how to conduct business practice in India in the early 2000s, it was necessary to analyse a range of areas from business etiquette through to Indian time keeping, corruption and bribery. One issue was the speed of response by the Indian Civil Service, the courts and legal system which, sometimes, makes geological time look as though it's proceeding at breakneck speed! Timekeeping and deadlines can be somewhat flexible and, if you are unused to working in India, drive you to distraction. However, and based on empirical experience, it's possible to state that those engaged in business, banking and law in India are some of the most dynamic, forward-thinking and innovative in the world (Budhwar and Varma, 2010).

So how do all these contradictions fit together to make the hugely internationally successful country one of the driving forces for growth and business development globally? In 1947, the government created what became known as the Licence Raj. This effectively created a straitjacket for Indian business and business development in that investment, diversification and innovation became subject to strict control. It's easy now to suggest that this was a huge mistake, but at the time, with a new nation, new ideas, the feeling of instability and the possibility that the biggest experiment in democracy that the world has ever seen might 'crash and burn', there were many justifications for caution, control and patience. It's also easy to underestimate political instability in India, with the strains of religious and caste divides causing further tension. There were also the geopolitical threats to India which successive governments saw as existential threats, not least aggression from China and questions about Pakistan's intent, particularly before East and West Pakistan became Bangladesh and Pakistan respectively.

Figure 18.1: Manmohan Singh in 2009

The Licence Raj caused the greatest pent-up frustration of course. With many industries being nationalised, it meant that the nascent government institutions were severely tested. In the early 1990s, two politicians emerged who purposely loosened the grip of the Licence Raj: Prime Minister P.V. Narasimha Rao and, more especially, Finance

Minister Dr Manmohan Singh. Under their reforms some of the loss-making nationalised industries were sold off or abandoned. Far more important was the vision behind the development of the already existing Indian Institutes of Management and Indian Institutes of Technology into world-class teaching and training organisations.

Crucial to the subsequent success of Indian business was the passionate belief and novel ideas of people such as F.C. Kohli, the father of Indian Information Technology (IT) and the founder of Tata Consultancy Services (Raianu, 2021). As a result, IT was fundamental to India's importance for the country to achieve an area of global dominance in business. Opening centres of excellence in IT and management were part of this process. Critics cited their belief that India's existing social and political problems of poverty, famine and disease were not given greater priority. However, the plan for business development was that it would provide the foundation for India's economic development (Raman, 2014). Undoubtedly those who believe in the 'trickle-down' effect of economic development think India is something of a disappointment. It has led to the creation of a successful middle class, which is now at 30% of the current population, and more people than there were Indians at the time of Independence.

Reflections on business development in India

In understanding how the focus on the development of the strongest IT capability in the world has transformed India's international standing in business, it's possible to identify particular changes in practice which facilitated an improved environment. Economic and policy reforms of the early 1990s greatly assisted. These enabled Indian IT companies to exploit the opportunities for rapid growth and technological innovation which were presented. At this point, it's important to contrast India's capabilities with its major rival in the 1990s and early 2000s: China (Sondhi et al., 2021).

While China may have possessed a sophisticated manufacturing capability, on which its rapidly developing economy was built, India had a number of advantages when it came to services. The first was that around 30% of India's population (almost 100% of its educated population) speak English as a second language. If you're selling a service, it is far more important over time to speak your customers' language than if you are offering widgets at 90% of the Western price. Secondly, though there may be corruption in India and its legal system works extremely slowly, there is an accepted rule of law. 'Thirdly,

Indian business' greatest advantage is its free and vibrant press. You might not be able to get legal redress quickly, but it's possible to shame wrongdoers very effectively!' Finally, and sometimes this may seem like a disadvantage when compared with the totally directed economy of China, India is the largest democracy in the world.

Democracy, regardless of however frustrated people may be with a legislature that has to achieve compromise, is a major advantage for business. You don't necessarily need to be a disciple of David Ricardo and his theory of relative economic advantage (Ricardo, 2004) to recognise that creating excellence within an economy and focusing more and more resources on those successful businesses will deliver greater growth and much more efficiency and effectiveness. India demonstrates this with considerable flair. With such advantages and the investment in IT skills, India in the 1990s was poised to take off as an international business powerhouse (Bagla, 2008).

Y2K, an opportunity India seized with gusto

A problem in Western IT systems was recognised early in the 1990s. This was that year-dates in nearly all software programs, from those that ran banks to those keeping aeroplanes in the air, were usually held as two digits. For example 1968 was stored as 68. This made sense in the 1960s when computers were first developed. Storing two digits was far more economical than four and storage space was expensive. However, as the year 2000 approached, it was accepted that 00 would not make it possible for computer systems to recognise that it wasn't 1900. For example, calculating interest on bank loans would be almost impossible.

This issue became know as the Y2K programme – or in India, the Y2K opportunity.

Analysts stressed that a huge amount of effort was going to be required to painstakingly examine literally hundreds of thousands of systems and recode the operating program, without any unintended consequences, to ensure no ambiguity or failure when the year changed from 1999 to 2000. This necessitated what's known as regression testing on a colossal scale. The effect on Indian IT companies was transformational in two distinct but important ways.

Firstly, the due diligence work and the recoding was relatively straightforward but required many thousands of skilled programmers.

With India's absolute economic advantage – wage rates were sometimes as low as 10% of equivalent Western rates – and a very large army of IT graduates, it made huge sense to 'offshore' this work to India. Not only was it cost-effective, but it was actually possible to get it done.

The second effect on Indian IT companies was that Western companies discovered that they now had access to, and confidence in, a pool of people with IT skills. So much more could be accomplished with IT systems. This unleashed a tidal wave of demand for new or improved systems. Who was best placed to develop these new programmes? The Indian IT companies.

As a direct result of these two developments, Indian IT companies quickly developed far more expertise than Western companies about the very systems that Western companies were using to run their own businesses. Indian companies quite quickly moved up the value chain, not only focusing on, say, regression testing, but also in producing IT architects, IT analysts and IT consultants. India's rapidly growing cadre of IT professionals were adept at spotting opportunities as well as carrying out analysis of business requirements and specifying IT systems with greater competence than their Western indigenous IT counterparts (Sridhar, 2011).

By moving Indian IT people into more creative roles inside Western companies, a pull was created which developed even more offshoring and outsourcing skills; at the same time there was a push from Western companies which allowed business process outsourcing (BPO) to be developed. Those Western countries and companies which embraced BPO early, such as the UK's insurance industry which had developed confidence in Indian expertise due to the Y2K programmes, were able to grow faster and much larger. This, of course, is an accepted 'acid test' of success in business. As a direct consequence, UK insurance companies were dominant in Europe prior to the UK's departure from the European Union. Crucially, the development of BPO produced a pull for the development of further Indian capabilities. As a result, India has become a global powerhouse in many other service sectors.

Conclusion

Things aren't perfect in India. There are still issues, some psychological as well as basic issues such as infrastructure impediments like poor roads and variability of utilities including electricity supply. Psychologically, it may be observed, Indian businesses haven't quite matured enough to have that degree of confidence, one might say arrogance, to realise that they have taken on the world and beaten it in so many areas. Large US computer companies still appear more dominant than their Indian competitors.

Such US companies are international companies which happen to be from the US originally International Indian IT companies happen to be international but remain Indian. In addition, Indian companies have no tradition of middle management. Despite what management consultancy McKinsey may suggest (Rasiel, 1999), every organisation needs an effective middle management layer.

Nonetheless, the way in which business has evolved in the last three decades is impressive. Though some suggest that change has been too slow and that poverty in India is still a significant challenge, it's necessary to reflect on the considerable progress achieved so far (Parkin et al., 2022). India is now probably the third-largest economy in the world, behind China and the US. It's expected to overtake the US within five years (IBEF, 2022). Not bad for a country that 75 years ago was even importing finished cotton goods from the UK!

References

Bagla, G. (2008), Doing Business in 21st Century India: How to Profit Today in Tomorrow's Most Exciting Market, Business Plus, New York

Budhwar, P.S. and Varma, A. (2010), Doing Business in India, Routledge, London

Davies, P. (2004), What's This India Business? Offshoring, Outsourcing and the Global Services Revolution, Nicholas Brealey International, London

Harris, J., Jeffrey, C. and Brown, T. (2020), India: Continuity and Change in the Twenty-First Century, Polity Press, Cambridge, UK

IBEF (2022), 'IT & BPM Industry in India', India Brand Equity Foundation Website, https://www.ibef.org/industry/information-technology-india.aspx, accessed 28 February

Parkin, B., Cornish, C. and Lockett, H. (2022), 'India ramps up spending to reclaim place as fastest-growing economy', Financial Times, 1 February, https://www.ft.com/ content/a0a6cf20-c4c0-43a0-a717-010167dbf1e7, accessed 28 February

Ricardo, D. (2004), The Principles of Political Economy, Dover Publications Inc, Mineola, New York

Raianu, M. (2021), Tata: The Global Corporation That Built Indian Capitalism, Harvard University Press, Cambridge, MA

Rasiel, E. (1999), The McKinsey Way, McGraw-Hill, New York

Sondhi, N., Panigrahi, R., Pang, M. and Chatterjee, R. (2021), Comparative Development of India & China: Economic, Technological, Sectoral & Socio-cultural Insights, Sage/Spectrum, Los Angeles

Sridhar, V. (2011), The Telecom Revolution in India: Technology, Regulation, and Policy, Oxford University Press India, New Delhi

Raman, S.V. (2014), Innovation in India: Combining Economic Growth with Inclusive Development, Cambridge University Press, Delhi

About the contributor

Dr Paul Davies is the founder of Bite-Sized Books and now chairman, having been CEO of Unisys India. He is the author of two books on Indian business, *What's This India Business?* and *New Business in India*, and created a successful consultancy business advising clients on offshoring and outsourcing, initially to India, but also taking in South Africa, Singapore, Egypt and a number of other developing outsourcing markets, including Eastern Europe. In his early career he gained a PhD focused on the novels of George Eliot – and it was only after a number of years teaching that he joined the IT industry, based in the Netherlands.

Chapter 19

Solar villages – a smart sustainable future for rural India

Cham Athwal

Summary

Post-independence India has achieved food security with the help of irrigation using highly subsidised electricity for pumping groundwater. However, currently powered by distant mostly coal burning power stations, this carries a huge cost in CO_2 production and groundwater depletion. Solarisation of irrigation pumps is posited as a sustainable pathway out of this dilemma... We propose that the excess electricity generated by the solar arrays at the irrigation pumps is used to power a smart village microgrid providing clean, local and reliable electricity for the energy transition.

Introduction

In 2020, 65% of India's population, that is around 900 million people, were to be found in rural areas and although this percentage is predicted to come down to 50% by around 2045, the absolute number of rural inhabitants is not expected to significantly decline over this period (The World Bank, 2022). About 70% of these rural households depend primarily on agriculture for their livelihood. The history of Indian agriculture is reviewed in chapter 20 in this book and an example of the contrast in the fortunes of the Indian population between the colonial era and post- independence is illustrated in Figure 19.1.

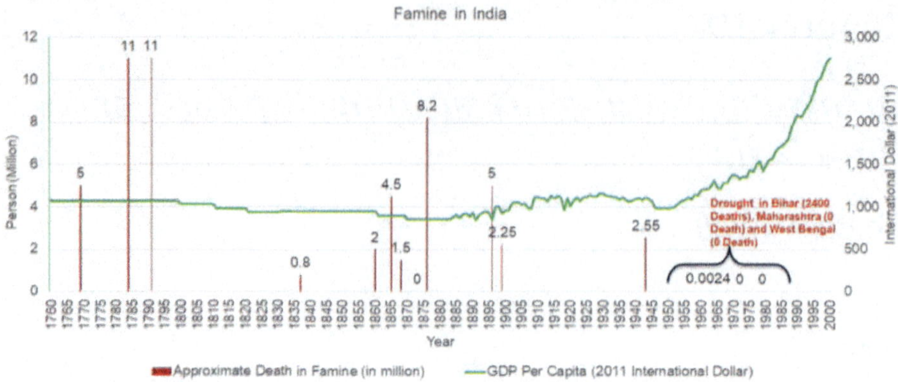

Figure 19.1: Timeline of famines and GDP per capita in India from 1760 to 2000 (Gulati, 2022).

After independence, India initially relied on imports and food aid to meet domestic requirements. However, after severe droughts in 1965 and 1966, India adopted bold, progressive policies that focused on the goal of food grain self-sufficiency. These ushered in the Green Revolution with adoption of hybrid seeds, inorganic fertilisers, pesticides and irrigation by electrically pumped groundwater. In 2021 India's food stocks (73 million tonnes (mt)) were more than three times the targeted reserve (21 mt) and agriculture exports greater than £30 billion per annum (Food Corporation of India, 2022). While these policies have served India well, they are now having a negative impact on groundwater resources, CO_2 mitigation and the financial health of the power sector.

Irrigation, subsidy and groundwater depletion

Successful farming in India usually requires irrigation; otherwise, there are very significant crop yield gaps. About 65% of irrigated agriculture is via groundwater, and over 85% of extracted groundwater is used for irrigation. Around 30 million tube wells are used to pump this water, of which 70% are powered by grid electricity (the rest mainly use diesel) consuming 234 TWh annually which is 18% of India's total electricity generation (cf. total electricity generation in the UK is 312 TWh annually). Since the Green Revolution, many states have supported greater adoption of irrigation by providing unmetered or concessional power supply for agriculture, such that the annual power subsidy for agriculture in India was £11 billion in FY 2018/19 (Ministry of Information and Broadcasting Government of India, 2021).

This subsidy helped to boost agricultural production but over the decades it has contributed to inefficient consumption of electricity, over-extraction of groundwater, and poor energy and subsidy accounting. It has added to the burden of state governments such that they are less able to adequately fund other services such as education and health. State electricity generation corporations (DISCOMs) have become financially distressed due to approximate estimations of subsidies and insufficient reimbursement by state governments leading to inadequate investment in maintenance and operational inefficiency in the power sector. Compounded by public procurement and minimum support price policies, the subsidy has also led to agroclimatically inappropriate crop choices in many states.

In 2017, India pumped 249 billion cubic metres of groundwater for irrigation, 25% of the total withdrawn in the world that year. This scale of pumping has led to large areas of the country being over-exploited (red on map in Figure 19.2) where replenishment is insufficient to match withdrawal.

Figure 19.2: Categorisation of degree of groundwater utilisation (Central Ground Water Board, 2020).

The depletion of groundwater has been especially acute in north-western states such as Punjab where the Water Department has predicted exhaustion of groundwater reserves to a depth of 300 m within the next 20 years. The provision of free power in Punjab since the early 1990s has led to a sharp increase in the number of grid-connected tube wells (up to 1.4 million in 2020). The use of electricity per hectare and depth of the water table is illustrated in Figure 19.3.

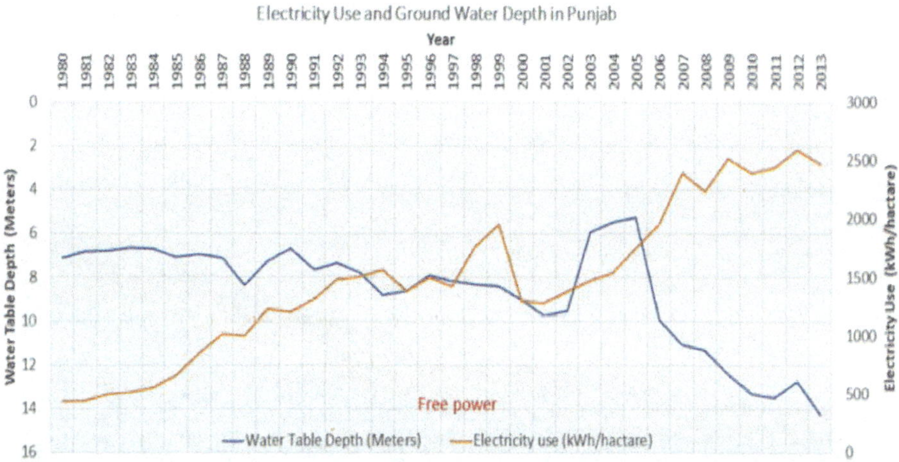

Figure 19.3: Timeline of agricultural electricity use and water table depth in Punjab (Gulati, 2022).

In 2016, Punjab (1.5% of India's area) produced 17% of India's wheat and 12% of rice, contributing 30% rice and 46% wheat to the Indian Central Pool that provides the government's food buffer and food for its welfare schemes. This feat has been achieved at the cost of excessive use of groundwater requiring periodic deepening of wells and consequent higher-power pumps and electricity usage. Farmers' vote bank prerogatives mean that it is not feasible for any democratic party to remove or reduce the free power subsidy. The main method to limit use of groundwater that has been adopted by many states, including Punjab, is rationing of electricity via the implementation of separate electrical lines and transformer stations (agricultural feeders) for irrigation pumps to those for the local village domestic supply. Commonly feeders for pumps are only live for eight hours a day and this is often during the night.

Solarisation of irrigation pumps contributing to India's COP26 commitments

Indian electricity generation is dominated by fossil fuels, especially coal (with around 73% of total generation), such that electricity for groundwater pumping produces around 400 mt of CO_2 per annum.

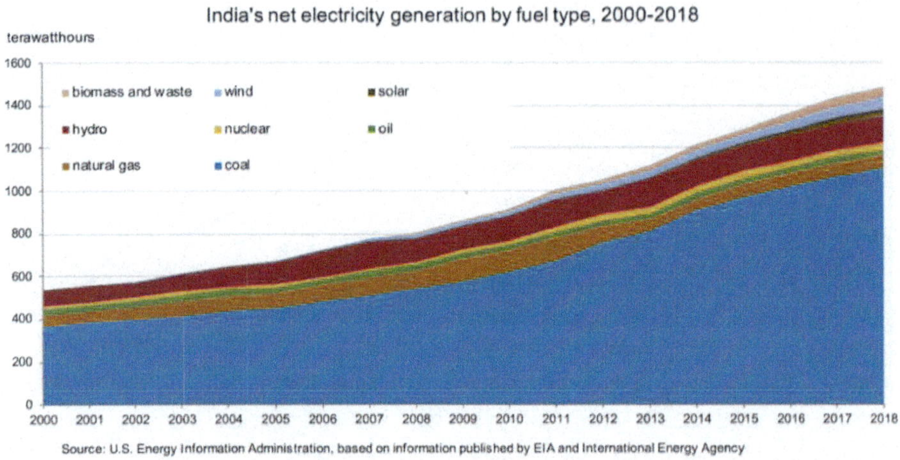

Figure 19.4: Timeline of India's net electricity generation by fuel type (U.S. Energy Information Administration, 2020).

India's COP26 commitments require 500 GW of power capacity from renewable sources by 2030; replacing all 30 million tube well pumps with on average 7 KW solar pumps could provide 210 GW of capacity. The Indian government has recognised this potential significant contribution to its renewable energy goals and in 2019 launched the Kisan Urja Suraksha Evam Utthaan Mahabhiyan (KUSUM) scheme. Component-C of this scheme makes provision for subsidising the solarisation of one million grid-connected pumps. Farmers will have to only contribute 10% upfront of the total expenditure to acquire and install a solar pump (Figure 19.5). The central and state governments will each provide 30% of the cost while the remaining 30% will be taken care of by a favourable bank loan to the farmer. At current costs this allows a farmer to install a 10 KW solar pump for an upfront cost of only £450 with good potential to recover this in one to two years.

Figure 19.5: External view of 15KW solar irrigation pump

Water-saving potential of grid-connected solar irrigation

Grid-connected solar irrigation pumps can also incentivise water saving if the farmer can sell electricity generated by the solar panels at an attractive rate. Then the farmer will have to choose between using electricity from the panels for irrigation or for earning direct income. This leads to the farmer having a market price for water without losing their historical access to 'free' electricity for irrigation. The feasibility of grid-connected solar pumps for incentivising water saving and increasing farmers' income was first demonstrated by the Dhundi pilot scheme in Gujarat that has been operating since late 2015. Figure 19.6 shows that the farmers on this scheme were significantly and increasingly incentivised to save electricity, and hence water, when rewarded by a feed-in-tariff of Rs 7 per KWh.

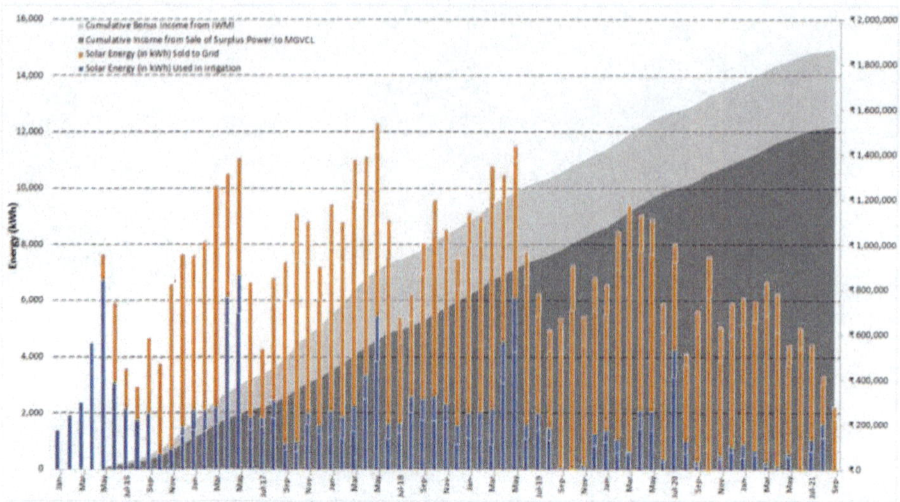

Figure 19.6: Comparison of electricity used for irrigation and sold to grid in Dhundi 2015 to 2021 (Verma, 2022).

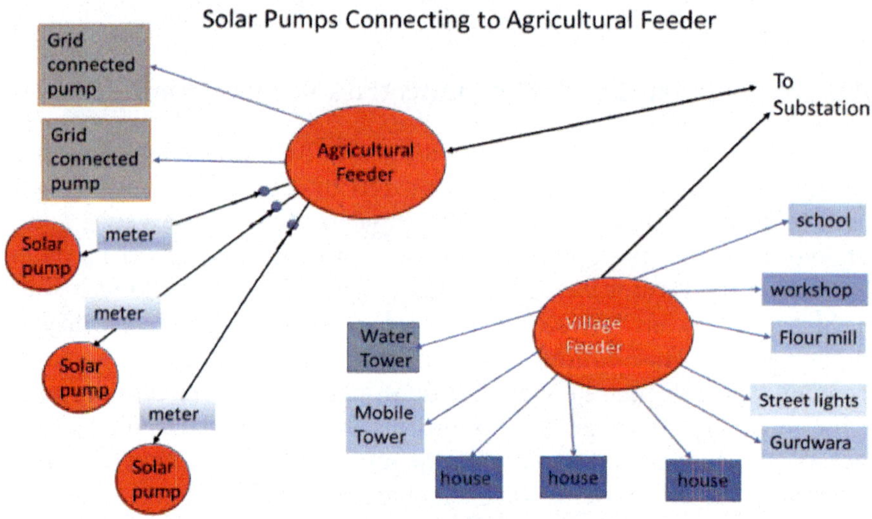

Figure 19.7: Village electricity schematic with solar pumps able to send electricity to the substation via an agricultural feeder.

The success of this pilot inspired the Gujarat government to launch the Suryashakti Kisan Yojana (SKY) initiative in late 2018, which by 2021 had achieved coverage of 90+ agricultural feeders and 4,000+ farmers, even under pandemic conditions (Verma, S. 2022). In this scheme (as well as for KUSUM Component-C more generally) the electrical topology that is realised at the village and its surrounding fields can be represented as in Figure 19.7, with the solar pumps able to supply electricity back to the grid via the agricultural feeder and farmers to be suitably recompensed.

In 2020, the World Bank published an exhaustive report analysing the business cases for implementing grid-connected solar pumps in Rajasthan (Gulati et al., 2020). Results of their analysis showed that a typical farmer would earn additional Rs 15,000/year during seven years of loan repayment and thereafter Rs 50,000/year. There is also a win-win for DISCOMs and state governments by elimination of the recurring power subsidy to agriculture, as illustrated in Figure 19.8, where ₹ Crore is equivalent to Rs 10M.

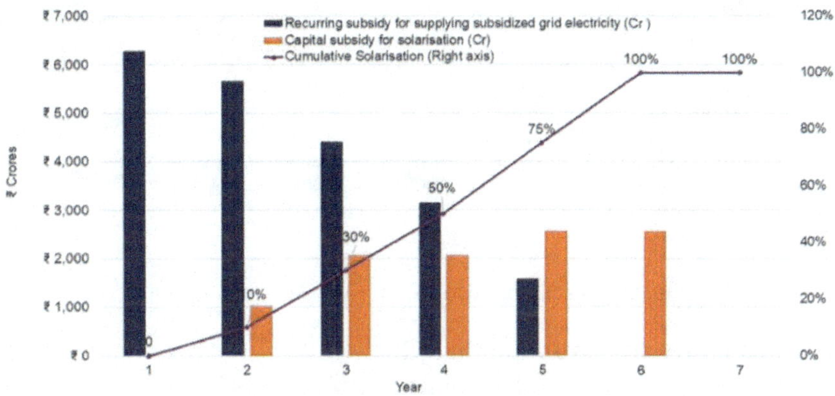

Figure 19.8: Impact of solarisation on recurring and capital subsidy (Ajmer and Jaipur DISCOMs only).

Solar pump-based village microgrid

Since 2019 researchers at BCU and Panjab University have proposed a range of alternative electrical topologies that allow additional benefits to arise for all stakeholders (Athwal, 2022; Verma, Y.P., 2022). These were based on the concept of microgrids. The US Department of Energy defines a microgrid as a group of interconnected loads and distributed energy resources within clearly defined electrical boundaries that acts as a single controllable entity with respect to the grid. A microgrid is geographically localised, can operate independently or connect to the wider grid and is intelligent. These characteristics match well with those of a typical Indian village, and analysis for Punjab shows that there is good parity between a village's power requirements and the generation capabilities from the solar arrays required for its irrigation pumps. In order to form a village microgrid, there will need to be a connection from the solar pumps to the village feeder. This could be achieved economically by using an additional electrical line from near the existing agricultural feeder to the village feeder (see Figure 19.8).

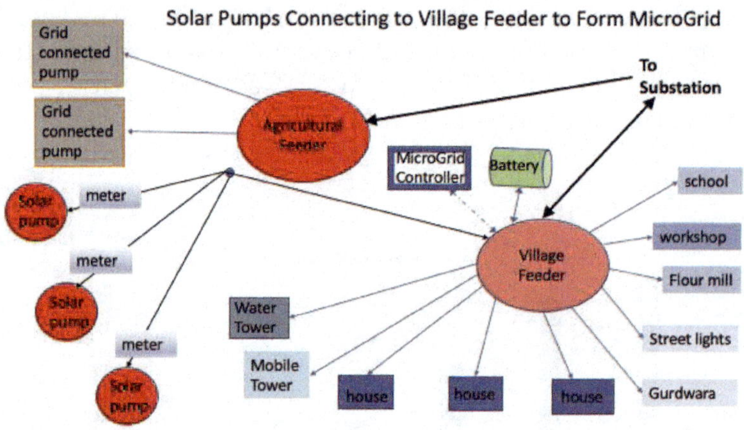

Figure 19.9: Electricity schematic for solar pump-based village microgrid.

Power outages are very frequent in Indian villages and the village-based battery storage can be used to supply power during these periods, especially at night-time or whenever power is not directly available from the solar panels. The battery can also provide a degree of power demand levelling by charging when excess local power is available and discharging when there is insufficient local power to meet demand. Sizing of the battery can be done on a village-by-village basis, with ease of adding additional battery storage if required.

The microgrid controller allows intelligent detection of outages and islanding of village feeder and associated control of battery charging/discharging. Weakly time-sensitive loads such as village water tower filling or operation of flour mills or cooling cycles of cold stores can also be controlled. Potential variable pricing based on availability of excess local power could be implemented via the controller accessing household-level smart meters if available or otherwise sending phone messages.

The microgrid concept seeks to maximise local (within the village) consumption of the locally generated electricity. This serves to minimise overall distribution and transmission losses which can be around 20% for the main grid and aids the resilience and balance of the village supply. Further benefits can be expected to arise in the future as electrification increases in transport and cooking, and air conditioning becomes more prevalent due to rising incomes. The availability of charging from the solar panels can further displace use of diesel and gas as innovations, such as electric tractors, electrification of other farm machinery and localised cold storage as well as electric two-wheelers and cars, become more prevalent. The use of localised intelligent control for the microgrid can act as a spur for or form part of further smart village initiatives; real-time local electrical power availability and pricing can be part of the local smart village app.

Conclusion

A few pilot schemes have demonstrated that farmer-owned grid-connected solar irrigation pumps can provide a low-carbon route out of the current inefficient use of groundwater for crop irrigation. Building on these, we have proposed the concept of solar village microgrids to drive further efficiencies and act as an enabler for a smart sustainable future for the many hundreds of millions living in rural India. Green power is democratised and literally placed in the hands of the people.

References

Athwal, C. 2022, Solar Village Microgrid Proposal: Overview and Potential Benefits, UKIERI-DST Partnership Development Workshop on Solar pump-based village microgrids-potential for tackling the energy/water/food nexus in Punjab

Central Ground Water Board, Department of Water Resources, Ministry of Jal Shakti, Government of India 2020, Master Plan for Artificial Recharge to Groundwater in India – 2020, http://cgwb.gov.in/Master Plan to GW Recharge 2020.pdf, accessed 8 May 2022

Food Corporation of India 2022. https://fci.gov.in/, accessed 8 May 2022

Gulati, M. 2022, Energy-Water-Agriculture Nexus in India: Lessons from Punjab and Rajasthan, UKIERI-DST Partnership Development Workshop on Solar pump-based village microgrids-potential for tackling the energy/water/food nexus in Punjab

Gulati, M.P., Priya, S. and Bresnyan, E.W. 2020. Grow Solar, Save Water, Double Farmer Income: An Innovative Approach to Addressing Water-Energy-Agriculture Nexus in Rajasthan. World Bank, Washington, DC. https://openknowledge.worldbank.org/ handle/10986/33375 License: CC BY 3.0 IGO, accessed 7 May 2022

Ministry of Information and Broadcasting Government of India 2021. PM KUSUM

Pradhan Mantri Kisan Urja Suraksha Evam Utthaan Mahabhiyan A New Green Revolution. https://mnre.gov.in/img/documents/uploads/file_f-1632204688401.pdf, accessed 21 October 2022

The World Bank 2022. Urban population (% of total population) – India. https://data. worldbank.org/indicator/SP.URB.TOTL.IN.ZS?locations=IN, accessed 21 October 2022

U.S. Energy Information Administration 2020. India Analysis. https://www.eia.gov/ international/analysis/country/IND, accessed 21 October 2022

Verma, S. 2022, SPaRC'ing agri-solarization through grid-connected SIPs, UKIERI- DST Partnership Development Workshop on Solar pump-based village microgrids- potential for tackling the energy/water/food nexus in Punjab

Verma, Y.P. 2022, Simulation of pilot solar village microgrid, UKIERI-DST Partnership Development Workshop on Solar pump-based village microgrids-potential for tackling the energy/water/food nexus in Punjab

About the contributor

Chamkour Singh Athwal is Professor of Digital Technology at BCU where he has been an academic for more than 30 years, most recently as the Faculty of Computing, Engineering and the Built Environment's Associate Dean for Research. With degrees in Physics at BSc, MSc and PhD level from the Universities of Manchester, London and Aston respectively, Cham has held postdoctoral research posts at Southampton and Lancaster Universities. Prior to joining BCU, Cham was a CERN Fellow in Geneva, Switzerland, for two years followed by five years of industrial experience at GEC Ltd. Professor Athwal has a wealth of experience in electrical and digital technologies, and also leveraging his heritage from Punjab's farming community he currently oversees the faculty's projects in India.

Chapter 20

Changing landscape of Indian farming: smart agriculture as a way forward

Navjot Sandhu, Javed Hussain and Shishank Shishank

Summary

This chapter provides an overview of the evolving nature, importance and context of the Indian farming sector. The onset of the Russian/Ukraine conflict has reinforced this sector's importance. The chapter considers government policy, practice and importance of smart technology to capitalise the full value of the sector. The analysis of the chapter concludes that the agricultural sector can benefit from innovative disruptive technologies to connect farming with consumers, eliminating intermediaries.

Introduction

The Indian agricultural sector has served the Indian economy well since the inception of the Green Revolution in the 1960s, helping to overcome food shortages and create employment opportunities. However, the agriculture sector share of GDP has declined, having consequences for poverty eradication and food security (Sandhu and Hussain, 2021; Sandhu, 2007, 2021; Jena and Bardhan, 2019; Sandhu et al., 2012, 2017). The agriculture sector is of national importance to sustain social cohesion in rural and urban areas and reduce migration and overcrowding in cities.

This chapter provides a brief historical context, explores emerging challenges and evaluates options for the Indian agriculture sector. We consider the use of disruptive technologies to empower farmers, enabling them to embrace smart technologies. The adoption of technologies to lessen the information asymmetry increasing farmer productivity and income to enhance their efficiency will be examined. The aim of this chapter is to initiate a dialogue among stakeholders for use of cutting-edge smart technologies.

Agriculture and economic growth

The economic growth of a country depends on the efficient functioning of all the sectors in the economy. Agriculture is the major contributor to economic growth in both developed and emerging countries (Sandhu and Hussain, 2021; Bharti, 2018: Misra et al., 2016; Eswaran and Kotwal, 2002). Prominent economists (Matsuyama, 1990; Rostow, 1990; Hayami and Ruttan, 1985; Jorgenson, 1961; Ranis and Fei, 1961; Nurkse, 1953) suggest that the agriculture sector is an essential component of the global economic development strategy (Suh, 2000). Nonetheless, industrial development is not possible without agricultural advances (Rostow, 1990; Nurkse, 1953). Matsuyama (1990) corroborated Rostow's proposition that the agriculture sector is a prerequisite for sustained economic growth (De La Escosura, 2022; Baek, 2018; Sandhu, 2007).

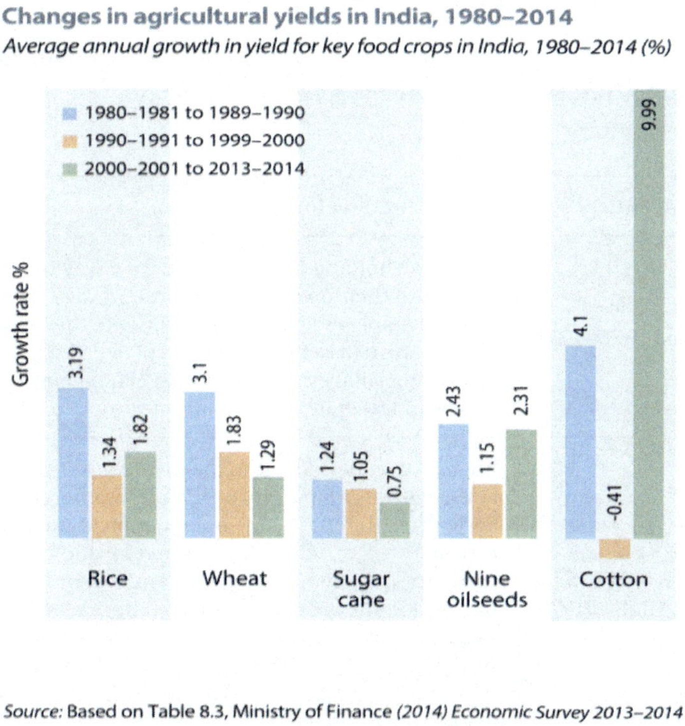

Figure 20.1: Changes in agricultural yields in India, 1980–2014 Average annual growth in yield for key food crops in India, 1980–2014.

Historically, all industrialised countries were once agrarian economies, as is the case today for developing countries. Indian agricultural predates the Indus Valley civilisation era, 9000 BC (Mulage, 2017), and today agriculture accounts for one-third of India's national wealth, 60% of total employment, contributing 18% to India's GDP Navjot Sandhu, Javed Hussain and Shishank Shishank (Sandhu and Hussain, 2021; Bharti, 2018: Misra et al., 2016). The arable land area in the country is the second-largest in the world after the United States. Approximately 38% of the land area in India is suitable for agriculture (Kanwal, 2022) though it is continuously declining due to urbanisation and population growth. India's farming output suffers from declining yields due to crop diseases, evolving weather conditions, inadequate irrigation systems, and lack of access to finance (Sandhu, 2021; Putsenteilo et al., 2020; Sidhu and Gill, 2006).

Evolution of Indian agriculture industry

Table 20.1 summarises the sector's development via an overview of the sector. **Table 20.1:** Evolution of farming policies and practices

Period	Important developments
Chola period (875–1279)	Collective holding of land slowly gave way to individual plots with their own irrigation system, also distribution of water by tank and channel networks to the drier areas. The pre-British period consisted of isolated and self-sustaining villages with underdeveloped markets and means of transport and communication.
British period (1757–1858 and 1858– 1947)	Anglo-Saxon period led to the disintegration of the village community partly by commercialisation of agriculture and partly by introduction of the new land revenue system, which led to untold exploitation of Indian peasantry plagued by frequent famines. However, during this period the growth of railways, spread of irrigation, the expansion of education, and creation of revenue settlements cannot be ignored. Nevertheless, the important contribution of this period is the establishment of local governments.
The British land system during 1793–1850	In 1793 Lord Cornwallis introduced the British land system in India and land revenue was a principal source of finance for East India Company administration. The new land system empowered revenue

	collectors and promoted them to private landlords (Zamindars). Zamindari (Bengal) and ryotwari (Bombay and Madras extended to north-eastern and western India) systems created a class divide and exploitation of poor farmers by charging exorbitant rent from them, which resulted in depressing agriculture and Indian peasantry.
Indus Valley civilisation (3300-1300 BCE)	An era of mixed farming innovation in irrigation. During this time, sophisticated irrigation, water storage systems including artificial reservoirs (3000 BC), and an early canal irrigation system (2600BC) were developed.
Vedic period (1500 BC to 500BC)	The importance of seeds was emphasised, with a specialised sequence of cropping practice and preparation of cow dung manure.
Mauryan period (322–185 BC)	Soils were categorised and meteorological observations were made for the agricultural use, construction and maintenance of dams and provision of horse-drawn chariots replacing traditional bullock carts.
Ancient South Indian agriculture (the century BC to the 3rd century CE)	Cultivated wide range of crops, introduced systematic ploughing, manuring, weeding and irrigation, and crop protection was practised for sustained agriculture.

Commercialisation of agriculture (1850–1947)	Between 1850 and 1947, government policy directed farmers to produce for sale rather than for personal consumption. Financial incentives were provided to cultivate cash crops. The policy had adverse outcomes that led to the fall in food production, leading to famine. The situation worsened with the ensuing Industrial Revolution, which improved rail and road links that were instrumental. Large exported quantities of wheat from Punjab, jute from Bengal and cotton from Bombay to England negatively impacted Indian agriculture and industrial development.
Era of stagnation in agriculture (1950–1960s)	A period marked by insignificant growth in agricultural production (low growth in crop and food grain production).
The Green Revolution (1960–1980)	A period of good transition from stagnancy to high agriculture production, characterised by shifting cultivation, conversion of forestland to agricultural land, mono-cropping and overgrazing; adaptation of high yielding varieties; the application of pesticides has shot up substantially over time; increased irrigation for rice-based

	cropping system further enhances the existing problem of water logging in coastal areas.
Surplus production and exports (1980–2000s)	India's transition from food security to surplus food production. The highlights of this period include expanding cereal production, economic reforms introduced that provided greater encouragement to export, and surplus of production of agricultural commodities over domestic demand. Augmented by an increase in population and strong income growth, India emerged as a net exporter of agricultural products.
Economic reforms, technological advancements and disruptive transformation: 2000 onwards	See the Economic Reforms (2000) report that provides a chronological account of the changes introduced by the successive governments from 2000 to 2021. 2000 and beyond saw a great push to agricultural production with the introduction of supporting reforms, new policies and adoption of technology by the successive governments from 2000 to 2021. Some key highlights from this period include better technology adoption, rise in institutional credit for agriculture, Schemes like National Horticulture Mission (NHM) and Bringing Green Revolution in Eastern India (BREI) that helped achieve record production, commodity exchanges that helped in fair pricing of commodities, small farmers agribusiness consortium (SFAC), horticulture mission for north east and Himalayan states (2001-2002), agricultural technology management agency (2005), national e-governance plan in agriculture (2006), national food security mission (2007), Rastriya Krishi Vikas yojana (2007), national crop insurance programme (2013-2014), Pradhan Mantri Krishi sinchai yojana (2015), paramparagat krishi vikas yojana (2015), pradan mantri fasal bima yojana (2016), eNam (2016), regional rural credit refinance fund (2016), agricultural produce market committee adopted cashless payment policy (2017), contract farming law (2017), agricultural export policy (2018), Pradhan mantri kisan maan dhan yojana/ samman nidhi yojana, (2019), digital initiatives by the Indian government (E-sagu, community radio, digital green, national agriculture market/ e-nam, the kisan call centre/ KCC (2020/21).

Figure 20.2: Source: Information compiled by author reviewing works of Mulage (2017); Datt et al. (2008); Sandhu (2007); Carter (1946); and Government of India (2022).

However, there is a growing acknowledgement among policymakers about the importance of the sector and the need to reform and adapt digital technologies. The Green Revolution in India was the catalyst for the upsurge in credit demand among farmers. It has transformed the country's agriculture sector from one of food deficiency to self-sufficiency. Sidhu (2001) attributed farmers' excessive borrowing to fund modern technology to enhancing productivity. Modern scientific techniques require adequate access to finance. However, farmers continue to experience financial constraints to meet the needs of the sector to purchase fertilisers, pesticides and quality seeds.

The emerging literature suggests that to sustain agricultural production, modern agricultural techniques and technologies are required to exploit the full potential. It is not possible without long-term subsidies; otherwise, it burdens farmers with unsustainable long-term indebtedness (Sandhu and Hussain, 2021; Sandhu, 2021, 2007; Pederson, 2004; Tokar, 2004). However, the government policy is to abandon protection and expose farmers to financial institutional demands, something that is neither practical nor politically viable as it will expose the sector to cyclical and market uncertainties, hence is not in the national interest. The sector is under sustained pressure as there is evidence of high suicide rates among farmers due to financial pressures and uncertainty relating to the agricultural yield.

The role of smart technologies in the agricultural sector

Indian agriculture techniques are considered outdated and need to be improved (Mulage, 2017; Carter, 1946) to cater for the modern world. Studies have examined structural issues in Indian agriculture, access to finance and information asymmetry (Gulati and Juneja, 2022; Sandhu and Hussain, 2021; Sandhu, 2020; Sandhu et al., 2017; Gulati et al., 2012). Nonetheless, the agricultural sector more specifically has suffered from market imperfections, underperformance and exploitation by intermediaries, threatening food security and migration towards urban cities. This neglect of farming communities has implications for government and the gross national product of India (Sandhu et al., 2017; Sandhu, Hussain and Matlay, 2012; Sandhu, 2007). The observed decline of the agricultural sector is evidence of market failure that has implications for food security and the well-being of the nation.

To innovate and address market supply chain imperfections, blockchain technology has the potential to provide solutions. Blockchain has gained momentum, proven its functionality and has been adopted by business organisations to reduce cost and streamline distribution (Sandhu and Hussain, 2021; Sharma et al., 2020; Kamilaris et

al., 2019). Blockchain has the potential to minimise cost and meet the culinary needs of the nation. The decentralised nature of blockchain ensures optimal utilisation of distribution systems and speedy access to consumers, resulting in a transparent market for high-end goods.

The use of artificial intelligence and digital smart farming systems such as smart sensors, drones, and unmanned mid-air vehicles can collect data to keep track of plant nutrition, soil composition, heating rate, dampness and other factors. The smart ecosystem will empower farmers so that they optimise the use of technology to enhance productivity. There is no doubt that the necessity of greater financing can broaden farmers' investment opportunities through the acquisition of effective technology, machinery, seeds and enhance the risk management tools.

Figure 20.3: Grape vineyards Viticulture Farming Sula winery Nasik Maharashtra India.

Recent developments

Three recent farm laws that were controversially repealed on 19 November 2021 are of significance. On 20 September 2020, the government of India promulgated three laws relating to agricultural marketing that represented a fundamental reorientation of the existing regulatory framework. The government had reforms similar to 1991, opening the Indian economy and linking it to globalised markets:

> The Farmers' Produce Trade and Commerce (Promotion and Facilitation) Act
>
> The Farmers (Empowerment and Protection) Agreement of Price Assurance and Farm Services Act
>
> The Essential Commodities (Amendment) Act

The Indian government proposed that the new laws will strengthen the farming sector's infrastructure through greater private investments and consequently private players would make agriculture profitable for farmers. However, these laws were passed without consulting the state governments or farmers and were later withdrawn due to resistance from farmers. The breakdown of trust and information asymmetry between policymakers and farmers led to agitation, unrest and the mass mobilisation of farming communities, invoking anxiety among those who supported agricultural reforms.

Marketing reforms, especially those that involve deregulation, need to be considered in the context of state intervention, especially regarding existing state support. This is especially important because at a time when most of the developed world is re- evaluating the sustainability of their agri-food supply chains, especially after Russia's invasion of Ukraine, India, as a nation of smallholders, has to take a strategic view to support a progressive high-tech agriculture sector. This requires strengthening farming organisations, enhancing supply chain mechanisms and supporting the modernisation of small and medium-scale local enterprises. Agricultural sector policies and practice in India have evolved since the Green Revolution. However, the policies require a critical overhaul to consider technological societal changes to ensure it remains a force for bettering the lives of farmers, promoting food and national security. The change will restore the confidence of farmers after the attempted abolishment of the minimum support price in 2020/21 that affected morale and destabilised the farming sector.

Conclusion

National security is linked with food security for all nations. Therefore, it is imperative to support agricultural productivity to improve quality of life for farmers. The Indian agriculture sector is predominately led by small landholders; therefore, strengthening and empowering small and marginal farmers is a necessity rather than serving predatory stakeholders. The legislative reforms need to reflect the on-the- ground realities of the farming community and empower them to adapt cost-saving technologies. Legislation needs to empower farmers to optimise commercial and social objectives. The regulatory framework needs to safeguard farmers from private players, informal and exploitative lenders, and intermediaries. Access to finance can encourage farmers to employ technologies to become competitive, safeguarding the nation's food and national security.

References

Baek, S. (2018). 'Theoretical Reshaping for the Augmented Inequality Dynamics', The Political Economy of Neo-modernisation, 1, 1, pp. 119–156.

Bharti, N. (2018). 'Evolution of Agriculture Finance in India: a Historical Perspective', Agricultural Finance Review, 78, 3, pp. 376–392.

Carter, G. (1946). Origins of American Indian agriculture. American Anthropologist, 48(1), pp.1-21. Available from https://www.deepdyve.com/lp/wiley/origins-of- american-indian-agriculture-1zOcDg0u2o (accessed 16 February 2021).

Datt, G. Mahajan, A. and Datt, S. (2008). Indian Economy, New Delhi: S. Chand & Company Pvt. Ltd., pp. 14–19.

De la Escosura, L. (2022). 'The Industrial Revolution, an Unintended Consequence of Self-defence?'. Journal of Global History, 17, 1, pp. 159–164.

Eswaran, M. and Kotwal, A. (2002). The Role of Agriculture in Development. Department of Economics, UBC. [Online]. Available from www.econ.ubc.ca/eswaran/441role.pdf (accessed 25 May 2020).

Government of India (2022). Agriculture [Online]. Available from: https://www. india.gov.in/topics/agriculture (accessed 12 March 2022)

Gulati, A. and Juneja, R. (2022). 'Transforming Indian Agriculture'. In Chand, R. Joshi, P. and Khadka, S. (Eds), Indian Agriculture Towards 2030 (pp. 9–37). Springer, Singapore.

Gulati, A. Kumar, A. Shreedhar, G. and Nandakumar, T. (2012). 'Agriculture and Malnutrition in India', Food and Nutrition Bulletin, 33, 1, pp. 74–86.

Hayami, Y. and Ruttan, V. (1985). Agricultural Development: An International Perspective. Baltimore and London: The John Hopkins University Press.

Hussain, J. and Matlay, H. (2007). 'Financing Preference of Ethnic Minority SMEs', Journal of Small Business and Enterprise Development, 14, 4, pp. 487–500.

Jena, S. and Bardhan, K. (2019). 'Resurrection of Indian Agriculture through Revolutionary Innovations of Science and Technology', Current Journal of Applied Science and Technology, 35, 6, pp. 1–10.

Kanwal, S. (2022). Agriculture in India – Statistics & Facts [Online Available from: https:// www.statista.com/topics/4868/agricultural-sector-in-india/#dossierKeyfigures (accessed 23 March 2022).

Kamilaris, A., Fonts, A. and Prenafeta-Boldu, P. (2019). 'The Rise of Blockchain Technology in Agriculture and Food Supply Chains', Trends in Food Science & Technology, 91, 1, pp. 640-652.

Matsuyama, K. (1990). 'Perfect Equilibria in a Trade Liberalisation Game', American Economic Review, 80, 1, pp. 480–492.

Misra, R. Chavan, P. and Verma, R. (2016). 'Agricultural Credit in India in the 2000s: Growth, Distribution and Linkages with Productivity', The Journal of Applied Economic Research, 10, 2, pp. 169–197.

Mulage, B. (2017). 'History of Agriculture System in India: A Legal Perspective', International Journal of Humanities Social Sciences and Education, 4, 7, pp. 25–30.

Nurkse, R. (1953). Problems of Capital Formation in Underdeveloped Countries. Oxford University Press: New York.

Pederson, P. (2004). 'India: Hunger rises as Agricultural Capital Boosts Yields, Profits', The Militant, 68, 27 [Online]. Available from: https://www.themilitant. com/2004/6827/682750.html (accessed 7 May 2021).

Putsenteilo, P. Klapkiv, Y. Karpenko, V. and Gvozdecka, I. (2020). 'The role of institutions in the development of agriculture', Bulgarian Journal of Agricultural Science, 26, 1, pp. 23–33.

Ranis, G. and Fei, J. (1961). 'A Theory of Economic Development', American Economic Review, 51, 1, pp. 533–565.

Rostow, W. (1990). The Stages of Economic Growth: A Non-Communist Manifesto. Cambridge University Press: Cambridge.

Sandhu, N. (2007). An Empirical Investigation of Financial Institutions' Lending Policies towards Agribusiness during the Post-Green Revolution in Punjab, India. Unpublished PhD thesis, BCU.

Sandhu, N. (2021). 'Dynamics of Banks' Lending Practices to Farmers in India', Journal of Small Business and Enterprise Development, 28, 1, pp. 102–120.

Sandhu, N. and Hussain, J. (2021). 'Entrepreneurship the Mediating Role of Finance and Entrepreneurial Education for Small Farmers in Developing Countries: Evidence from India', International Journal of Entrepreneurial Behavior & Research, 27, 6, pp. 1403–1422.

Sandhu, N., Hussain, J. and Matlay, H. (2015). 'Informal Lenders and Small/Marginal farmers in India: An Unregulated Sociological Symbiotic Relationship?', In Hussain, J. and Scott, J. (Eds) International Research Handbook on Entrepreneurial Finance (pp. 206-228). Cheltenham: Edward Elgar.

Sandhu, N., Hussain, J. and Matlay, H. (2012). 'Barriers to Finance Experienced by Female Owner/Managers in India', Journal of Small Business and Enterprise Development, 19, 4, pp. 640–655.

Sandhu, N., Scott, J., Hussain, J., Gibb, J., Sinha, P. and Akoorie, M. (2017). Women Entrepreneurs, Informal Finance and Microenterprise Growth in Rural India: An Exploratory Study. Measuring an Entrepreneurial Ecosystem. Edward Elgar: Cheltenham.

Sharma, A., Jhamb, D. and Mittal, A. (2020). 'Food Supply Chain Traceability by using Blockchain Technology', Journal of Computational and Theoretical Nanoscience, 17, 6, pp. 2630–2636.

Sidhu, J. (2001). 'Green Revolution' in India has Farmers under Severe Debt. [Online]. Available from www.mindfully.org/Farm/India-Green-Revolution.htm (Accessed 27 October 2021).

Sidhu, R. and Gill, S. (2006). 'Agricultural Credit and Indebtedness in India: Some issues', Indian Journal of Agricultural Economics, 61, 1, pp. 11–35.

Suh, J. (2000). Agricultural Development and Structural Change in the Context of General Economic Growth. Unpublished PhD Thesis, University of Maryland

Tokar, B. (2004). 'The World Bank and the Next Green Revolution'. [Online]. Green Tide, 17, 4. Available from: http://www.zmag.org/ZMagSite/Apr2004/tokarpr0401. html (accessed 27 October

About the contributors

Dr Navjot Sandhu is Associate Professor within the Birmingham City Business School. She has published extensive research within the domain of financing marginal farmers. Dr Sandhu's PhD thesis was in the area of farming that examined financing and growth of marginal farmers in Punjab, India. In addition, she has extensive lived experiences of farmers in India and has networks with minority farmers in Canada, the USA and the UK. Dr Sandhu has experience of supervising and examining PhDs nationally and internationally. She has collaborated in Fintech and disruptive technologies from Said Business School, University of Oxford.

Professor Javed Hussain is an academic with over 31 years' experience. He has conducted research within the broader domain of ethnic entrepreneurship within the UK and agriculture industry within India, Africa, Pakistan and Malaysia. Professor Javed Hussain has participated in 3 Research Excellence Frameworks (REFs) and a Research Assessment Exercise (RAE) in 1996. He has successfully supervised to completion over 27 PhDs.

Dr Shishank Shishank is Senior Lecturer in Operations Management and is currently supervising four PhD students. He has a background in operations management, supply chain and disruptive technologies and applications for competitive performance. He is a certified Blockchain Strategist from Said Business School, University of Oxford.

Chapter 21

The National Innovation System of India: historical perspective and key characteristics

Danilo Spinola and Rituparna Kaushik

Summary

This chapter presents a brief review of the evolution of the Indian National Innovation System (NIS), from its historical formation to its current challenges from a systemic perspective. Since its independence in 1947, India went through a fast economic development, moving from a rural agricultural-based economy to an industrialised urban economy with a robust high-tech service sector. Indian NIS characteristics qualitatively changed from a fully public-oriented, closed, and inward-oriented system to a mixed open system in which the public sector plays a central role alongside large firms/conglomerates in crucial sectors, resulting in a relatively developed but still heterogeneous and imbalanced innovation structure.

Introduction

Economic growth relies on sustaining technological progress, which increasingly depends on the produced scientific knowledge leading to innovation. Furthermore, innovation ideally needs to be disseminated through recognised channels to the general public. This dissemination channel is vital for the industry to grow and support growth. In this aspect, the existence of a recognised NIS becomes of utmost importance. The primary goal of a NIS is to translate basic research into innovation, benefiting the interests of the wider public (Dodgson et al., 2011). Lundvall (1992, p.2) describes the NIS as 'The elements and relationships which interact in the production, diffusion and use of new, and economically useful, knowledge ... and are either located within or rooted inside the borders of a nation state' (p.2).

The NIS approach highlights the multiple relationships between different actors, such as the flows of technology and information among people, enterprises and institutions, which are essential to the innovative process (Lundvall, 2007). A well- defined NIS consists of sectors such as government entities, universities and research institutes, industry and their environment. Discussions regarding innovation in many emerging nations are becoming more dominant, and the innovation 'buzzword' is of central interest today, however, with many different uses.

Figure 21.1: INS Sindhudhwaj being presented with the Best Innovation Trophy by Prime Minister Narendra Modi.

Innovation in India became a topic of central national importance only in the 21st century[8] (Prabhu and Jain, 2015). Although innovation refers to the 'welfare of the general public', the Indian NIS has emerged with multiple glitches on its way. The Indian innovation system today is highly complex and imperfect, with multiple tangles of user segments and income disparities leading to highly differentiated markets (Bound and Thornton, 2012). This created tussle and struggles among the policymakers and the business leaders.

8. India has had science and technology policy documents since the 1950s, but those were just *pro-forma*. There was no stress on R&D; innovation only became a buzz recently.

This chapter describes the evolution of the Indian NIS as a historical process in which the different periods and stages continuously shape the trajectory of the system. Most of the articles in the literature focus on the radical break between an inward- looking strategy of import substitution and post-1990 with a more market and outward-oriented approach. In this chapter, the focus is on the break. Our objective is to describe how the distinct periods shaped the current Indian NIS: a strong but highly heterogeneous system – in terms of sectors, institutions and market structure.

Historical development of the Indian innovation system

1. Inward-oriented period (1947–1985)

India became an independent nation in 1947 with severe socio-economic constraints, in a period between the end of World War 2 and the first stages of the Cold War. This geopolitical condition split the world into two main blocks, represented by a capitalist US-centric West and a Communist USSR-centric East. Post-independence India's first Prime Minister, Jawaharlal Nehru, politically adopted a non-alignment policy. In terms of economic policies, nevertheless, India was influenced by USSR's development strategies.[9] The Indian economic policies were centred around the role of a developmentalist state in an import substitution strategy, in which the central administration was involved in virtually any economic decision (Chacko, 2015). From 1947 to 1964, India had fast growth in the state's organisational density in terms of states roles and responsibility (Mukherji, 2009).

The policy framework until the mid-1980s followed five-year economic plans as the main policy-making instrument, with the government performing a central role in the coordination of the economic system. The initial shape of the Indian NIS can be represented as a radial network with the national government in its centre. It was an inward-looking strategy in which the private sector played only a very small role. This economic system aimed to address the country's military needs: the Indian NIS profile was very much oriented to the nuclear, space and defence industries, which guided the development of strategies, capabilities, and R&D expenditure (Gonzalo et al., 2022).

9. The initial aim was to industrialise at a faster pace ignoring the dominant agrarian nature of the economy, which failed miserably. Then the focus shifted to agriculture.

This framework was responsible for the industrialisation of India, creating a pool of educated workers for industrial and technology activities (Lall, 1992; Krishna, 2022). However, it also resulted in a system with an outdated productive structure, with imbalances that would remain in the future constitution of the Indian NIS (Ghosh and Kumar, 1991).

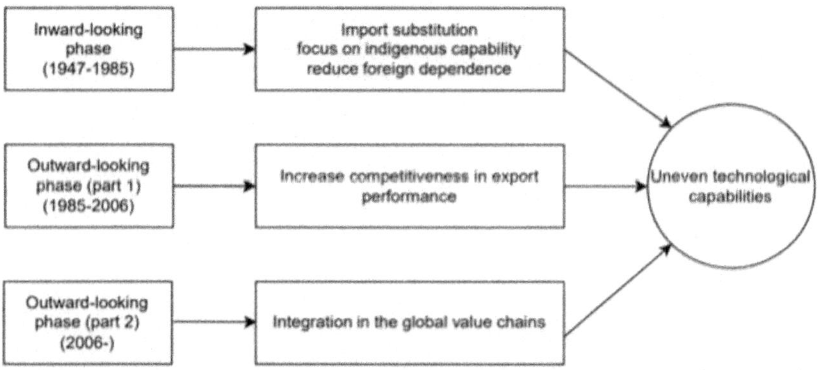

Figure 21.2: Phases of Indian NIS development; source: own elaboration, based on Baskaran and Muchie (2007).

In institutional terms, during the inward-oriented phase (1947–1985), a number of Science and Technology (S&T) agencies were created.[10] (Krishna, 2013), as well as universities, institutes of technology and finance institutions.[11] (Nayyar, 2015), shaping the institutional framework and forming the basis for the development of a strong scientific and technology infrastructure (Nassif, 2007; Gonzalo, 2018). These institutions were instrumental in creating a platform for knowledge creation (Rajan, 2012; Krishna, 2022).

10. R&D labs, such as the Council of Scientific and Industrial Research, government departments, such as the Department of Science and Technology (DST) and Indian Council of Medical Research, and autonomous bodies, such as the National Institute of Design.

11. Such as Industrial Finance Corporation of India.

An important mechanism for technology transfer was the use of joint ventures between state-owned groups (origin of the large conglomerates) and foreign companies, especially Japanese (as per the pioneering case of Suzuki) (Kaushik and Paul, 2021). The joint ventures demanded significant investments in education, in particular S&T, which created a human capital basis for future technological developments.

Nevertheless, even with such policies, the lack of endogenous incentives led the Indian NIS to be characterised by low volumes, obsolete technology and fragmented supply (Rao, 2008).

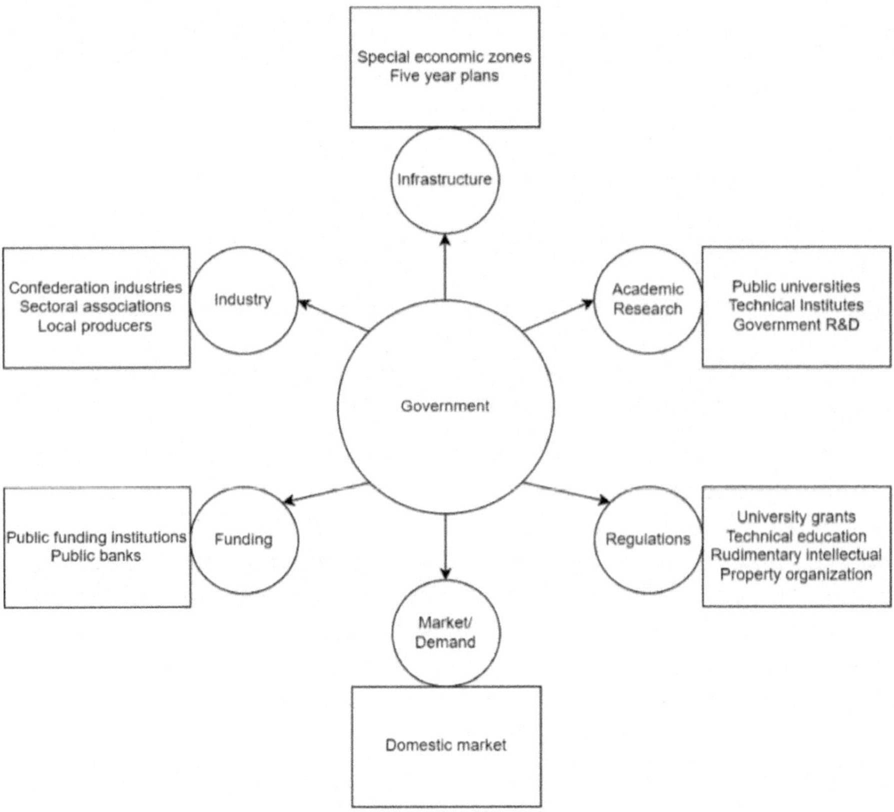

Figure 21.3: India's NIS in the inward-looking phase; source: own elaboration inspired by Sharma et al. (2012) and Edquist and Hommen (2009).

2. Outward-oriented approach before India joined the TRIPS[12] Agreement (1985–2006)

To avert a balance of payment crisis, India has gone through a process of pro- market reforms since the end of the 1980s. This process of liberalisation changed the international position of India towards an outward-guided approach. The reforms aimed at giving the private sector a stronger role in the economy and started reshaping the Indian NIS, tackling the issues and imbalances created during the import substitution era. The Indian economy then started integrating itself into the global value chains.

The post-liberalisation reforms[13] resulted in the steady emergence of a private sector able to develop itself in the form of conglomerates, which prioritised technological and process upgrading. Nevertheless, this rapid development was uneven and concentrated on the development of some strategic sectors. With the increasing importance of the private sector in the post-liberalisation period, private research institutes, as well as private industry, were also adjusted to the NIS network. India's DST describes this system as a layered one, where public and private entities get featured simultaneously (Figure 21.3).

The Indian National Innovation System (NIS) today (since 2006)

India has been recently touted to be a hub of innovation among emerging economies. Despite the positive atmosphere, R&D expenditure in both the private and public sectors has been increasing at a sluggish rate (Mehta, 2018). The macro innovation data shows modest changes in the proportion of GDP spent on R&D, in who spends on R&D, and in which sector it is done. The DST's R&D statistics for 2019–20 suggest that the share of India's R&D expenditure has never exceeded 1% of GDP, in contrast to countries like Taiwan, China and Brazil, which have been spending more than 1% of their GDP on R&D for over half a decade.

12. The Agreement on Trade-Related Aspects of Intellectual Property Rights (TRIPS) is an international legal agreement among the members of the World Trade Organization (WTO). The agreement establishes the common international standards for intellectual property.

13. The New Industrial Policy of 1991 focused on integrating India into the world by removing licensing restrictions and incentivising foreign investment, technology transfer and industrial development, while limiting the role of the public sector (Ghosh and Kumar, 2021).

Figure 21.4 shows that though the R&D expenditure has been increasing since 1995, its share in GDP has been declining since 2010, finally stagnating at 0.7% since 2012.

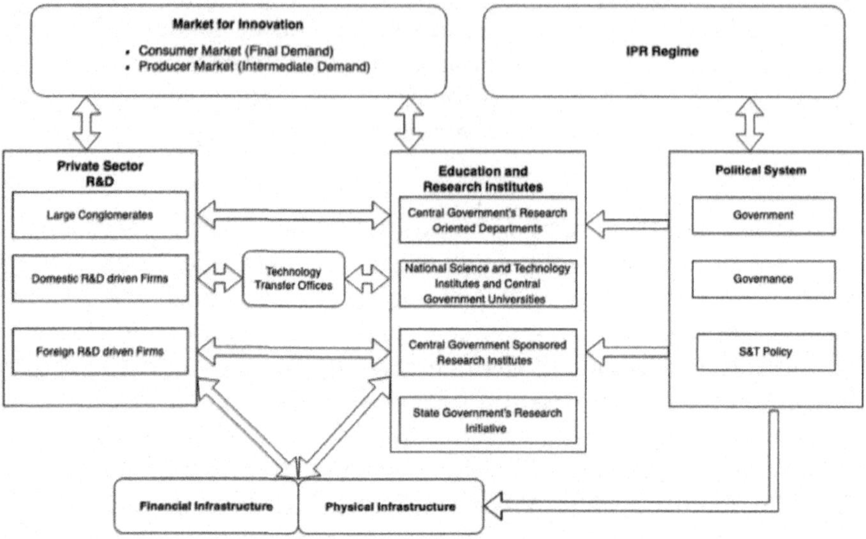

Figure 21.4: Indian NIS in the outward-looking phase; source: own elaboration.

Public vs private innovation

In terms of who performs R&D, i.e., the public or the private sector, there have been few changes since liberalisation. The public sector continues to dominate India's R&D initiative. That dominance, with less support for business sector R&D in India, has historically given the impression that research is an activity that only the government should engage in (Fan, 2011). While the share of R&D in the private sector has increased since 1991, it has been experiencing a decline since reaching a high of 37.7% in 2015 (Figure 21.5).

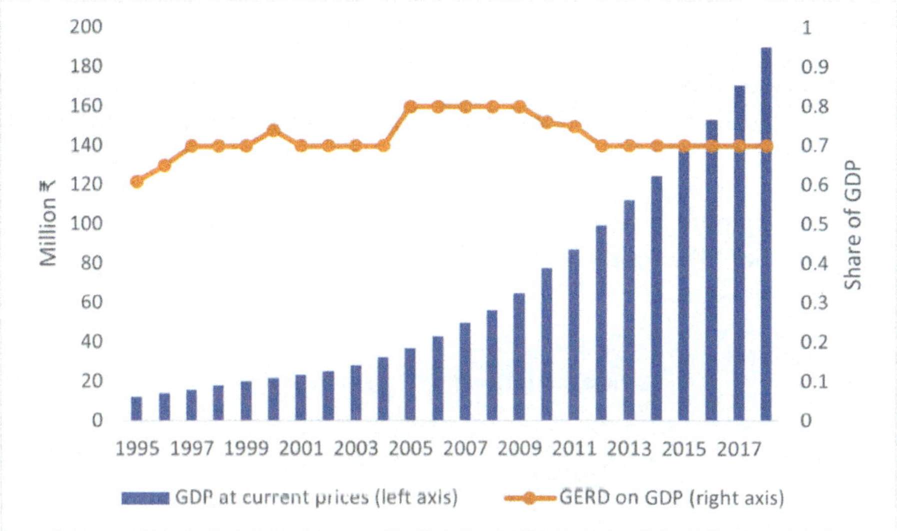

Figure 21.5: National R&D expenditure and its percentage with GDP from 1990/91 to 2018/19; source: DST's R&D statistics, 2019–20. GERD = Gross Expenditure on R&D.

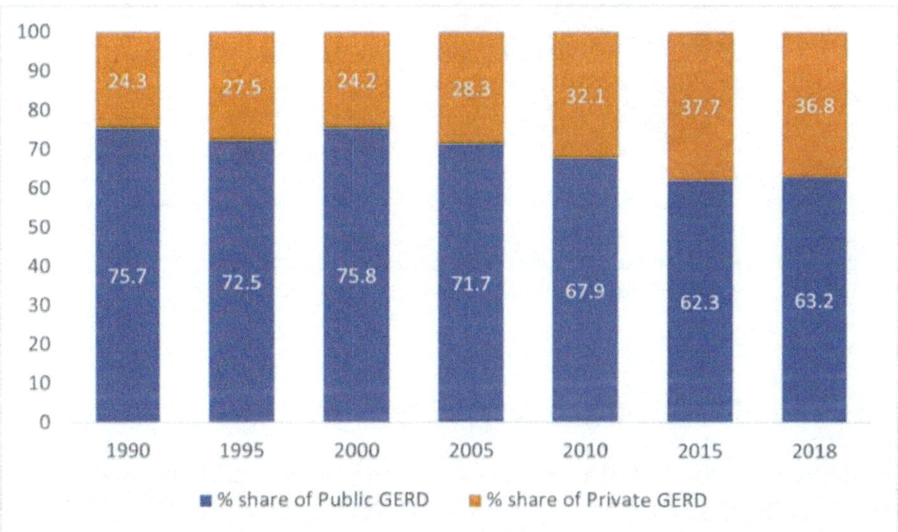

Figure 21.6: Share of public and private sector spend in gross national R&D expenditure from 1990 to 2018; source: DST's R&D statistics, 2019–20.

Research and Development (R&D) per industry

According to the 2019–20 R&D report by the Ministry of Science and Technology, health (18.59%), defence (17.15%) and development of agriculture, forestry and fishing (12.6%) are the sectors with highest proportion of expenditure on R&D (see Figure 21.7). India has a significant global presence in these industries, hosting many leading international firms dedicating significant investment on R&D.

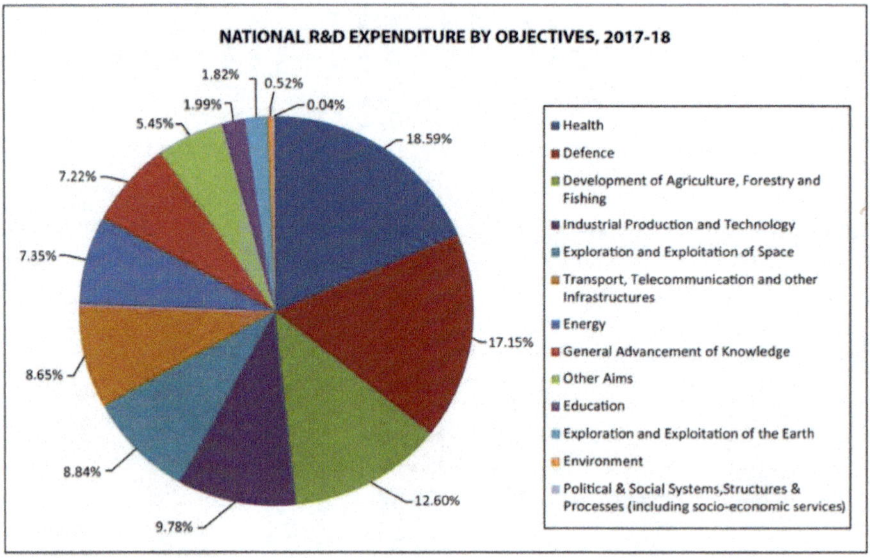

Figure 21.7: R&D expenditure per sector (as a share of total R&D) 2017-18; source: Government of India DST's R&D statistics, 2019–20.

Science and Technology (S&T) policy

India's relationship with S&T policy dates back to 1958, consisting of a short document with loopholes and no clear guidelines to achieve the R&D targets (Rao, 2008). After the failure of that policy, India turned its back on the S&T policy for three decades. In 1983, India had its first science policy with structured objectives, focusing on priority areas and acquisitions of new technology to attain technological self-reliance and competence. Over the years, the next two S&T policies, i.e., 2003 and 2013, led to greater investment and R&D activities. In recent years, a sense of acknowledgement about the importance of the private sector emerged, which was reflected in the S&T policies of 2013 and 2020. These current S&T policies also reflected the need to improve the "Intellectual Property Rights" (IRP) regime of India, drawing attention to modifying the IPR norms for the social goods to promote balanced growth. Despite the significant improvement, scientists in India argued that "Science Technology and Innovation" (STI) policies lacked clear-cut direction and guidance (Naik, 2021). Even though the case for economic development through S&T is discussed widely, it lacks the necessary guiding direction on how India can exploit the benefits.

Conclusion

From a historical analysis, the Indian NIS traditionally followed a specific, relevant, but still narrow view on innovation, prioritising public departments and institutes. Many contend that the private sector was side-lined due to the closed nature of the economy and fear of the private sector. Since liberalisation, the private sector has emerged, but its growth in R&D and innovation, despite increasing, remains very slow and uneven. The result is a relatively developed, strong, but still heterogeneous and unequal structure of NIS.

Heterogeneity marks today's Indian NIS. On the one hand, the system is strong and dynamic in some selected sectors, being on the international technological frontier, with important innovation hubs and regional clusters. On the other hand, there is a strong sectoral unevenness, with many challenges, such as the concentration of R&D on large firms, the gap in the innovative abilities of small and medium enterprise (SMEs), and the low value added on manufactured products (focused on assembling and sales). Finally, we highlight the relevant role of innovation policy with a systemic perspective, which is central to facing those many challenges, addressing the imbalances, and fostering and focusing on the gains generated by a solid and complete innovation system (Joseph et al., 2021).

References

Baskaran, A. and Muchie, M., 2007. The Making of the Indian national innovation systems: lessons on the specific characteristics of the domestic and the external co- evolution of technologies, institutions and incentives. Paper presented at the 4th ASIALICS International Conference, Kuala Lumpur, Malaysia (July). Available at: https://eprints.mdx.ac.uk/4201/1/Baskaran_-Mammo__DIIPER_Working_Paper_ 2007-02.pdf

Bound, K. and Thornton, I.W., 2012. Our frugal future: Lessons from India's innovation system. London, NESTA

Chacko, P., 2015. The new geo-economics of a 'rising' India: state transformation and the recasting of foreign policy. Journal of Contemporary Asia, 45(2), pp. 326–344

Department of Science and Technology (DST), India R&D Statistics 2019–20. December 2020

Dodgson, M., Hughes, A., Foster, J. and Metcalfe, S., 2011. Systems thinking, market failure and the development of innovation policy: The case of Australia. Research Policy, 40(9), pp. 1145–1156

Edquist, C. and Hommen, L. eds., 2009. Small country innovation systems: globalization, change and policy in Asia and Europe. Edward Elgar Publishing. Cheltenham

Fan, P., 2011. Innovation capacity and economic development: China and India. Economic Change and Restructuring, 44(1), 49–73

Ghosh, R.N. and Kumar, U., 2021. A Critical Study on The New Industrial Policy of India 1991. International Journal of Humanities, Engineering, Science and Management, 2(01), pp. 76–93

Gonzalo, M. 2018. A Long-term Narrative on India from Latin America: Peripherization, National System of Innovation and Autonomous Expenditures. PhD Thesis. Instituto de Economia/Universidade Federal do Rio de Janeiro, Rio de Janeiro, Brazil. Available at: https://www.ie.ufrj.br/images/IE/PPGE/teses/2018/ MANUEL%20GONZALO.pdf

Gonzalo, M., Guimaraes Alves, N., Federico, J., Szapiro, M. and Kantis, H., 2022. Venture capital industry emergence and development in India and Brazil: the role of the state and challenges for the Global South countries. Innovation and Development, pp. 1–22

Joseph, K.J., Kakarlapudi, K.K. and Arun, T., 2021. Reconciling higher productivity with innovation paradox: mode of learning and innovation in India's manufacturing sector. Innovation and Development, 11(2–3), pp. 323–342

Kaushik, R. and Paul, S.B., 2021. Strategic Interactions, Bargaining Power and Stability of Joint Venture in an Emerging Nation. Journal of Industry, Competition and Trade, 21(4), pp. 543–564

Krishna, V. 2013. 'India'. In Scerri, M. and Lastres, H. (eds.) The role of the state, BRICS – National systems of innovation. New Delhi: Routledge, pp. 138–187

Krishna, V.V., 2022. India@ 75: Science, Technology and Innovation Policies for

Development. Science, Technology and Society. 27(1), pp. 113–146

Lall, S., 1992. Technological capabilities and industrialization. World Development, 20(2), pp. 165–186.

Lundvall, B.-Å., 1992. National Innovation Systems: Towards a Theory of Innovation and Interactive Learning, Pinter, London

Lundvall, B. Å., 2007. National innovation systems–analytical concept and development tool. Industry and Innovation, 14(1), pp. 95–119

Nassif, A., 2007. National innovation system and macroeconomic policies: Brazil and India in comparative perspective. UNCTAD Discussion Papers 184, United Nations Conference on Trade and Development

Nayyar, D., 2015. Birth, life and death of development finance institutions in India. Economic and Political Weekly, 50(33), pp. 51–60

Mehta, S., 2018. National innovation system of India: An empirical analysis. Millennial Asia, 9(2), pp. 203–224

Mukherji, R., 2009. The state, economic growth, and development in India. India Review, 8(1), pp. 81–106

Naik, S., 2021. STIP2020: A wish-list, not a policy. 20 February 2021. Available at https://indiatogether.org/science-policy-society. Accessed on 10th June, 2022.

Prabhu, J. and Jain, S., 2015. Innovation and entrepreneurship in India: Understanding jugaad. Asia Pacific Journal of Management, 32(4), pp. 843–868

Rajan, Y.S., 2012. Shaping the national innovation system: The Indian perspective. The Global Innovation Index, pp. 131–141

Rao, C.N.R., 2008. Science and technology policies: The case of India. Technology in Society, 30(3–4), pp. 242–247

Sharma, P., Nookala, S.B. and Sharma, A., 2012. India's national and regional innovation systems: challenges, opportunities and recommendations for policy makers. Industry and Innovation, 19(6), pp. 517–537

About the contributors

Dr Danilo Spinola has a PhD in Economics of Innovation from the United Nations University (UNU-Merit) where he is an affiliated researcher, part of the research team on Innovation, Structural Change and Economic Complexity. He has experience working as a consultant for international organisations, such as the Economic Commission for Latin America and the Caribbean and for the Interamerican Development Bank. Dr Spinola's research is currently focused on three pillars: innovation processes in complex systems; structural change, economic dynamics and economic resilience; and economic Growth and income/wealth distribution.

Dr Rituparna Kaushik holds a PhD in the area of Innovation Economics from the Indian Institute of Technology, Delhi (IIT Delhi). Currently he is working in FLAME University, Pune as Assistant Professor of Economics. Rituparna's work broadly focuses on firm-level innovation and R&D effort in the context of India. He is working on measuring the efficiency of the nation's innovation system and gender bias in innovation in India.

Chapter 22

The Indian automotive industry, an overview

Alex De Ruyter

Summary

This chapter provides an overview of the evolution of the Indian automotive sector over the past 75 years. It looks at how changing policy regimes (from protectionist to modest liberalisation measures in the 1990s, through to the current Modi government's stance) have influenced the make-up and evolution of the sector. Importantly, the chapter looks at how varying policy regimes at provincial level have shaped the internal evolution of investment and production decisions. Finally, the chapter briefly explores the prognosis for the sector going forward. With India predicted to become the third-largest automotive market by volume in the world by 2026, it considers some of the problematic issues facing an emerging economy such as India, in the transition to low-carbon vehicles as part of a green economy.

Introduction

The automotive industry is one of India's key manufacturing sectors and has experienced significant growth over recent decades. Globally, Indian firms such as Tata Motors (the owners of UK brand Jaguar Land Rover) have increasingly become significant players in the international market. As of 2021, the manufacture of transport equipment accounted for some 10–12% of Gross Value Added within India's manufacturing sector (Chhibber and Gupta, 2021). While the Covid-19 pandemic has posed severe challenges to manufacturing within India, the automotive industry is expected to provide major growth opportunities over the coming years, with 65 million new jobs expected in the sector by 2026 as companies boost production (ibid.).

Until the 1940s, India was an importer of cars; automotive production commenced in India in 1942, with the manufacture of automobiles by Hindustan Motors (or HM, a now defunct firm, see Martin, 2022). Independence in 1947 ushered in a period of high trade barriers, as the Indian government attempted to promote the development of domestic industry behind a high tariff wall. As such, production was severely limited, with a system of industrial licensing put in place, which often favoured companies politically connected to the ruling Congress Party (Black et al., 2020).

Figure 22.1: Hindustan Motors Ambassador Avigo 4281.

However, the consequence of this was a closed market with a limited choice of low- quality and expensive makes and models, with the domestic market dominated by firms such as HM, Premier, Mahindra and Mahindra, and Ashok Leyland (Martin, 2022). As such, Black et al. (2020, p. 13) argue that protectionist measures at this time 'proved to be a mixed bag, with some policies encouraging learning and others stymieing growth'. Moreover, they argued that growth in the automotive sector was driven 'not by upgrading and learning, but by the capture of the licences and protection from international competition' (ibid.).

However, this broad approach to industry and trade policy continued until the 1980s, when changes started to occur with the formation of a joint venture between Suzuki and Maruti Udyog, a state-owned company (Black et al., 2020: 14). Suzuki saw a clear market potential here. Moreover, Suzuki had played a pivotal role in the development of a cluster of suppliers around Delhi by training local component makers to be compliant with its own quality requirements (ibid.). As such, this venture soon came to dominate the Indian passenger vehicle market, capturing some 70% of the market by the 1990s. Then in 1992 a period of economic liberalisation set in. Delicensing of the sector occurred by 1993 and this period saw the entry into India of major global vehicle manufacturers such as Ford, Toyota, GM, Honda and Hyundai (IBEF, 2009). However, it was only in 2001 that the import of motor vehicles and engines was finally permitted by the Indian government (ibid.).

Globally, India is now the fourth-largest producer of passenger vehicles, having overtaken Germany and only being eclipsed by China, the US and Japan, as shown in Table 22.1. In an era of FDI, India offers location advantages in terms of a large (and rapidly growing) domestic market, and also a low-cost but highly skilled workforce which allows global players to use it as a platform to produce small cars for export (Black et al., 2020). Domestically, the Maruti Suzuki joint venture company remains by far the largest producer in India, with approximately 48% of the market share in the Indian passenger vehicle market, while Hyundai is the second-largest car manufacturer in India. Other significant players include Tata Motors, Mahindra and Mahindra, and Honda (Reliance General Insurance, 2022).

However, the automotive industry in India continues to enjoy substantial protections from international trade. Indeed, India (along with Brazil and China) had the second-highest number of barriers to trade of all countries surveyed by the Trade and Investment Barriers Report 2016 (European Commission, 2017: 7). This, it's speculated by commentators, is intended to achieve protection and, indeed, trade-distorting measures have continued to be an active policy tool for the Indian government (ibid.: 15).

These measures include substantial non-tariff barriers on the import of motor vehicles. In particular, they can only be imported direct from the country of manufacture (thus preventing storage or warehousing of cars on route) and can only be imported via the naval docks located in Chennai, Mumbai and Kolkata; furthermore, cars with an engine capacity of 1,000 cc to 2,500 cc are banned from import to India (Team ACKO, 2022). Restrictions on importing used vehicles are yet more stringent: all vehicles have to comply with the Indian Motor Vehicles Act

1988. India's infrastructure is also extremely poor, most notably with regards to transportation (The Economic Times, 2016).

Furthermore, India's automotive lobby, the Society of Indian Automotive Manufacturers (SIAM), remains vociferously opposed to reducing customs duties on imported cars and engines (The Hindu, 2021). As such, cars, buses, trucks, bikes and engines are all on the list of items that SIAM seeks to exclude from free trade agreements (SIAM, 2022). Thus, going forward, the Indian government faces a challenge. Does it continue to protect the domestic automotive sector behind a tariff wall and other non-tariff trade barriers? Or does it embrace trade liberalisation and thereby provide a spur for the domestic sector to become more internationally competitive and thereby encourage increased innovation and quality for its domestic market?

UNIT	2019	2020	2021
China	25,750,650	25,225,242	26,082,220
United States	10,892,884	8,821,026	9,167,214
Japan	9,684,507	8,067,943	7,846,955
India *	4,524,366	3,381,819	4,399,112
South Korea	3,950,614	3,506,774	3,462,404
Germany (cars & Light Commercial Vehicles only)	4,947,316	3,742,570	3,308,692
Mexico	4,013,137	3,177,251	3,145,653
Spain	2,822,632	2,268,185	2,098,133
Thailand	2,013,710	1,427,074	1,685,705
Russia	1,719,146	1,435,551	1,566,317
WORLD TOTAL	**92,183,011**	**77,711,725**	**80,145,988**

Table 22.1: Motor vehicles – top ten countries by production; source: OICA (2022).

*for India - Cars: Audi, BMW, Jaguar Land Rover, Mercedes not reported; commercial vehicles: since 2015.

Conclusion

Finally, going forward, in common with the rest of the world, there is a need to transition the sector towards the use of zero-carbon technologies, which includes electric vehicles (EV) and hydrogen-powered vehicles. At present EVs are in limited supply in India and not readily available on the market (Khurana et al., 2020). However, the Indian government has declared its intention to shift towards net zero after 2030 and has been examining options to increase the uptake of EVs, such as 'battery swapping', although this faces challenges in terms of battery size and power. Certainly, there is a clear, recognised imperative in the shift to EV (with EV sales penetration expected to rise to over 40% of the total by 2040) as being key to reducing the severe air pollution in major Indian cities, although the lack of charging infrastructure also remains a problem (ibid.).

The continued viability of the domestic automotive sector will thus form a key part of the Indian government's aspirations to make the country a high-tech global manufacturing hub. However, challenges remain as to how this will be achieved. Key will be ensuring that smaller firms in the supply chain secure the benefits of innovation and technology transfer (Sudan and Taggar, 2022).

References

Black, A., Roy, P., El-Haddad, A. and Yilmaz, K. (2020). The political economy of automotive industry development policy in middle income countries: A comparative analysis of Egypt, India, South Africa and Turkey. ESID Working Paper No. 143. Accessed on August 23rd 2022 at https://eprints.soas.ac.uk/32972/1/Final%20 ESID%20WP%20No%20143.pdf

Chhibber, B. and Gupta, N. (2021). The Indian automotive industry: From resilience to resurgence? McKinsey report. Accessed on October 25th 2022 at https://www. mckinsey.com/industries/automotive-and-assembly/our-insights/the-indian- automotive-industry-from-resilience-to-resurgence

European Commission (2017). Report from the Commission to the European Parliament and the Council on trade and investment barriers 1 January – 31

December 2016. Accessed on October 24th 2022 at https://trade.ec.europa.eu/doclib/docs/2017/ june/tradoc_155642.pdf

India Brand Equity Foundation (IBEF) (2009). Profile of Indian Automotive Industry. Accessed on October 23rd 2022 at https://www.ibef.org/download/ Automotive_171109.pdf

Khurana, A., Ravi Kumar, V. and Sidhpuria, M. (2020). 'A Study on the Adoption of Electric Vehicles in India: The Mediating Role of Attitude', Vision, 24 (1), pp. 23–34. Accessed on October 24th 2022 at https://journals.sagepub.com/doi/pdf/10.1177/0972262919875548

Martin, L. (2022). The Evolution of the Automobile Industry in India. Symbo Insurance blog. Accessed on October 16th 2022 at https://www.symboinsurance.com/ blogs/car-insurance/evolution-automobile-industry-india/

OICA (International Organization of Motor Vehicle Manufacturers) (2022). Correspondents Survey: World Production of Motor Vehicles by Country and Region. Accessed on October 23rd 2022 at https://www.oica.net/wp-content/uploads/ By-country-region-2021.pdf

Reliance General Insurance (2022). Top Car Manufacturing Companies in India. Accessed on October 23rd 2022 at https://www.reliancegeneral.co.in/Insurance/ Knowledge-Center/Blogs/Top-Car-Manufacturing-Companies-in-India.aspx

SIAM (Society of Indian Automotive Manufacturers) (2022). SIAM Sensitive List. Accessed on October 22nd 2022 at https://www.siam.in/cpage. aspx?mpgid=16&pgid1=26&pgidtrail=73

Sudan, T. and Taggar, R. (2022). 'COVID-19 Induced Supply Chain Disruptions and Automotive Industry: A Case Study of Maruti Suzuki India Limited and Mitigation Strategies'. Global Economics Science, Accessed on October 23rd 2022 at file:///C:/ Users/ID124562/Downloads/nadia,+GES-1095-v3i1-35-52.pdf

Team ACKO (2022). How To Import Foreign Cars To India – Procedure, Guidelines. Accessed on October 24th 2022 at https://www.acko.com/car-guide/how-to-import- foreign-cars-to-india-procedure-guidelines/

The Economic Times (2016). India's poor infrastructure biggest roadblock to 'Make in India': S&P. Accessed on October 24th 2022 at https://economictimes.indiatimes. com/news/economy/infrastructure/indias-poor-infrastructure-biggest-roadblock- to-make-in-india sp/articleshow/53508076.cms

The Hindu (2021). SIAM warns against duty cut on car imports from EU. The Hindu. Accessed on October 23rd 2022 at https://www.thehindu.com/business/Industry/ siam-warns-against-duty-cut-on-car-imports-from-eu/article4595339.ece

About the contributor

Dr Alex De Ruyter is a Professor and Director of the Centre for Brexit Studies at BCU. He has published over 70 research outputs in the time since he completed his PhD in 2002 and been the recipient of funding from various research bodies, including the British Academy. He has published in leading international journals such as Regional Studies, Urban Studies and the European Journal of Industrial Relations, presented at numerous international conferences and is a Fellow of the Regional Studies Association. Alex's main research interests are in labour markets, globalisation, Brexit and economic development. He is regularly invited to comment in the media on these issues.

Chapter 23

Reflecting on India's economic and technological revolution

Vicky Pryce, Steven McCabe and Beverley Nielsen

Introduction

With India being the fifth-largest country in the world, with a population of 1.38 billion, and with a large and growing middle class, it's not surprising it was regarded as an economy with immense potential in 2001 by, then Goldman Sachs' Chief Economist, Jim (now Lord) O'Neill who coined the acronym BRICS, comprising Brazil, Russia, India, China and, later, South Africa. India may be regarded as the star performer as a country with potential for investment and further trade links. Nonetheless, the path to India's current position has not been without challenges and setbacks. As this chapter describes, India's economic and technological development since independence has been achieved through a series of political interventions, many of which, certainly in the first decades after 1947, did not provide the anticipated outcomes.

The Challenge of post-colonial economic management

Previous chapters have presented a range of analyses on the way in which India has developed as a country since gaining independence in August 1947. Given the tumultuous nature of its birth as a new state, particularly in experiencing the human tragedy of the largest recorded migration of people in history which resulted in 15 million displaced and up to two million deaths, it's hardly surprising that India's first decades as an independent nation were characterised by enduring instability. For any nation facing immediate challenges post-colonialism, those vested with control, the government, must attend to the reality of making offices of state operate effectively.

Following the end of British rule, Indian citizens, largely dependent on subsistence wages in agriculture and not having benefited from the industrialisation so crucial in creating Britain's prosperity, not to forget the exploitation which came with Empire, faced a range of problems which stymied Nehru's vision, proclaimed on the eve of independence, of ending poverty, ignorance, disease and inequality. In 1700, though India's share of world income was 22.6%, marginally below that of Europe at 23.3%, by 1952 this had shrunk to a mere 3.8% (Maddison, 2001). Manmohan Singh, Indian economist and former prime minister between 2004 and 2014, spoke for many in contending that the fate of his country had by the turn of 20th century become, in terms of per capita income, one of the poorest in the world.

Recognising the structural difficulties undermining India's economy as well as the majority of citizens suffering abject poverty, only one in six being literate, India's first prime minister, Jawaharlal Nehru, accepted that the vision he'd articulated on 14 August would require the state to engage in considerable intervention. The Indian state, Nehru believed, would be the main provider of not only the conventional paraphernalia of government - transport infrastructure, health, education and military - but also of finance to private businesses. In order to implement what resonated with a socialist approach to achieving economic development that would produce justice and massive reduction in inequality and poverty, central planning would be required. Accordingly, in 1950 the National Planning Commission was established.

In an approach to economic management that would largely continue until the implementation of neoliberal policies in the 1990s, the first-year plan for India's development, launched in 1951, was primarily based on increasing self-sufficiency in food through raising yields from growth of grains through investment in irrigation. Correspondingly, this plan used the principles of the Harrod–Domar model, which was proposed by Roy Harrod in 1939 and independently developed by Evsey Domar in 1946. The underpinning theory of this model is based on the Keynesian idea of exogenous growth through increased savings and investment. Crucially, it assumed that the growth rate is determined by the savings rate divided by the capital/output ratio, so 'If the capital/output ratio is given, you need to increase the savings rate to raise growth rate, which in turn will increase investment rate' (Debroy, 2021). Initially, the plan appeared to work as India's economy grew at an average annual rate of 3.6% during the plan period, which exceeded the 2.1% target.

India's second five-year plan (1956–61) effectively created the basis of the country's long-term growth through a desire to invest in industrialisation to serve domestic consumption as citizens' income increased (thereby reducing imports) and, eventually, earn much-needed revenue from exports. This plan, referred to as 'The Mahalanobis Plan' in honour of Prasanta Chandra Mahalanobis, a scientist and statistician who was chief adviser to the National Planning Commission from 1955, was hugely influential in its objectives and widely acknowledged as an 'invocation of the spirit of swadeshi or self-reliance' (Debroy, 2021).

The 1956 Plan and Industrial Policy Resolution provided a clear direction which the Indian government wished to take with regards to the development of the public sector. Equally important, it introduced what was known as the Licence Raj, a system of licences and regulations that critics argued were harmful to the establishment of private business. When the second national plan was published it attracted critics. One, B.R. Shenoy, a neo-libertarian economist who'd studied under F.A. Hayek, argued that India's dependence on deficit financing to achieve 'heavy industrialisation' as well as slavish adherence to market intervention would lead to internal problems and undermine dynamic entrepreneurialism which critics of centralised planning asserted was critical to improving the country's economic prospects. Shenoy's criticism proved prescient more quickly than even he might have imagined as, in 1957, India experienced a balance of payment (BoP) crisis (Malenbaum, 1957).

The 1957 BoP crisis, the first of many economic crises following decades, saw negative growth which coincided with rapidly rising costs for imports which had increased by over 50%. As a consequence of India's trade deficit increasing from $0.1 billion in 1955 to almost $0.9 billion in 1957, and its gold stock and foreign reserves being halved, the government was forced to confront the reality that centralised planning did not automatically lead to the desired objectives. Though reconsideration of this approach was contemplated, the pervading wisdom was to continue with the philosophy which appeared to have worked so well in the first five- year plan.

India's economy from 1960 to 1990: recurrent emergencies

Though space does not allow a detailed analysis of the period from 1960 to the 1990s, it's useful to be aware that India's geopolitical situation did not assist its economic progress and quest to achieve a more balanced mixture of activities. As explained by Lieutenant General Vijay

Oberoi (2020), border disputes with neighbours China and Pakistan have meant India is required to spend almost 3% of GDP on defence, which was as high as US$76.6 billion in 2021, the third highest in the world. At the same time, the quest to make India a dominant manufacturing economy which would create well-paid jobs needed to constantly be balanced against the immediate priority of ensuring citizens did not starve during the transition.

Nehru's sudden death on 27 May 1964 was a blow to India's quest to achieve change. He was replaced by Lal Bahadur Shastri who'd served in his cabinet with a number of portfolios including for railways and as Home Minister. Shastri was immediately confronted by persistent food shortages which he believed were being exacerbated by centralisation and price controls. Arguably, Shastri's tenure as Indian prime minister is remembered for his advocacy of high-yield variety seeds for grain (particularly wheat) coupled with environmentalism and biodiversity policies now considered mainstream. This approach was termed an 'evergreen revolution'. Indeed, building on the success of this approach, Shastri developed what's become known as the 'white revolution' based on a cooperative arrangement of farmers and dairies. Amul, a huge state-controlled cooperative society based in Anand in Gujarat and one of India's best-known brands, was part of this revolution.

Many considered that Shastri's leadership in achieving victory against Pakistan in the war in 1965 allowed him the political freedom to ensure more involvement by private enterprise and overseas investment that would eventually become the mainstream orthodoxy a quarter of a century later. However, like his predecessor, Shastri was not to live to see his policies flourish as he died on 11 January 1966. This inevitably meant a new leader for India. However, the third person to hold the office of Indian prime minister was significant in that as well as being a woman, she was the daughter of Nehru. Indira Gandhi's surname resulted from marriage to Feroze Gandhi in 1942, who'd actually been born Ghandy but, inspired by Mahatma Gandhi's leadership for independence, changed it.

***Figure 23.1**: Indira Gandhi*

Indira Gandhi became an utterly dominant Indian political figure both domestically and internationally. Her initial zeal in achieving the vision set out by her father was unquestionable. As such she was willing to implement a series of economic measures which aimed to stimulate growth but explicitly intended to also improve the prosperity of India's citizens. However, progress against a backdrop of continuing poverty was painfully slow. A devaluation of the rupee by Gandhi in June 1966 resulting a reduction of 4.76 50 the dollar to 7.50. Ostensibly to deal with India's latest BoP crisis by making exports more attractive, and this meant imports increased in price. India's inflation rate increased. Following the 1967 election, her Congress Party suffering a reduced majority and loss of power in seven states, Gandhi nationalised 14 banks in July 1969 to stimulate lending to small farmers.

India's economy in the 1970s continued to suffer from continued financial crises and a struggle to make the progress desperately needed to raise living standards of the poorest. Following conviction for electoral fraud by Allahabad High Court which stripped Gandhi of office and banned her from running for any political office for six years, her reaction was to appeal to the Supreme Court and following unrest, to impose a state of emergency on 25 June 1975 which lasted 21 months until Gandhi's Congress Party was defeated in 1977 by the Janata alliance of opposition parties. Imposition of draconian laws and censorship during the state of emergency period presented the impression of a country with severe problems undermining confidence by investors. Closure of operations by IBM and Coca-Cola because of imposition of the Foreign Exchange Regulation Act which meant that foreign investors could not own over 40% in Indian enterprises in the late 1970s consolidated concerns as to India's immediate economic prospects.

The 1980s saw sustained economic progress. Failure and internal division among the Janata opposition meant Gandhi was returned to power in January 1980. She implemented a series of eye-catching but expensive reforms to improve the Indian economy and its competitiveness as part of the country's sixth five-year plan. Price controls were abandoned, fiscal reforms implemented, and reform of the public sector commenced coupled with a reduction in import duties as well as delicensing of domestic industry. As an indicator of increased self-confidence, in November 1983, the Maruti 800, an Indian 'People's Car', was made in collaboration with Suzuki of Japan.

Unfortunately, 1984 was a year in which two major events in India caused many to ask whether the country could ever achieve the sort of economic goals long promised by politicians and urgently required by the majority of citizens who wished to see progress for themselves and their children. The assassination of Indira Gandhi on 31 October 1984 by two of her Sikh bodyguards as a consequence of her decision to storm the Golden Temple in Amritsar in the Punjab produced internal tumult and a sense of international panic. Equally, the accidental release of methyl isocyanate gas from the American-owned Union Carbide plant in Bhopal, on 3 December 1984, which caused the deaths of at least 3,800 people and resulted in significant morbidity and premature death for many thousands more, was another blow to Indian confidence.

Indira Gandhi undoubtedly engaged in nepotism in promoting the political careers of her two sons Sanjay and Rajiv. The former, regarded as her heir apparent, died in an air accident in 1980. Rajiv, who considered himself apolitical, was encouraged to follow in his brother's 'footsteps'. After his mother's death, he was perceived as the natural successor as leader of the Congress Party in a continuation of the Nehru– Gandhi political dynasty. Though not without criticism, Rajiv, through economic reforms contained in the 1985–86 budget, oversaw reduced direct taxes for companies and increased exemption limits for income tax. Crucially, Rajiv Gandhi is widely acknowledged as having fostered the IT and telecom revolutions considered critical to India's current success. Sadly, like his grandfather and mother, Rajiv would not live to see the full benefits of overseas investment in the IT sector. On 21 May 1991, in the village of Sriperumbudur, about 40 km (25 miles) from Madras (now Chennai), Rajiv was assassinated by a member of the Liberation Tigers of Tamil Eelam.

Conclusion – so, you want a revolution! India's economic transformation in the 1990s to the present day

According to the Confederation of Indian Industry (2022), the introduction of the 1991 Industrial Policy allowed India to engage in 'major economic reform'. Most particularly, it allowed much greater private sector involvement in industry than had been possible previously. Importantly, the licensing system which had been in place, which heavily prescribed and regulated what was required by businesses wishing to engage in industry, was abandoned. Many point out that this approach was very much what had been recommended by Padma Desai and her co-author (and husband) Jagdish Bhagwati in their book *India: Planning for Industrialization: Industrialization and Trade Policies Since 1951* published two decades earlier. Finance Minister in 1991, Manmohan Singh, who became India's prime minister in 2004, admitted as much.

Much of that change followed a series of crises which required selling off India's reserves of gold coupled with a devaluation of the country's currency twice in two days in early July 1991. These changes were at the heart of the economic liberalisation regarded as being fundamental to underpinning the ability of India to transform its fortunes. Indeed, as is central to the current Indian government's economic stance (and policies), there should be as few restrictions on business as possible to facilitate investment and the entrepreneurial dynamism that is essential to wealth creation which will produce the revenue to allow spending on citizens' well-being.

There has been a vast increase in 'start-ups' in India, most particularly in the digital sector, which has attracted international corporations to locate their operations in the country. This has provided massive opportunity for well-educated young people with relevant qualifications who, crucially, from the perspective of such footloose investors, speak English and can easily communicate with other businesses in their supply chain as well as customers. Very importantly, the exponential growth in fledgling businesses has ensured the development of an ecosystem of angel and venture funding as well as incubators and accelerators. In turn, demand within India and internal consumption has increased. The result, and despite ambivalence during much of modern India's development over the extent that it favoured trade openness or not (Baru, 2022), has been, as the CII contends, that contemporary India is a major player in global trade with exports now in excess of US$350 billion compared to US$0.1 billion in 1950–51.

So now India has the ambition to be a global power rivalling China in East Asia. It has the distinction of being the largest democracy in the world, though various religious and ethnic factions feel disenfranchised. But it is true that the steady business operating environment since 1991 is being credited for the long period of growth, which has, if anything, accelerated in recent years, helped by rising globalisation. Of course, this was interrupted by the impact of the global financial crisis in 2008 and also more recently by Covid.

Huge problems in terms of inequality in India still exist. At the same time, despite the rapid industrialisation and diversification of the economy and the rise in services, including in the IT and telecoms sectors, agriculture remains a major part of GDP at 16.38% in current prices (Ministry of Statistics and Programme Implementation, 2021; see Figure 23.2). It's to be noted that food prices are a major contributor to price inflation and living standards (Times of India, 2022).

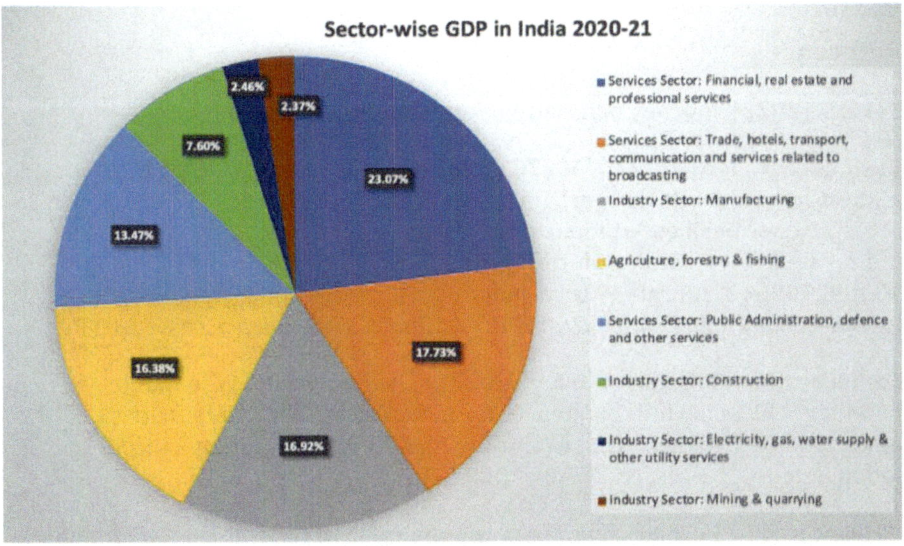

Figure 23.2: Sector-wise GDP in India 2020-21; source: Ministry of Statistics and Programme Implementation, 2021

On the positive side, the economy bounced back strongly, growing by 8.7% in Fiscal Year 2021/22 after the sharp 6.6% drop in 2020-21 (India Briefing, 2022). The International Monetary Fund estimated over 7% growth in 2022/23 which if realised will be among the highest in the world. Circumstances have changed recently, with higher energy costs and drought during 2022 affecting agricultural yields and food prices rising sharply globally. India is embarking on signing up new

FTAs, the basis of which is openness to trade and investment, which will underpin its industrial policy and avoid any temptation to reengage in protectionism.

However, uncertainties remain in terms of India's longer-term position as a global power. Indeed, India and China are the two big countries singled out for not taking part in Western sanctions against Russia following its invasion of Ukraine and now being in receipt of cheaper Russian oil diverted from Europe or other 'unfriendly' nations. And yet for India, continued and improved trade and investment relationships with the West and a fight against the retrenchment of globalisation that is now threatened are a must for its wider economic and industrial ambitions to be realised.

References

Baru, S. (2022), Journey of a Nation, Rupa Publications, India

Business Standard (2022), 'At $76.6 bn, India's military spending third highest in world: SIPRI report', Business Standard Website, 26 April, https://www.business-standard.com/ article/current-affairs/at-76-6-bn-india-s-military-spending-third-highest-in-world- sipri-report 122042500616_1.html#:~:text=India's%20military%20expenditure%20 increased%20to,Institute%20(SIPRI)%20on%20Monday, accessed 10 July

Confederation of Indian Industry (2022), 'The Evolution of the Indian Economy 150 since Independence', Confederation of Indian Industry, https://www.ciiblog.in/the- evolution-of-the-indian-economy-since-independence/, accessed 27 July 2022

Debroy, B. (2021), 'Five-Year Plans and the myth of Harrod-Domar', Indian Express, 18 September, https://www.newindianexpress.com/opinions/2021/sep/18/five-year-plans-and-the-myth-of-harrod-domar-2360256.html, accessed 10 July

Desai, P. and Bhagwati, J. (1970), India: Planning for Industrialization: Industrialization and Trade Policies Since 1951, Oxford University Press, India

India Briefing (2022), India's GDP Grows 8.7% in FY 2022, 6 June, https://www.india- briefing.com/news/indias-gdp-grows-8-7-percent-in-fy-2022-25216.html/, accessed 30 August

Maddison, A. (2001), The World Economy: A Millennium Perspective, Organisation for Economic Co-operation and Development (OECD), Paris, France

Malenbaum, W. (1957), 'The Economic Crisis in India', The Economic Weekly, 6 July, pp. 840–843

Ministry of Statistics and Programme Implementation (2021), Sector-wise GDP of India, 17 June 2021, https://statisticstimes.com/economy/country/india-gdp- sectorwise.php, accessed 19 August

Oberoi, V. (2020), India's Wars since Independence: A Concise History, United Services Institute, December, https://usiofindia.org/publication/usi-journal/indias- wars-since-independence-a-concise-history/#:~:text=The%20Indian%20 Military%20has%20fought,the%20Kargil%20war%20in%201999., accessed 10 July

Times of India (2022), 'State of the Indian Economy' 21 June, https://timesofindia. indiatimes.com/business/india-business/budget/data/state-of-indian-economy, accessed 30 August

About the contributor

Vicky Pryce is an international economist, currently Chief Economic Adviser and board member at the Centre for Economics and Business Research. She is a former Joint Head of the UK Government Economic Service and Visiting Professor at BCU and King's College, London. She was previously Partner and Chief Economist at KPMG and for a while also head of International Privatisations for the firm working in Eastern Europe, Africa, the Middle East, India, Bangladesh and China. Earlier in her career she had senior economic positions in banking and the oil sector and was educated at the German School of Athens and the London School of Economics.

Chapter 24

Conclusion – What's the future for India?

Makhan Singh, Steven McCabe and Beverley Nielsen

Ruchir Sharma, chair of Rockefeller International, writing in the *Financial Times* on 15 August 2022, the 75th anniversary of India's independence, accepted that the country is no richer 'relative to the rest of the world' than when Nehru took over amid the toxicity of violence and turmoil but with the euphoria of freedom from British rule. However, though India may not have achieved the rapid economic progress and social transformation envisaged by its political leaders at partition, its achievements have, given the not inconsiderable impediments endured, been impressive. One of the greatest challenges India has had to confront is that its population has quadrupled since 1947 having overtaken China's in 2023 (Ellis-Petersen, H., 2023). More crucially, average income remains roughly where it was at independence, 18% of the world average.

Nehru's quest of addressing inequality, which was admirably ambitious and not assisted by its natural resources having been systematically plundered during colonisation, was made all the more difficult by population growth as rapid as that experienced by India in the last 75 years. It's hardly surprising that the average income enjoyed by India's citizens has declined and, latterly, merely matches 1947. Clearly, it should be acknowledged that developing India's economy and achieving social transformation was always going to be a long-term project. As the chapters in this book describe, there's been considerable progress in recent years. Indeed, India's prospects for the future are immensely positive.

Abundant physical resources, vastly improved infrastructure and development of education provision for all in recent decades, combined with a strategy to utilise industrial expertise and exploit innovative capability, indicate that India's economy will continue to grow. Investment in establishing India as a global leader in information and digital technology demonstrates that Indian citizens can compete with the best in the world. *Make in India,* an initiative first announced by current Prime Minister Narendra Modi in September 2021, has been vital to such progress. Providing government support and financial incentives for entrepreneurial companies in creating and developing domestically produced goods, *Make in India* is essential to reducing India's reliance on imports as well as boosting exports.

Figure 24.1: Narendra Modi launches Make in India.

Rapidly rising energy prices will continue to impact on global 'value chains' and provide added stimulus to discussions concerning reshoring and 'proximity manufacturing'. Indeed, 'globalisation', always contingent on peace and cheap energy, is now under threat. In a world in which global brands are dominant and distance to market is no barrier, actively competing in manufacturing is the bedrock of any developed country. To be regarded as such and to shake off the tag of being a 'developing nation' was explicitly referred to by Prime Minister Modi in his speech to mark India's 75th anniversary of independence from New Delhi's 17th-century Mughal-era Red Fort (Guardian, 2022).

Consultation of data shows that India's future through invention and ingenuity in Science and Technology is on assured ground by being a fundamental part of government policy. That the Nobel Prize has been won three times by Indians since independence – Har Gobind Khorana for medicine in 1968, Subrahmanyan Chandrasekhar for physics in 1983 and Venkatraman Ramakrishnan in 2009 for chemistry – provides demonstrable evidence of success which will undoubtedly continue. That India, despite domestic economic constraints, has been able to launch space probes and develop its nuclear capability is testament to dedicated and passionate staff working in R&D within the country's universities and entrepreneurial companies. India's current standing in the Global Innovation Index at 46th, having been 81st as recently as 2015, is proof positive of such commitment.

As way of further indication of India's phenomenal trajectory in science and technology, which, vitally, will underpin its economic and social development, it is constructive to refer to the fact that in March 2022, Toyota launched its Mirai hydrogen fuel cell car in India with the Indian Oil Corporation supplying hydrogen power for the vehicle. In IT, already a success story, the country's most influential IT companies, TCS, Infosys, Wipro, HCL and Tech Mahindra, increased their workforces by more than 122,000 in the first six months of 2022. Further, during the pandemic, India's pharma industry played its part in supplying vaccines and enjoyed growth of almost 15% in 2021.

Across a range of sectors in India, government investment in the innovation and entrepreneurship ecosystem has ensured there is financial support and expert advice to the thousands of start-up companies which will provide valuable employment and goods required by citizens. The fact that between 2014 and 2021, there was a 572% growth in patent approvals in India indicates tremendous success in this regard. The role of academia is seen as crucial in the quest to inculcate ever greater innovation and ingenuity. In August 2021, INDIAai and NASSCOM unveiled the first Lab2Market programme intended to enhance industry–academia collaboration. The following month, the Patents Rules (2021) bill was proposed which will reduce fees paid to protect new ideas by 80% for educational institutions. Crucially, over the next five years, Indian academic institutes will receive almost US$ 2.68 million in funding to carry out research into developing energy (especially green), healthcare improvement and aviation.

The importance of India's culturally diverse and eclectic heritage, including songs, music, dance, theatre, folk traditions, performing arts, rites and rituals, paintings and writings, needs no elaboration. In looking forward it is axiomatic that culture, arts and tourism will play a major role in India's continued economic and cultural transformation as part of Prime Minister Modi's pledge made at the 75th anniversary of independence that India should become a developed country within 25 years. As chapters in this book demonstrate, the international relationships forged between India and with organisations, business and education providers in the UK, particularly BCU, have proven to be symbiotic and delivered demonstrable benefit to all concerned.

As appreciation of culture has deepened, it becomes possible to identify further potential for collaboration offering opportunities for mutual improvement. This includes the Munjal Birmingham Centre for Innovation and Entrepreneurship (MBCIE) in Ludhiana involving BCU as well as other partner higher education institutions. This provides a location for individuals to develop new business ideas and existing organisations to grow their offer as well as a place for entrepreneurs to collaborate. MBCIE is intended to act as an Indian counterpart to BCU's new STEAMhouse facility in Birmingham which explicitly includes the arts as part of the traditional technical subjects of science, technology, engineering and maths in the teaching curriculum.

In a post-pandemic world, in which every country suffered from the impact of the virus which caused death and suffering as well as temporary closure of vast swathes of economic activity, India is extremely well placed to take advantage of the reopening of international markets. This provides the prospect of India being able to enjoy a higher rate of economic growth than international competitors. Indeed, as Ruchir Sharma contends, India is likely to be a 'breakout star' and 'on track to surpass the UK, Germany and Japan to become the third-largest economy by 2032.' We absolutely agree with Sharma's conclusion that India is moving in the right direction.

References

Ellis-Petersen, H., (2023) 'India overtakes China to become world's most populous country', The Guardian 24th April 2023

Hegarty, S. (2022), 'World Population Day: India will overtake China in 2023, says the UN', BBC Science and Environment, 11 July, https://www.bbc.co.uk/news/science- environment-62126413, accessed 19 August

Guardian (2022), 'Modi pledges to make India a developed country in 25 years on partition anniversary', Guardian, 15 August, https://www.theguardian.com/ world/2022/aug/15/modi-pledges-to-make-india-a-developed-country-in-25-years- on-partition-anniversary, accessed 20 August

Sharma, R. (2022), 'At 75, India is finally ready to join the global party', Financial Times, 15 August, https://www.ft.com/content/dec674c5-9009-4da1-a857-c2e68473c9ae, accessed 19 August

Image Information

India flag photo

Matthew T Rader https://matthewtrader.com, CC BY-SA 4.0 <https://creativecommons.org/licenses/by-sa/4.0>, via Wikimedia Commons

Introduction - *Anita Bhalla*

Introduction by Anita Bhalla, OBE, Chair, Birmingham City University (BCU). Source: Anita Bhalla

Patronage - *Caroline Rowett, Dr Andrew Fleming.*

Patronage for this book by partners of Birmingham City University. Dr. Andrew Fleming and Caroline Rowett. Images source: British High Commission in Chandigarh

Acknowledgments - *Makhan Singh, Dr Steven McCabe and Beverley Nielsen*

Foreword - *Pankaj M. Munjal*

Foreword by Pankaj M. Munjal, Chairman, Hero Cycles Source: Pankaj M. Munjal

Opening Thoughts - *Manoj Ladwa*

Shri Manoj Ladwa presents a book edited by him, "Winning Partnership - INDIA - UK Relations Beyond Brexit", to the Prime Minister, Shri Narendra Modi. Government Open Data License – India (Wikimedia)

Special Message - *Rowan Kennedy*

Special message by Rowan Kennedy, former Acting Country Director, British Council India. Source: British Council India

1.1 *Makhan Singh, Steven McCabe and Beverley Nielsen* - Map of the British Indian Empire from Imperial Gazetteer of India Source: Edinburgh Geographical Institute; J.G. Bartholomew and Sons, Oxford University Press).

1.2 Source: www.outlookindia. com/website/story/opinion- india-of-2019-would-have- shocked-nehru-and-gandhi- not-so-much-jinnah/344819 accessed 8th July). Source: www.outlookindia. com/ website/story/opinion- india-of-2019-woulG14d-have- shocked-nehru-and-gandhi- not-so-much-jinnah/344819

1.3 Earl Mountbatten of Burma, KG GCB OM GCSI GCIE GCVO DSO KStJ ADC PC FRS. Allan Warren , CC BY-SA 3.0, via Wikimedia Commons

1.4 States and Union Territories Source & credit: Mapsofindia.com

1.5 Population of India by age group (2020). Source & credit: Encyclopaedia Britannica

2.1 *Christian Wolmar* - Matheran Steam Railway. Source: Wikimedia - public domain

2.2 New Delhi Railway station board in English, Hindi and Urdu. MikeLynch, CC BY-SA 3.0, via Wikimedia Commons

2.3 A Train at Kanpur Central Railway Station, Kanpur. KpinfomediaIndia - Creative Commons Attribution-Share Alike 4.0 International license

3.1 *Ventakesh Vijay, Makhan Singh, Pratik Dattani and P. Jagadeesh* - Science and Technology Heritage of India Gallery - Science Exploration Hall - Science City - Kolkata. Biswarup Ganguly - Creative Commons Attribution 3.0 Unported license

3.2 Green energy, windmills – panoramio. Rajaraman Sundaram - Creative Commons Attribution 3.0 Unported license

3.3 The Crew Escape System test Satish Dhawan Space Centre, Sriharikota, Andhra Pradesh. India Department of Space - Government Open Data License – India

3.4 The Secretary, Department of Space, Chairman, Space Commission and Chairman, Indian Space Research Organisation (ISRO), Shri A.S. Kiran Kumar releasing the Compendium on Indian Space Industry. India Department of Space - Government Open Data License – India

3.5 Dr. Vikram Sarabhai Jigneshnat - public domain

4.1 *Natasha Carr, Maggie Prain, Inderjeet Kaur and Radha Reddy*
Taking a detailed history to risk assess, plan, and provide appropriate maternity care.
Source: The Fernandez Foundation, Hyderabad, India

4.2 Midwives and educators at Fernandez Foundation. Source: The Fernandez Foundation, Hyderabad, India

4.3 Facilitating family-centred care and education; note partner involvement. Source: The Fernandez Foundation, Hyderabad, India

4.4 Indie Kaur, Director of Midwifery
Source: The Fernandez Foundation, Hyderabad, India

4.5 Dr Evita Fernandez and members of medical staff at the Fernandez Foundation. Source: The Fernandez Foundation, Hyderabad, India

4.6 Educating, empowering and advocating for women. Source: The Fernandez Foundation, Hyderabad, India

4.7 Caring for mum and baby in the postnatal period; part of the midwife's role. Source: The Fernandez Foundation, Hyderabad, India

5.1 *Anita Virk and Swadhin Padhy*. Anita Virk, aged 11, with the famous Bollywood superstar Sanjay Dutt and her older sister Rajan – Mumbai 1982. Copyright is of the author

5.2 R–L: Anita Virk with Gopi Puthran (film director – Mardaani 2) and Swadhin Padhy (Ronkel Media Education & Research Institute) Visit to BCU in February 2020 as part of an India–UK arts knowledge exchange project. During their visit, the university hosted the screening of Mardaani 2 at the Midlands Arts Centre (MAC), Birmingham. The film marked the directorial debut of Gopi, who was the writer of the first Mardaani film, produced by Yash Raj Films. Copyright is of the author

5.3 Shuddhi: A New Beginning (official poster) Copyright is of the author

5.4 Road to Reform (official poster) Copyright is of the author

6.1 *Mark Jeffreys* India national team at Olympics 1948. The Hindu - public domain

6.2 XIX Commonwealth Games-2010 Delhi Winners of Discus (Women's) Krishna Poonia of India (Gold), Harwant Kaur of India (Silver) and Seema Antil of India (Bronze) during the medal presentation ceremony of the event. Ministry of Youth Affairs and Sports, India - Government Open Data License

6.3 The Minister of State for Youth Affairs and Sports and Information and Broadcasting (IC), Col. Rajyavardhan Singh Rathore withthe Indian Kick Boxers, who represented India at the 2018 World Championship in Argentina, in New Delhi. Attribution: Ministry of Youth Affairs and Sports (GODL-India) - Pradeep Kumar

6.4 Indian cricket players - Lensbug Chandru – Creative Commons Attribution 2.0 Generic license

7.1 *Andrew Trujillo* - Puneeth and Nethravathi, 2021. Source: Puneeth and Nethravathi, 2021

8.1 *Anne Phillips, Wasim Hanif, Martha Stewart, Jayne Robbie and Theresa Smyth* - Dr J.P. Bose. Source: Journal of The Association of Physicians of India

8.2 Young Bengali girl being treated with insulin by Dr Bose. Source: Journal of The Association of Physicians of India. Photograph of a child with type 1 diabetes treated by Dr Bose: Kumudini, Bengali Hindu female, aged 12, admitted to Carmichael Hospital for Tropical Diseases on 23rd June 1929. The photo on the left is Kumudini before treatment with insulin, and the one on the right is after treatment.

8.3 Dr Viswanathan Mohan. Source: Dr Viswanathan Mohan

9.1 *Louise Lansdown, Lamberto Coccioli and James Bunch* - A R Rahman - Creative Commons Attribution 3.0 Unported license

9.2 Anthony Alcock and Srinivasa Murthy during rehearsals of the Sunshine Orchestra. © A R Rahman Foundation

9.3 Louise Lansdown coaching the Sunshine Orchestra's string players. © A R Rahman Foundation

9.4 Anthony Alcock coaching the Sunshine Orchestra's string players. © A R Rahman Foundation

10.1 *Vivek Sachdeva and Gregory Leadbetter*. World Poetry Day Celebrations (2018) in Ravindra Bharathi. Pranayraj 1985 - Creative Commons Attribution-Share Alike 4.0 International license

10.2 Harmeet Vidiarthy Stalinjeet - Creative Commons Attribution-Share Alike 4.0 International license

11.1 Panchalingam Suntharalingam. Percentage of student enrolment by levels (AISHE, 2019–20). Data adapted from All India Survey on Higher Education (AISHE) 2019-2020

11.2 Percentage enrolment in private and state higher education (AISHE, 2019–20). Data adapted from All India Survey on Higher Education (AISHE) 2019-2020

11.3 Enrolment by level in different types of universities (AISHE 2019–20). Data adapted from All India Survey on Higher Education (AISHE) 2019-2020

11.4 BCU in-country 2016 convocation. BA(Hons) Interior Architecture and Design graduates with Dr Panchalingam Suntharalingam (second left from the front row). Source: ICAT Design and Media College, Chennai, India (2016)

12.1 *Sam Coley, Arul Aram and Lavanya Rajendran* - Community Radio Station, HAU. Attribution: World Development Foundation, New Delhi, India

12.2 Community members during programme production (photograph courtesy: Anna Community Radio). Photograph courtesy: Anna Community Radio.

13.1 Anna Community Radio Signage (photograph courtesy: S. Coley).

13.2 More memories of Mumbai, India
Photograph - India own private collection, J. Norton, 2013

13.3 Memories of Chennai, India. Photograph - India own private collection, J. Norton, 2018

13.4 Memories of Coimbatore, India: visit to SASI Creative Colleges [photograph] (India own private collection, J., Norton, 2019). Pictured left to right: Prof Mohammed Ali Sharieff, Principal/ Director, SCSA; Shaswati Choudhury, SASI Academic Consultant; Dr Baskaralingam Vaseeharan, Director – Collaborative Programmes, Alagappa University, Karaikudi (visiting external adviser); Jackie Norton, Associate Professor International and Deputy Director of International Partnerships (ADM); Marlene Little, Associate Professor and Link Tutor; Mr Rajdeepan Swaminathan, Managing Trustee SASI Creative Colleges. Photograph - India own private collection, J. Norton, 2019

13.5 Defining generations (Francis and Hoefel, 2018).
Source: True Gen: Generation Z and its implications for companies - Francis and Hoefel, 2018

14.1 *Dharmesh Rajput*. BBC Pebble Mill, Birmingham. Robin Vanags - Creative Commons Attribution-Share Alike 2.0 Generic license

14.2 Waldorf Cinema. Mick Turner / Balsall Heath Local History Society

14.3 Bobby film poster. Credit: Dharmesh Rajput

15.1 *Jasbir Kaur*. Sikh woman wearing a turban and salwaar kameez. Author: Jaskaur - Creative Commons Attribution-Share Alike 4.0 International license

15.2 Vaani Kapoor walked the ramp at the Lakme Fashion Week 2018. Source: Hungama Digital Media Entertainment - Creative Commons. Attribution 3.0 Unported license

15.3 Rituparna Sengupta – Kolkata. Author: Biswarup Ganguly - Creative Commons Attribution-Share Alike 4.0 International license

15.4 Alia Bhatt at graces Vogue India's Fashion's Night Out Attribution: Bollywood Hungama - Creative Commons Attribution 3.0 Unported license

15.5 *Beverley Nielsen* - Census of India 2021 - Source: 2011 Census of India

16.2 Smriti Irani addressing people at the launch of the National Web Portal for Apprenticeship Training Scheme, implemented by the Ministry of Human Resource Development through Boards of Apprenticeship Practical Training, in New Delhi. Licensed under the Government Open Data License - India (GODL)

17.1 *Imran Mogra* - Husain Ahmad Madani 2012 stamp of India. India Post, Government of India - licensed under the Government. Open Data License - India (GODL)

17.2 Amjad Khan – Bollywood actor. Source: Wikipedia – Fair Use. International license

17.3 The President, Dr. A.P.J. Abdul Kalam addressing the nation on the eve of 58th Republic Day, in New Delhi on January 25, 2007. Source: President's Secretariat - Wikimedia Commons

18.1 *Paul Davies and Steven McCabe* - Manmohan Singh in 2009. The White House from Washington, DC. Source: Official White House Photo by Pete Souza

19.1 Cham Athwal - Timeline of famines and GDP per capita in India from 1760 to 2000 (Gulati, 2022). Gulati, M. 2022, Energy-Water-Agriculture Nexus in India: Lessons from Punjab and Rajasthan, UKIERI-DST Partnership Development Workshop on Solar pump based village microgrids-potential for tackling the energy/water/food nexus in Punjab

19.2 Categorisation of degree of groundwater utilisation (Central Ground Water Board, 2020). GROUND WATER YEAR BOOK INDIA 2019-20, Government of India - licensed under the Government Open Data License - India (GODL)

19.3 Timeline of agricultural electricity use and water table depth in Punjab (Gulati, 2022). Gulati, M. 2022, Energy-Water-Agriculture Nexus in India: Lessons from Punjab and Rajasthan, UKIERI-DST Partnership Development Workshop on Solar pump-based village microgrids-potential for tackling the energy/water/food nexus in Punjab

19.4 Timeline of India's net electricity generation by fuel type (U.S. Energy Information Administration, 2020). Graphic created by author based on data from U.S. Energy Information Administration 2020. India Analysis. https://www.eia. gov/international/analysis/country/IND, accessed 21 October 2022

19.5 External view of 15KW solar irrigation pump

Comparison of electricity used for irrigation and sold to grid in Dhundi 2015 to 2021 (Verma, 2022). Verma, S. 2022, SPaRC'ing agri-solarization through grid-connected SIPs, UKIERI-DST Partnership Development Workshop on Solar pump-based village microgrids-potential for tackling the energy/ water/food nexus in Punjab

19.6 Village electricity schematic with solar pumps able to send electricity to the substation via an agricultural feeder. Copyright is of the author

19.7 Impact of solarisation on recurring and capital subsidy (Ajmer and Jaipur DISCOMs only). Gulati, M.P., Priya, S. and Bresnyan, E.W. 2020. Grow Solar, Save Water, Double Farmer Income: An Innovative Approach to Addressing Water-Energy-Agriculture Nexus in Rajasthan. World Bank, Washington, DC. https://openknowledge.worldbank.org/handle/10986/33375 License: CC BY 3.0 IGO,

19.8 Electricity schematic for solar pump-based village microgrid. Copyright is of the author

20.1 *Navjot Sandhu, Javed Hussain and Shishank Shishank*
Changes in agricultural yields in India, 1980–2014 Average annual growth in yield for key food Source: Mulage (2017)

20.2 Source: Information compiled by author reviewing works of Mulage (2017); Datt et al. (2008); Sandhu (2007); Carter (1946); and Government of India (2022). Source: Author's own elaboration inspired by Mulage (2017), Datt et al., 2008, Carter (1949) and Government of India (2022)

20.3 Grape vineyards Viticulture Farming Sula winery Nasik Maharashtra India. Author: Pablo Ares Gastesi - Creative Commons Attribution-Share Alike 2.0 Generic license

Printed in Great Britain
by Amazon

36518099R00165